Foreign D
on the Silk Road

FOREIGN DEVILS ON THE SILK ROAD

The Search for the Lost Cities and Treasures of Chinese Central Asia

PETER HOPKIRK

The University of Massachusetts Press

Amherst

Library of Congress Cataloging in Publication Data
Hopkirk, Peter.
Foreign devils on the silk road.
Bibliography: p.
Includes index.
1. Asia, Central—Antiquities. 2. Silk Road.
I. Title.
DS786.H6175   1984   951'.6   83-24092
ISBN 0-87023-435-8

Contents

Illustrations

PLATES

MAPS *between pp. 12 and 13*

SOURCES OF ILLUSTRATIONS

Acknowledgements

In piecing together this little-known episode in Central Asian history I have drawn on many sources, written and unwritten, published and unpublished. All written sources, save for one or two contemporary newspaper reports and obituaries, are listed in the bibliography. But it is to four men, now all dead, that I owe my greatest debt. Without them – and the detailed accounts of their exploits which they left – there would be no book. These four are Sven Hedin, Sir Aurel Stein, Albert von Le Coq and Professor Langdon Warner, all of whom played leading roles in this narrative. All four wrote vividly and entertainingly, but their books are long out of print and difficult – and expensive – to obtain. These long-forgotten works are listed separately in the bibliography with their publishers. I am particularly grateful to the Stein Trustees for permission to quote extensively from Sir Aurel Stein's own writings.

A most valuable source has also been Jeannette Mirsky's recent biography of Stein – the outcome of many years' work, particularly on his previously unpublished correspondence.

In writing this book I owe a great deal, too, to my wife Kath who did much of the initial research, helped me with my enquiries in Peking, Tokyo and Delhi, translated the Pelliot material, made many improvements in the text and much else besides. I am indebted also to the following distinguished scholars who helped me with matters of fact, but who are in no way responsible for the use I have put these to. What views I have expressed are entirely my own. In Peking: Professor Hsia Nai, Director of the Institute of Archaeology. In West Berlin: Prof. Dr Herbert Härtel, Director of the Museum of Indian Art. In Leningrad: Mme Natalia Diakonova of the

Hermitage Museum. In Tokyo: Dr Jiro Sugiyama, Curator of Oriental Art at the National Museum. In Delhi: Dr P. Bannerjee, Curator of the Indian National Museum.

My gratitude is also due to the following individuals: William St Clair who persuaded me that it was time to write something more lasting than newspaper articles. John R. Murray, my publisher (and editor), whose family have a long and distinguished tradition of producing classic works on Central Asia, and without whose personal interest in the subject and unflagging encouragement this book would have remained no more than an idea.

I also owe thanks to David Loman and Christer von der Burg, both oriental booksellers, for finding me rare and little-known items of source material. My gratitude is due, too, to Simon Scott Plummer, a colleague at *The Times*, who tracked down the Otani murals for me in Seoul and discovered there the answers to two other mysteries. Again, without the interest of Frances Wood and Howard Nelson of the British Library I would never have found out what became of the long-forgotten forgeries of Islam Akhun.

The following have also assisted me with various matters Chinese and Japanese: Verity Wilson, now of the Victoria and Albert Museum, Annette Lord (currently of Peking), Kate Owen (formerly of the Contemporary China Institute) and Michiyo Sawada (of Kyoto). I must thank, too, Heidi St Clair who helped me with German translations, Diana Balfour who typed every word of this book, and Libby Perkins and Tessa Hughes who both read the typescript. Finally I am grateful to the staff of those two vast repositories of oriental intelligence, the India Office Library and the Library of the School of Oriental and African Studies.

P.H.

Note on Place Names

Apart from the different ways of romanising Chinese and Turkic place names (Tun-huang, Touen-houang, Dunhuang), some towns and villages possess several totally different names – a Turkic one, a Chinese one, a Mongolian one and sometimes one or more historic titles. Thus Urumchi (Wulumuchi) is sometimes called Tihwa by the Chinese, also Bung Miao Tze, Bashbalikh and Peitin – the last two being ancient names. Kashgar is also known as Kashi Shi, Yarkand as Shache, Hami as Kumul, and so on. All this can be extremely confusing to a reader who turns to other sources, whether books or maps. I have used, throughout, the name by which a place is best known, or was known at the time by those who visited it in the course of this narrative.

Prologue

'The Chinese complain, and the foreigner cannot well deny it, that caravan-loads of priceless treasures from the temples, tombs and ruins of Chinese Turkistan have been carried off to foreign museums and are for ever lost to China.' So wrote Sir Eric Teichman in *Journey to Turkistan*, an account of his travels along the old Silk Road on a Foreign Office mission in 1935. It made the Chinese 'boil with indignation,' he added, 'to read in the books of foreign travellers descriptions of how they carried off whole libraries of ancient manuscripts, frescoes and relics of early Buddhist culture in Turkistan'.

My aim in this book is to tell the story of these long-range archaeological raids made by foreigners into this remote corner of Central Asia during the first quarter of this century. It is primarily about six men – Sven Hedin of Sweden, Sir Aurel Stein of Britain, Albert von Le Coq of Germany, Paul Pelliot of France, Langdon Warner of the United States, and the somewhat mysterious Count Otani of Japan.

Between them, until the Chinese finally put a stop to it, they removed wall-paintings, manuscripts, sculptures and other treasures literally by the ton from the lost cities of the Silk Road. Today, to the bitter chagrin of the Chinese and the exasperation of scholars, this great Central Asian collection is scattered through the museums and institutions of at least thirteen different countries. Some of it, through inattention or lack of funds, is crumbling away. Much also has disappeared or been destroyed. To see everything that has survived one must be prepared to travel to India, Japan, Russia, America, Taiwan, South Korea, Sweden, Finland, East and West Germany, Britain, France and China, and to visit over thirty institutions.

The men who carried off all these treasures had few qualms about the rightness of what they were doing. Nor, it should be said, did the governments or institutions (including the British Museum) which sent them. At the time they were lionised and honoured for their remarkable discoveries and unquestionable contributions to the scholarship of Central Asia and China. Stein and Hedin, neither of whom was British born, even received knighthoods. The Chinese, on the other hand, view their archaeological activities in a very different light, although they did nothing to prevent them at the time. To the Chinese, 'so-called scholars' like Stein, Pelliot and von Le Coq were no more than shameless adventurers who robbed them of their history. It is an issue, moreover, on which they are not entirely without allies in the West.

In 1956, some thirty years after Teichman, another rare British traveller to the region passed along the ancient Silk Road and at Bezeklik was shown the blank walls which had once borne brilliant murals. In *Turkestan Alive*, Basil Davidson recounts how the official conducting him around the cliff-hewn temples pointed to each of the gaps in turn and uttered the one word 'Stolen!' Davidson, who leaves us in no doubt where his own sympathies lie, goes on: 'He said it wherever we came across a large and painful excision; and he said it often.' It was echoed each time, first by the girl from the antiquities department who accompanied them, and then by the driver. 'They felt aggrieved; and they were right,' Davidson adds.

He himself felt aggrieved when, on returning to London, he saw how Sir Aurel Stein's collection was displayed in the British Museum – 'tucked away in a corner with little room to explain or reveal its unique value'. Even today, perhaps in deference to Chinese feelings, there is nothing to indicate that almost everything in the small Central Asian section was acquired through the prodigious, if (to some) questionable, efforts of one man. Perhaps out of similar deference to our feelings, at Bezeklik and elsewhere the Chinese today no longer point accusingly at the incisions left by von Le Coq and his rivals.

For starting what he calls the 'international race for antiquities from Chinese Turkestan', Davidson blames Hedin and Stein, the first men to realise the archaeological possibilities of the region. He goes on: 'The Germans sent out four expeditions between 1902 and 1914; the French sent expeditions; the Russians and Japanese sent expeditions. These bold scholars staked out "spheres of influence" and "fields of discovery" and quarrelled vigorously over the one and the other.' He concludes: 'Nowadays it is a sad and weary sight to stare at rock-temple frescoes where these ruthless old collectors used their knives. Many of the frescoes had survived for over a thousand years: had they managed to survive a bare half-century longer they would be there to this day.'

But not everyone would agree with Davidson's confident assertion. For a start, was the damage always inflicted by those 'ruthless old collectors'? It certainly seems not if one is to accept the accounts of earlier eye-witnesses. One British traveller, Colonel Reginald Schomberg, who passed that way in 1928, reported that most of the frescoes from one site had been removed by von Le Coq, but added: 'providentially so, for nearly all the remaining ones had been shamelessly defaced by the local Mohammedans'. He went on: 'It cannot be too often emphasised that it is solely due to European archaeologists that any of the Buddhist treasures of Turkestan have been saved from Turki fanaticism and vandalism.' Of another site he wrote: 'The damage done to the pictures was lamentable, for the faces of the Buddha had been slashed across or scarred and the few remaining statues almost destroyed.' Those who have been privileged to visit the great monastery of Bezeklik, near Turfan, will testify to the destruction wrought by religious vandals (and possibly by Red Guards) before, belatedly, the Chinese authorities took it upon themselves to protect the few surviving frescoes.

Iconoclasm, however, was not the only threat to the survival of these treasures. Those remarkable missionaries Mildred Cable and Francesca French, in their book *The Gobi Desert* published nearly forty years ago, describe the casual damage they witnessed in progress not far from Bezeklik at the ancient walled city of Karakhoja. 'Destruction of the buildings had been going on for a long time,' they reported, 'and we saw farmers at work with their pickaxes pulling down the old ruins and probably destroying many relics in the process.' The farmers found the old earth valuable for enriching their fields. They furthermore ploughed up the land within the enclosure and sowed crops round the old monuments. Cable and French add: 'Unfortunately the irrigation which is necessary for raising crops is fatal to structures made of earth, to mural decorations and to all other remains which depend on the dryness of desert conditions for their preservation.'

Professor von Le Coq, who himself dug extensively at this site, reported that between the first and second German expeditions – a period of some eighteen months – 'the locals have destroyed a very great deal by their constant digging'. In his *Buried Treasures of Chinese Turkestan* he explains that the local farmers scraped off the brightly coloured pigment from the frescoes, regarding this as a particularly powerful fertiliser. Ancient beams from ruined temples, moreover, preserved for centuries by the moistureless climate, were especially prized, either as fuel or for building in a region where wood was so scarce. The wall-paintings, he explained, were 'an abomination to Moslems, and hence wherever they are found they are damaged – at all events on their faces'. Chinese officials, he claimed, made no attempt to stop them, being Confucians and despising Buddhism.

He was told of one villager who, pulling down a wall, had unearthed cartloads of manuscripts, many decorated in colour, including gold. As a Moslem he dared not keep them lest the mullah should punish him for possessing infidel books, so he had thrown the whole lot into the river. Le Coq himself reports stumbling upon another ancient library which, together with frescoes of once-exquisite quality and quantities of textiles, had been totally destroyed by irrigation water.

Other hazards included earthquakes and local treasure-hunters. Professor von Le Coq recalled that many of the temples from which he had removed wall-paintings as late as 1913 were destroyed by earthquakes three years later. As Stein ruefully discovered, native treasure-seekers were particularly active along the southern arm of the Silk Road, a factor in the Germans' decision to concentrate their resources on the sites around Turfan and Kucha, which lie on the northern arm. The eagerness shown by western travellers to purchase old manuscripts and other antiquities during the closing years of the nineteenth century undoubtedly encouraged treasure-hunters to pillage important sites which might otherwise have remained intact. It was also to encourage enterprising local forgers whose often ingenious counterfeits were to baffle seasoned orientalists.

But such hazards were by no means purely local, as the Chinese are quick to point out. On seven terrible nights in World War II, more masterpieces of Central Asian art were wiped out in Berlin than tomb-robbers, farmers, irrigation schemes or earthquakes could have accounted for in many years. It is to these treasures, lost for ever when the old Ethnological Museum was destroyed by Allied bombing, that the Chinese inevitably refer if one tries to argue that men like Stein and von Le Coq were doing no more than rescue for posterity what otherwise would have perished anyway. Nor were the Berlin frescoes the only Central Asian treasures which might have fared better if they had been left where they were found. A large part of the collection of Buddhist art brought back from Chinese Turkestan by Count Otani's three expeditions has not been seen since World War II, and Japanese scholars have so far been unable to trace it.

The whole question of the Turkestan treasures, and in particular the thousands of manuscripts from Tun-huang, now divided between London and Paris, remains a highly emotive one. It is one which still greatly exercises the Chinese, as I found in Peking when I discussed it at length with Dr Hsia Nai, Director of China's Institute of Archaeology, and himself a veteran Silk Road excavator. Sir Aurel Stein of Britain is unquestionably regarded as the most villainous of the foreign archaeologists, followed closely by Professor Pelliot of France. For their removal of the so-called 'secret' library from the Caves of the Thousand Buddhas at Tun-huang is something that the Chinese can never forgive. Sven Hedin of Sweden, who dug up highly important historical documents from sand-buried Lou-lan, comes third on their blacklist. From this it will be seen that it is the loss of the written evidence of their past which (to use Sir Eric Teichman's phrase) causes the Chinese to 'boil with indignation', even more than the removal of the great wall-paintings and other works of art.

Just how many of these paintings, sculptures and manuscripts would have survived had they been left *in situ* and not been the victims of what Davidson calls 'archaeological theft', the reader must decide for himself. He must also judge for himself the morality of depriving a people permanently of their heritage, however sound the motives for 'rescuing' it may have seemed at the time. The question of why the Chinese allowed the treasures to be removed in the first place must likewise be considered. But that is not what this book is about. My purpose is to put together – for the first time – the story of these expeditions and to show what it was that drew such very different men to this remote and extremely inhospitable corner of China, at grave risk to their healths and frequently to their lives.

At the time of writing, most of Chinese Central Asia, except (for a lucky few) Tun-huang, Urumchi and the Turfan region, is still closed to foreign visitors. But if the present thaw continues, and Sino-Soviet relations do not worsen, it may not be very long before the reader will be able to follow in the footsteps of Stein and Hedin, von Le Coq and Pelliot, Langdon Warner and the Japanese, and see many of the Silk Road oases and sites for himself. But in the meantime he must remain content with maps and photographs. So let us turn to the map of modern China and find the two adjoining regions of Sinkiang and Kansu. For it is there that virtually the whole of this story takes place.

1. The Rise and Fall of the Silk Road

In Central Asia's back of beyond, where China tests her nuclear weapons and keeps a wary eye on her Russian neighbours, lies a vast ocean of sand in which entire caravans have been known to vanish without trace. For well over a thousand years the Taklamakan desert has, with good reason, enjoyed an evil reputation among travellers. Apart from the handful of men who have crossed its treacherous dunes, some of which reach a height of three hundred feet, caravans throughout history have always skirted it, following the line of isolated oases along its perimeter. Even so, the ill-marked tracks frequently became obliterated by wind-blown sand, and over the centuries a sad procession of merchants, pilgrims, soldiers and others have left their bones in the desert after losing their way between oases.

Surrounding the Taklamakan on three sides are some of the highest mountain ranges in the world, with the Gobi desert blocking the fourth. Thus even the approaches to it are dangerous. Many travellers have perished on the icy passes which lead down to it from Tibet, Kashmir, Afghanistan and Russia, either by freezing to death or by missing their foothold and hurtling into a ravine below. In one disaster, in the winter of 1839, an entire caravan of forty men was wiped out by an avalanche, and even now men and beasts are lost each year.

No traveller has a good word to say for the Taklamakan. Sven Hedin, one of the few Europeans to have crossed it, called it 'the worst and most dangerous desert in the world'. Stein, who came to know it even better, considered the deserts of Arabia 'tame' by comparison. Sir Percy Sykes, the geographer, and one-time British Consul-General at Kashgar, called it 'a Land of Death', while his sister Ella, herself a veteran desert traveller, described it as 'a very abomination of desolation'.

Apart from the more obvious perils, such as losing one's way and dying of thirst, the Taklamakan has special horrors to inflict on those who trespass there. In his book *Buried Treasures of Chinese Turkestan*, von Le Coq describes the nightmare of being caught in that terror of all caravans, the *kara-buran*, or black hurricane.

> Quite suddenly the sky grows dark ... a moment later the storm bursts with appalling violence upon the caravan. Enormous masses of sand, mixed with pebbles, are forcibly lifted up, whirled round, and dashed down on man and beast; the darkness increases and strange clashing noises mingle with the roar and howl of the storm ... The whole happening is like hell let loose. ... Any traveller overwhelmed by such a storm must, in spite of the heat, entirely envelop himself in felts to escape injury from the stones dashing around with such mad force. Men and horses must lie down and endure the rage of the hurricane, which often lasts for hours together.

Several other European travellers, including Hedin, who lived through such storms left similar descriptions. The vital thing was to keep your head. A caravan of sixty horsemen escorting a consignment of silver ingots to the oasis of Turfan in 1905 perished when they were struck by a *buran* so powerful that it overturned the heavily laden carts. 'The sixty Chinese horsemen', von Le Coq relates, 'galloped into the desert where some of the mummified bodies of men and beasts were found later on, while the others had utterly and entirely disappeared, for the sandstorm likes to bury its victims.' Clearly it was a case of panic, by the horses if not also by the riders. But in Chinese minds such happenings were caused by the demons which they believed inhabited the desert and lured men to thirsty deaths.

Hsuan-tsang, the great Chinese traveller, who passed through the Taklamakan on his way to India in the seventh century, describes these demons. 'When these winds rise,' he wrote, 'both man and beast become confused and forgetful, and there they remain perfectly disabled. At times, sad and plaintive notes are heard and piteous cries, so that between the sights and sounds of the desert, men get confused and know not whither they go. Hence there are so many who perish on the journey. But it is all the work of demons and evil spirits.'

Sir Clarmont Skrine, who served as British Consul-General at Kashgar in the 1920s, has left a vivid description of the desert's appearance in his book *Chinese Central Asia*. 'To the north in the clear dawn the view is inexpressively awe-inspiring and sinister. The yellow dunes of the Taklamakan, like the giant waves of a petrified ocean, extend in countless myriads to a far horizon with here and there an extra large sand-hill, a king dune as it were, towering above his fellows. They seem to clamour silently, those dunes, for travellers to engulf, for whole caravans to swallow up as they have swallowed up so many in the past.'

Skrine, who for two and a half years manned this sensitive listening post where three empires met – those of China, Russia and Britain – recalled speaking with an old Chinese traveller who arrived in Kashgar from 'China proper' via the Gobi and Taklamakan deserts. On one lonely stretch of this journey he had marched for fifty days, he told Skrine, without seeing a soul.

Another traveller who, nearly forty years earlier, covered the three thousand five hundred miles from Peking to Kashgar was Colonel Mark Bell, V.C., Director of Military Intelligence of the Indian Army. His secret purpose in making the journey was to assess whether the Chinese would be able to resist an encroachment by the Russians through Central Asia towards India. He and a young companion, Lieutenant (later Sir Francis) Younghusband, raced one another from Peking to India by different routes, Bell winning by five weeks.

Afterwards Bell wrote somewhat dismissively of the Gobi. 'Water can be readily obtained and is often close to the surface,' he reported. 'Travellers like to make much of crossing the desert, but it has few hardships; and before we left Kashgaria we had reason to think the Gobi days pleasant in comparison with the Kashgarian desert hills and flats. . . .' By the latter, of course, he meant the fringes of the Taklamakan which he, like most other travellers, carefully skirted.

Over the years this little-known region of China has, on the maps of the day and in the memoirs of travellers, borne numerous different names. In vogue at various times were Chinese Tartary, High Tartary, Chinese Turkestan (sometimes spelt Turkistan), Eastern Turkestan, Chinese Central Asia, Kashgaria, Serindia and Sinkiang. The earlier their use, the vaguer were their boundaries, although all included the Taklamakan. Some Victorian travellers called it High Asia, though this appears to have included Tibet – 'the most stupendous upheaval to be found on the face of our planet', as Sven Hedin once described it.

Ancient Han records show that two thousand years ago the Chinese knew the Taklamakan as the *Liu Sha*, or 'Moving Sands', for its yellow dunes are ever in motion, driven by the relentless winds that scour the desert. Present-day hydrographers and climatologists refer to it more tamely as the Tarim basin after the glacier-fed river which flows eastwards across it to shallow Lop-nor lake, the mystery of whose apparent 'wandering' would finally be solved by Sven Hedin. On the map of modern China the Taklamakan (meaning, in Turki, 'go in and you won't come out') is shown by a large egg-shaped blank in the heart of what is now officially termed the Sinkiang-Uighur Autonomous Region.

The Taklamakan and its oases are protected on all four sides from any but the most determined of intruders. To the north

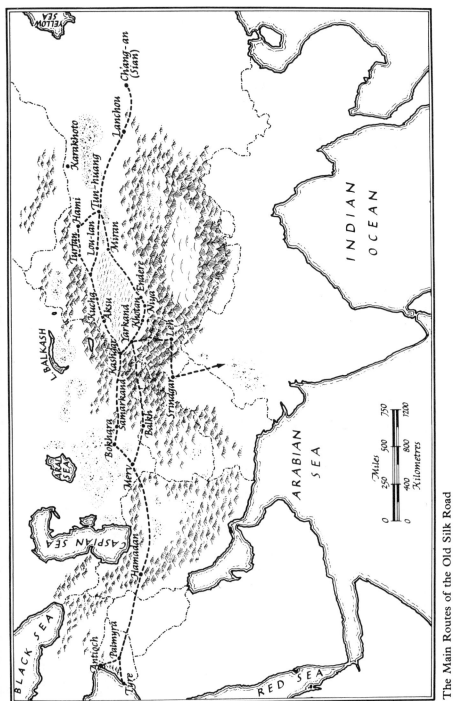

The Main Routes of the Old Silk Road

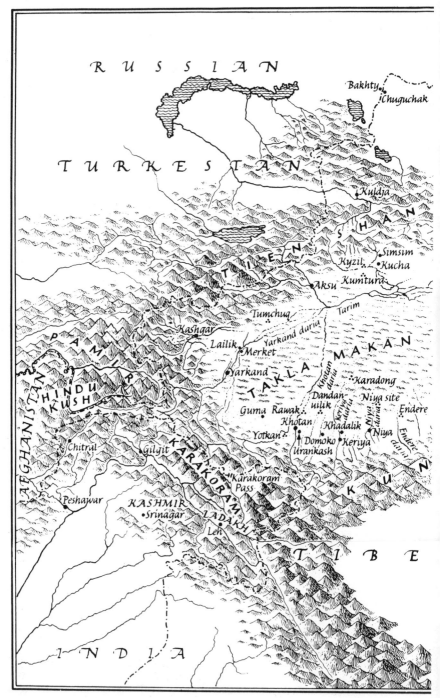

Chinese Turkestan and Adjacent Areas

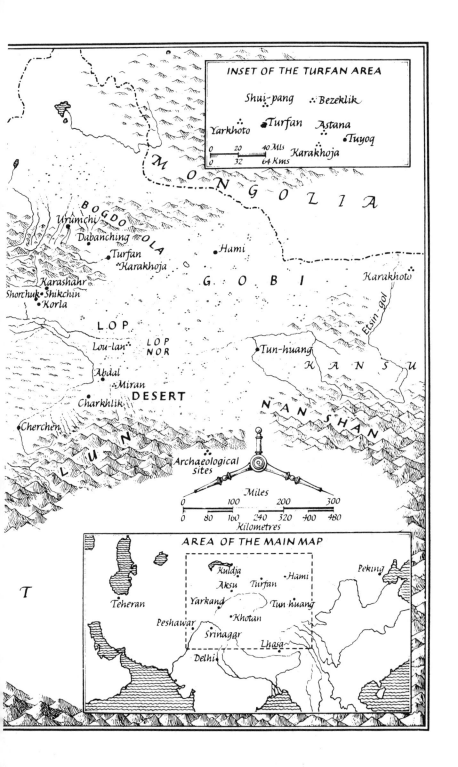

INSET OF THE TURFAN AREA

Shui-pang · .·. Bezeklik

Yarkhoto ·.·.· ●Turfan Astana
Karakhoja ●Tuyoq

0   20   40 Mls
0   32   64 Kms

MONGOLIA

BOGDO OLA
Urumchi
Dabanching
Turfan
Karakhoja
Karashahr
Shorchuk ●Shikchin
Korla

Hami

GOBI

Karakhoto

Etsin-gol

LOP

Lou-lan
LOP
NOR

Tun-huang
KANSU

Abdal
Miran
Charkhlik
DESERT

NAN SHAN

Cherchen

KUN LUN

Archaeological
sites

Miles
0   100   200   300
0   80   160   240   320   400   480
Kilometres

AREA OF THE MAIN MAP

Kuldja
Aksu   Turfan   ●Hami
Peking

Teheran   Yarkand
Tun-huang

Peshawar   ●Khotan

Srinagar   Lhasa

Delhi

T

rise the majestic T'ien Shan. To the west lie the Pamir – 'The Roof of the World'. To the south stretch the Karakoram and Kun Lun ranges. Only the east is free of mountains. But there nature has placed two further obstacles, the Lop and Gobi deserts. Most British travellers (Bell and Younghusband excepted) have approached Chinese Central Asia from India via the Karakoram passes which in places reach nineteen thousand feet. Hedin describes this bleak route as a 'via dolorosa' because of the many lives it has claimed, both human and animal. As recently as 1950 a traveller wrote: 'Never once until we reached the plains were we out of sight of skeletons. The continuous line of bones and bodies acted as a gruesome guide whenever we were uncertain of the route.' In *The Lion River*, a history of the exploration of the Indus river, Jean Fairley writes: 'Nothing grows along the Karakoram route and the traveller must carry all the food he needs for himself and his beasts. Pack animals, overloaded with trading goods at the expense of fodder, have died in this pass in their millions.' Sir Aurel Stein, on the other hand, dismisses the Karakoram route somewhat mischievously as 'a tour for the ladies'.

During the nineteenth century, however, there was one hazard which could not be shrugged off so lightly – the risk of being murdered. Any trespasser in this mountainous badland was regarded as fair game by local tribesmen (even in 1906 Stein took a small armoury with him). This lawlessness was to cost several European travellers, including Dalgleish, Hayward and Moorcroft, their lives. Not that this deterred anyone. Such perils were part of the challenge of Central Asia. Today, with the building of a new two-way highway across the Karakoram, the era of hiring mules and ponies, cooks and coolies, of clinging dizzily to mountain ledges, dodging rockfalls and bullets – the very stuff of Central Asian travel – is finally at an end.

But the men whose exploits concern us here belonged to the earlier age (although Sven Hedin, the first of them, died only in 1952). To achieve their purpose they were willing to endure great hardship, frequent danger and, if necessary, death in this grim Asiatic backwater. What was it that drew them so powerfully to the Taklamakan with its cruel winters and sweltering summers? To understand this it is necessary to turn back the pages of China's history some two thousand years.

★   ★   ★

A century before the birth of Christ an adventurous young Chinese traveller called Chang Ch'ien set out across China on a secret mission to the then remote and mysterious regions of the west. Although its immediate purpose ended in failure, it proved to be one of the most important journeys in history, for it was to lead to China discovering Europe and the birth of the Silk Road. Chang, who was renowned for his strength and daring, was sent on his trail-blazing journey by Wu-ti, the Han Emperor, who found himself facing increasing harassment from China's ancient foes, the Hsiung-nu. These warlike people, Huns of Turkic stock, were eventually destined to appear in Europe as the ravaging Huns of our own history books. Their raids on China had begun during the period of the Warring States (476–206 BC) and in 221 BC the Emperor Shi Huang-ti had built the Great Wall in an effort to keep them out.

Emperor Wu-ti, or the Son of Heaven as he was officially known, had learned from Hun captives that some years earlier they had defeated another Central Asiatic people, the Yueh-chih, made a drinking vessel from the skull of their vanquished leader and forced them to flee far to the west, beyond the Taklamakan desert. There, he was informed, they were waiting to avenge their defeat, but first sought an ally. Wu-ti immediately decided to make contact with the Yueh-chih with the aim of joining forces with them and making a simultaneous attack on the Hsiung-nu from both front and rear.

He therefore sought a suitable volunteer for this dangerous

mission – dangerous because an emissary from China to the Yueh-chih would first have to travel through Hun-held territory. Chang Ch'ien, an official of the imperial household, volunteered and was accepted by the Emperor. In the year 138 BC he set out with a caravan of one hundred men determined to run the Hun gauntlet. But in what is now Kansu they were attacked by the Hsiung-nu and the survivors taken prisoner, remaining captive for ten years. Chang was well treated, however, and even provided with a wife. With the aim of eventually making his escape and continuing his journey westwards, he managed to retain Wu-ti's ambassadorial token – a yak's tail – throughout his captivity. One day, after their captors had allowed them more and more liberty, Chang and the remnants of his party managed to slip away and set out once again on their mission.

They finally reached the territory of the Yueh-chih (who later became the Indo-Scythian rulers of north-west India), only to discover that in the years that had passed since their defeat by the Huns they had become prosperous and settled and had lost all interest in avenging themselves on their former foes. Chang remained with them for a year, gathering as much information as possible about them and other tribes and countries of Central Asia. While journeying home through Hun territory he was again captured. As luck would have it, civil war broke out among his captors, and in the confusion he managed to escape once again. Finally, after thirteen years away, and long assumed to be dead, he reached Ch'angan, the Han capital, to report to the Emperor. Of his original party of one hundred men only one, besides himself, reached home alive.

The intelligence that Chang Ch'ien brought back – military, political, economic and geographical – caused a sensation at the Han court. From his emissary the Emperor learned of the rich and previously unknown kingdoms of Ferghana, Samarkand, Bokhara (all now in Soviet Central Asia) and Balkh (now in Afghanistan). Also for the first time the Chinese learned of the existence of Persia and of another distant land called Li-jien. This, present-day scholars believe, was almost certainly Rome. But of more immediate importance was the discovery in Ferghana of an amazing new type of warhorse which, Chang reported, was bred from 'heavenly' stock. Fast, large and powerful, these were a revelation to the Chinese whose only horses at that time were the small, slow, local breed today known as Prejevalsky's Horse, and now only to be found in zoos.

Wu-ti, realising that the Ferghana horses would be ideal for cavalry warfare against the troublesome Huns, was determined to re-equip his army with them. He sent a mission to Ferghana to try to acquire some, but it was wiped out on the way there, as were successive missions. Finally a much larger force, accompanied by vets, was sent to lay siege to Ferghana. However, the inhabitants rounded up their horses and drove them into the walled city, threatening to kill themselves and the horses if the Chinese came any closer. At last an honourable surrender was arranged and the Chinese left for home with their chargers. Although now long extinct, these 'heavenly horses' have been immortalised by Han and T'ang sculptors and artists. The most splendid example is the world-famous bronze 'Flying Horse' excavated by Chinese archaeologists on the Silk Road in 1969 near Sian, Wu-ti's one-time capital, and cast by an unknown sculptor some two thousand years ago.

Greatly pleased with his emissary who had shown such determination on this epoch-making journey, Emperor Wu-ti bestowed upon him the title 'Great Traveller'. Many further expeditions followed, for Wu-ti was now determined to expand his empire westwards. One of these was again led by Chang, this time in 115 BC to the Wu-sun, a nomadic people who lived along the western frontier of the Hsiung-nu, whom Wu-ti hoped to gain as allies against the Huns. Again Chang failed to enlist their aid, for they were too afraid of their powerful neighbours and China seemed far off. Not long after his return from this mission, the Great Traveller died, greatly honoured by his emperor, and still revered in China today. It was he who had blazed the trail westwards towards Europe which was ultimately to link the two superpowers of the day – Imperial China and Imperial Rome. He could fairly be described as the father of the Silk Road.

*   *   *

Although one of the oldest of the world's great highways, the Silk Road acquired this evocative name comparatively recently, the phrase being coined by a German scholar, Baron Ferdinand von Richthofen, in the last century. As a description, moreover, it is somewhat misleading. For not only did this great caravan route across China, Central Asia and the Middle East consist of a number of roads, but it also carried a good deal more than just silk. Advancing year by year as the Han emperors pushed China's frontiers further westwards, it was ever at the mercy of marauding Huns, Tibetans and others. In order to maintain the free flow of goods along the newly opened highway, the Chinese were obliged to police it with garrisons and watchtowers. As part of this forward policy they built a westward extension to the Great Wall, rather like the Roman *limes*.

The Silk Road (sometimes known as the Silk Route) started from Ch'ang-an, present-day Sian, and struck north-westwards, passing through the Kansu corridor to the oasis of Tun-huang in the Gobi desert, a frontier town destined to play a dramatic role in this story. Leaving Tun-huang, and passing through the famous Jade Gate, or Yu-men-kuan, it then divided, giving caravans a choice of two routes around the perimeter of the Taklamakan desert.

The northern of these two trails struck out across the desert towards Hami, nearly three weeks distant. Then hugging the foothills of the T'ien Shan, or 'celestial mountains', it followed the line of oases dotted along the northern rim of the Taklamakan, passing through Turfan, Karashahr, Kucha,

Aksu, Tumchuq and Kashgar. The southern route threaded its way between the northern ramparts of Tibet and the desert edge, again following the oases, including Miran, Endere, Niya, Keriya, Khotan and Yarkand. From there it turned northwards around the far end of the Taklamakan to rejoin the northern route at Kashgar. From Kashgar the Silk Road continued westwards, starting with a long and perilous ascent of the High Pamir, the 'Roof of the World'. Here it passed out of Chinese territory into what is now Soviet Central Asia, continuing via Khokand, Samarkand, Bokhara, Merv, through Persia and Iraq, to the Mediterranean coast. From there ships carried the merchandise to Rome and Alexandria.

Another branch left the southern route at the far end of the Taklamakan and took in Balkh, today in northern Afghanistan, rejoining the west-bound Silk Road at Merv. An important feeder road, this time to India, also left the southern route at Yarkand, climbed the hazardous Karakoram passes, the 'Gates of India', to the towns of Leh and Srinagar, before beginning the easy ride down to the markets of the Bombay coast. There was yet another branch at the eastern end of the trail known to the Chinese as 'the road of the centre'. After leaving the Jade Gate, this skirted the northern shore of Hedin's 'wandering lake' at Lop-nor and passed through the important oasis town of Lou-lan before rejoining the main northern route.

The Silk Road was entirely dependent for both its existence and survival upon the line of strategically situated oases, each no more than a few days' march from the next, which hugged the perimeter of the Taklamakan. In turn, these depended for their survival upon the glacier-fed rivers flowing down from the vast mountain ranges which form a horse-shoe around three sides of the great desert. As the Silk Road traffic increased, these oases began to rank as important trading centres in their own right and no longer merely as staging and refuelling posts for the caravans passing through them. Over the centuries the larger and more prosperous oases gained sway over the surrounding regions and developed into independent feudal principalities or petty kingdoms.

This made them an increasingly attractive target for Huns and others greedy for a share of the Silk Road profits. Because this trade was beginning to bring considerable wealth to Han China, a ceaseless struggle now ensued between the Chinese and those who threatened this economic artery. Periodically the Chinese would lose control of the Silk Road and it would temporarily fall into the hands of the barbarian tribes or to some independent feudal ruler. The new overlord would then demand tribute for allowing the safe-passage of goods in transit, or simply pillage the caravans, until the Chinese managed to regain control of the route by force of arms, treaty or savage reprisals. Even when the Silk Road was firmly under Chinese control, caravans rarely travelled unarmed or unescorted for there was also always the risk of being attacked by brigands (particularly Tibetans skulking in the Kun Lun) on one of the more lonely stretches of the trail. All this made the journey a costly one, ultimately encouraging the development of sea routes, but in the meantime adding greatly to the price of the goods. Nonetheless, despite these hazards and interruptions, the Silk Road continued to flourish.

*   *   *

The Romans firmly believed that silk grew on trees. As Pliny wrote: 'The Seres are famous for the wool of their forests. They remove the down from leaves with the help of water. . . .' Virgil too described how the 'Chinese comb off leaves their delicate down'. The Chinese, moreover, had no intention of dispelling such myths. Although willing enough to sell their silk, whose secret they themselves had discovered a thousand years before, they were determined to maintain their monopoly of the trade. This they managed to do for a further six centuries, until the first silkworm eggs were smuggled out of China to Byzantium, supposedly by Nestorian monks who, it is said, concealed them in a hollowed-out wooden staff.

The first Romans to encounter this revolutionary new material were the seven legions of Marcus Licinius Crassus. It happened when they were pursuing the Parthians eastwards across the Euphrates in 53 BC. Suddenly, at Carrhae, the fleeing Parthians wheeled their horses, discharging backwards a deadly hail of arrows – the original Parthian shot. It broke the Roman formation, transfixing men two at a time and nailing the hands of others to their shields. Even so the steadfast legionaries might still have held their ground had it not been for what followed. Screeching their barbaric war-cries the Parthians suddenly unfurled great banners of silk in the blazing sunlight in the faces of their already demoralised foes. The Romans, who had never seen anything like it before, turned and fled, leaving some twenty thousand dead behind.

The Parthians, the Romans knew, were a warlike and unsophisticated people, quite incapable of inventing or manufacturing this astonishing material which was 'as light as a cloud' and 'translucent as ice'. But where had they got it from? Roman Intelligence soon found out. It had come from the 'silk people', a mysterious tribe living on the far side of Central Asia. For one of the Emperor Wu-ti's early trade missions, following in the footsteps of Chang Ch'ien, had penetrated as far as Parthia where it had bartered a quantity of silk for an ostrich egg and some conjurers, both of which, according to Chinese annals, had delighted the Son of Heaven.

In no time the Romans had managed to obtain samples of the new material, so alluring to the eye and delicate to the touch, and were eager for more. At the same time it dawned on the Parthians that there were fortunes to be made as middlemen in this new traffic. Before very long the wearing of silken garments by both sexes had become the rage in Rome – to such an extent that in AD 14, fearing that it was becoming an instrument of decadence, Tiberius banned men from wearing it. Pliny wrote disapprovingly of the new see-through garments which 'render women naked' and blamed Roman women for the drain on the nation's economy that their thirst for silk imposed.

But despite official disapproval the trade flourished, and by the year 380 a Roman historian reported that use of silk 'once confined to the nobility, has now spread to all classes without distinction, even to the lowest'. It had become so expensive, however, that it is said to have changed hands for its exact weight in gold, although some scholars have questioned this. Anyway Rome had to pay for it in gold, and as the demand continued to grow this began to have increasingly serious consequences for the economy. Much of the profit was going into the pockets of the middle-men of the now flourishing Silk Road rather than to its weavers, the 'Seres', in far-off China. As early as the first century AD, some enterprising Roman merchants had tried to by-pass the avaricious Parthians by sending agents to explore new routes, and by the second century bales of silk were already beginning to reach Rome via the sea route from India, thus making considerable savings. To try to preserve their valuable monopoly, the Parthian merchants spread abroad terrifying tales of the dangers of the sea journey, and we know that at least one Chinese mission to the West was successfully deterred by these.

But the Silk Road carried much else besides silk. The China-bound caravans were laden with gold and other valuable metals, woollen and linen textiles, ivory, coral, amber, precious stones, asbestos and glass which was not manufactured in China until the fifth century. Caravans leaving China bore furs, ceramics, iron, lacquer, cinnamon bark and rhubarb, and bronze objects such as belt buckles, weapons and mirrors. Not all these goods travelled the whole length of the Silk Road, many of the items being bartered or sold at the oases or towns on the way, where they were replaced with other goods, such as jade, on which a profit could be made further on. Indeed, few if any of the caravans ever travelled the whole way, some nine thousand miles there and back. Chinese merchants were never seen in Rome, nor

Roman traders in Ch'ang-an. For a start, it would not have been in the Parthians' interest to allow this. They had every reason for preventing the recipients of a commodity which passed through their territory from discovering its original cost. Moreover, it is unlikely that any pack animal – and these included camels, horses, mules, donkeys, bullocks and (in the Pamir and Karakoram passes) yaks – could have lasted this distance. The system was for caravans to take on fresh animals at regular staging posts. Even so, thousands of beasts were lost every year on this gruelling trail.

*   *   *

This great trans-Asian highway carried yet another commodity which was to prove far more significant than silk. It was to revolutionise art and thought not only in China but throughout the entire Far East. This was the gentle creed of Buddhism, which preached compassion to all living creatures, an idea born in north-east India in the sixth century BC. King Ashoka's conversion in the third century BC had led to its adoption as the official religion of his empire which then comprised almost all of India. Buddhism first reached China, according to legend, as a result of a dream by the Han Emperor Ming-ti in the first century AD. In this he saw a golden figure floating across the room in a halo of light. Next morning he summoned his wise men and demanded an interpretation. After deliberating among themselves they decided that he must have seen the Buddha (for the new faith had already been heard of in China). An envoy was immediately dispatched to India to find out more about Buddhism and its teaching. After a long absence he returned to the Han court not only bearing sacred Buddhist texts and pictures, but also bringing with him Indian priests who had agreed to explain their religion to the Chinese emperor. Legend or not, it is certain that from about this time onwards missionaries and pilgrims began to travel between China, Central Asia and India. In addition to sacred books and texts they brought with them examples of the art of the new religion, never before seen in China, which was to astonish and delight the aesthetically conscious Chinese.

The penetration of China by Buddhism not only gave the Chinese a new religion but, of central importance to this narrative, it gave to the world an entirely new style of art which has come to be known as Serindian. This term is coined from the two words Seres (China) and India. Logically it should have been simply a fusion of Indian Buddhist art and the art of contemporary Han China. It almost certainly would have been had it not been for the great Himalayan massif which so effectively isolated China from all direct contact with India. But faced by this impenetrable barrier, the gospel of Buddhism together with its art came to China by a round-about route, gradually absorbing other influences on its way. Its real point of departure was not India proper but the Buddhist kingdom of Gandhara, situated in the Peshawar valley region of what is now north-western Pakistan. Here another artistic marriage had already taken place. This was between Indian Buddhist art, imported by the ruling Kushans (descendants of the Yueh-chih) in the first century AD, and Greek art, introduced to the region four hundred years earlier by Alexander the Great.

The most revolutionary product of this Graeco-Buddhist, or Gandharan, school was the depiction of Buddha in human form, for it was the first time that artists anywhere had allowed themselves to show him thus. As a being who had ceased to exist, theologically speaking, by achieving Nirvana and thus escaping the endless cycle of rebirth, he had always been por-trayed before by means of a mystical symbol such as a single footprint, a wheel, a tree, a stupa or Sanskrit characters. But the Gandharan Buddha is shown by sculptors with straight, sharply chiselled nose and brow, classical lips and wavy hair – all Hellenistic influences. Another obvious Mediterranean introduction is the diaphanous, toga-like robe he wears in place of the expected loin cloth. But his eyes are heavy-lidded and protruding, the lobes of the ears elongated, and the oval-shaped face fleshy – all characteristics of Indian iconography. The stretched ear lobes symbolise Buddha's casting away of the heavy, jewelled and worldly earrings that he had worn as a wealthy prince before his conversion to a life of self-denial and teaching.

The first western travellers to reach the Gandhara region from India during the nineteenth century were astonished at the sight of this art, so different from 'the squat, contorted and grimacing forms' of the Indian religious art they were used to. In the rush to obtain examples of it for museums and collections dreadful and irreparable damage was inflicted on temples and sites there. The climate, moreover, had expunged the wall-paintings. For this reason the genius of these Graeco-Buddhist artists is known to us almost entirely through their sculpture, cut from the grey schist of the region.

It was this Gandharan art therefore which, instead of the original Buddhist art of India, travelled over the northern passes with the revolutionary message of Buddhism into Chinese Central Asia. From there it moved slowly eastwards along the newly founded Silk Road, following in the footsteps of missionaries, merchants and returning pilgrims, and gradually absorbing new influences, including those of China. The progress of the new religion through the oases around the Taklamakan desert resulted in a proliferation of monasteries, grottoes and stupas. These received rich patronage from the local ruling families and also from wealthy merchants anxious to invoke protection for their caravans or to give thanks for their safe return. Such gifts and donations were considered to be an act of merit which might enable the donor to escape further rebirth into this world. In many of the wall-paintings discovered in chapels and shrines along the Silk Road their donors or benefactors, both male and female, are depicted (as in Christian Renaissance works) in pious attitudes, and even by name.

As the new faith gathered converts, pilgrims in search of

its original sources, scriptures and holy sites set out westwards along the Silk Road. They crossed over the Karakoram and Pamir passes to Gandhara, by now a second Holy Land to the Buddhist faithful, and thence to India itself. Several of them left detailed descriptions of life in the by now flourishing oasis towns of the Taklamakan desert. One of the earliest of these travellers was Fa-hsien, who journeyed most of the way on foot. He left a vivid account of the Kingdom of Khotan, on the southern arm of the Silk Road, as he saw it in AD 399.

Fa-hsien's highly important travelogue, first translated into English in 1869, records: 'This country is prosperous and happy; its people are well-to-do; they have all received the faith and find their amusement in religious music. The priests number several tens of thousand.' He describes a monastery which deeply impressed him with its splendour, called the King's New Monastery, which had taken eighty years and three reigns to build. 'It is about two hundred and fifty feet in height, ornamentally carved and overlaid with gold and silver, suitably finished with all the seven preciosities. Behind the pagoda there is a Hall of Buddha which is most splendidly decorated. Its beams, pillars, folding doors and windows are all gilt. Besides this, there are apartments for priests, also fitly decorated beyond expression in words.' The seven preciosities he refers to were gold, silver, lapis lazuli, crystal, ruby, emerald and coral.

Fa-hsien, who stayed at Khotan for three months, records that there were fourteen large monasteries in the kingdom 'without counting the smaller ones'. Before the door of every house stood a pagoda, 'the smallest of which would be about twenty feet in height'. The inhabitants, he found, were generous and hospitable. 'They prepare rooms for travelling priests, and place them at the disposal of priests who are their guests, together with anything else they may want.'

He describes a Buddhist festival in which the royal court took part. 'Beginning on the first day of the fourth moon, the main streets inside the city are swept and watered, and the side streets decorated. Over the city gate they stretch a large awning with all kinds of ornamentation, under which the king and queen and court ladies take their places.' A procession followed, led by the priests of the monastery where the king had lodged Fa-hsien. A mile or so outside the city a float had been prepared 'over thirty feet in height, looking like a movable Hall of Buddha, and adorned with the seven preciosities, with streaming pennants and embroidered canopies'. A figure of Buddha was placed on this 'four-wheeled image car', with two attendant Bodhisattvas and devas following behind. 'These are all beautifully carved in gold and silver and are suspended in the air,' Fa-hsien notes. The ceremony proceeded, and when the images had approached to within one hundred paces of the city gate the king removed his cap of state and donned new clothes. 'Walking barefoot and holding flowers and incense in his hands, with attendants on either side, he proceeds out of the gate,' Fa-hsien records. 'On meeting the images, he bows his head down to the ground, scatters the flowers and burns the incense.' The whole ceremony was spread over fourteen days, as each of the major monasteries had its own day for the procession as well as its own Buddha-bearing float. At the end of it the king and queen returned to their palace, and Fa-hsien continued on his pilgrimage via the Kingdom of Kashgar, where the northern and southern branches of the Silk Road reunited.

The Buddhist faith gave birth to a number of different sects or 'schools' in Central Asia. Two of these – the 'Pure Land' and Ch'an (or Zen) sects – eventually reached Japan where they still flourish today. It was ostensibly to search for the long-lost holy sites and relics of the 'Pure Land' sect that the Japanese Count Otani mounted his three expeditions to Chinese Central Asia. These were also to serve, some would maintain, as a cover for something altogether more secular.

But Buddhism was not the only foreign-born religion to reach China via the Silk Road. Two others, together with their art and literature, also established themselves around the Taklamakan. These were Nestorian Christianity and Manichaeism. The Nestorians, who denied that Christ could be simultaneously human and divine, were in the year 432 outlawed in the West at the Council of Ephesus. Many adherents of this sect fled eastwards to the Sassanian empire in what is present-day Iran. From there its merchant-missionaries carried its beliefs, and also its art, into China where the first Nestorian church was consecrated at Ch'ang-an in 638. It reached there via the northern branch of the Silk Road and Nestorian communities grew up in many of the oases. Numerous Nestorian manuscripts were discovered in the early years of this century both at Turfan and also in the walled-up library at Tun-huang. Because so many Nestorians were both merchants as well as missionaries, the creed eventually took root along all the caravan trails of Chinese Central Asia, also reaching southwards into Tibet. Neither the banning of all foreign religions from China in the year 845 under the T'ang Dynasty nor the bloody conquest of Chinese Central Asia by the followers of Mohammed in the eleventh century managed to extinguish it completely. Marco Polo, the Venetian traveller, found many Nestorians at Kashgar and Khotan when he passed by there at the end of the thirteenth century.

Manichaeism, born in Persia in the third century, was based on the opposing 'Two Principles' – Light (the spirit) and Darkness (the flesh). The disciples of Manes were ruthlessly persecuted by the Christians in the West at the end of the fifth century. Fleeing eastwards they eventually reached Chinese Central Asia and China proper where they became firmly established under the Sui (589–618) and T'ang (618–907) dynasties. Until the Germans began to unearth whole Manichaean libraries in the Turfan region, this creed appeared to have no literature, and was known chiefly by the violently hostile writings of its opponents, notably St Augustine.

The Uighur Turks encountered Manichaeism around the

year 762 when they pillaged Ch'ang-an, the T'ang capital, and became converts to it soon after. This outlandish creed, which borrowed from the conflicting beliefs of Christianity and Zoroastrianism, enjoyed its heyday in the tenth century. Thereafter it suffered a decline, eventually disappearing from China. In the western oases of the Silk Road it was violently extinguished and supplanted by the tidal wave of Islam, while further east it was replaced by Buddhism. Proof of the latter can be seen at Karakhoja, at the north-eastern end of the Tak-lamakan, where beautiful Manichaean wall-paintings were discovered by von Le Coq concealed behind later Buddhist ones. However, it was the art of Buddhism which left the most powerful and enduring monuments along the Silk Road, although both Nestorian and Manichaean artists and scribes also left behind them ample evidence of their own remarkable achievements.

The art and civilisation of the Silk Road, in common with that of the rest of China, achieved its greatest glory during the T'ang Dynasty (618–907), which is generally regarded as China's 'golden age'. During the long periods of peace and stability which characterise this brilliant era, prosperity reigned throughout the empire. Its capital Ch'ang-an, the Rome of Asia and point of departure for travellers using the Silk Road, was one of the most splendid and cosmopolitan cities on earth. In the year 742 its population was close on two million (according to the census of 754, China had a total population of fifty-two million, and contained some twenty-five cities with over half a million inhabitants). Ch'ang-an, which had served as the capital of the Chou, Ch'in and Han dynasties, had grown into a metropolis measuring six miles by five, surrounded by a defensive wall. The gates were closed every night at sunset. Foreigners were welcome, and some five thousand of them lived there. Nestorians, Manichaeans, Zoroastrians, Hindus and Jews were freely permitted to build and worship in their own churches, temples and synagogues. An endless procession of travellers passed through the city's gates, including Turks, Iranians, Arabs, Sogdians, Mongolians, Armenians, Indians, Koreans, Malays and Japanese. Every known occupation was represented: merchants, missionaries, pilgrims, envoys, dancers, musicians, scribes, gem dealers, wine sellers, courtiers and courtesans. Dwarfs, gathered from all over Asia, were particularly popular among the Chinese as jugglers, dancers, actors and entertainers. Entire orchestras were brought from distant towns along the Silk Road and from elsewhere in Asia to entertain the imperial court.

A remarkably accurate record of the origins and occupations of these foreigners is found in the terracotta tomb figures discovered around Ch'ang-an (today called Sian) in graves dating from that era. Many of these *ming-chi*, or tomb furnishings, clearly depict foreigners whose race or country of origin scholars have been able to determine from their physiognomy or dress. In addition to the continuous procession of travellers, a cornucopia of luxuries and everyday goods emptied itself daily into the capital's many bazaars. Among the more exotic commodities, many of which arrived via the Silk Road, were cosmetics, rare plants (including the saffron crocus), medicines, aromatics, wines, spices, fragrant woods, books and finely woven rugs. In addition to the 'heavenly horses' from Ferghana, some of which were trained to dance to music, there were peacocks, parrots, falcons, gazelles, hunting dogs, the occasional lion or leopard, and that two-legged marvel (to the Chinese) the ostrich. These latter creatures, two of which reached China in the seventh century, were first known to the Chinese as 'great sparrows' and later as 'camel birds', a description borrowed from the Persians. One of these was reputed to be able to run three hundred Chinese miles in a day, and to digest copper and iron.

Despite their insatiable appetite for these exotic imports, the Chinese nevertheless regarded the foreigners who brought them as *Hu*, or barbarians. Indeed, such was their deeply rooted sense of superiority that they regarded all foreigners with contempt. Gifts from foreign rulers were accepted by the imperial court as tribute and visiting princes and envoys received as vassals.

*   *   *

Under the T'ang Dynasty the Silk Road may have enjoyed a golden age, but the fortunes of both the dynasty and its principal trade route were firmly bound together. When the dynasty began to decline, so too did the civilisation of the Silk Road. It was a process which was to end in the ultimate disappearance, together with their monasteries, temples and works of art, of many flourishing towns. Indeed, so completely did all traces of this once-glorious era vanish that it was not until the nineteenth century that it was rediscovered. The reasons for its disappearance are complex, and the process was spread over several centuries. But there were two principal causes. One was the gradual drying up of the glacier-fed streams which supplied the oasis towns. The other was the sudden arrival, sword in hand, of the proselytising warriors of Islam from far-off Arabia.

Ever since man first moved into the oases of the Taklamakan, back in the mists of Central Asian pre-history, it had been a struggle for survival. Not only against marauding Huns, Tibetans and others, but against death by thirst or starvation. Indeed, survival would have been impossible in this barren landscape but for the streams cascading down from the mountains and spilling into the desert. By skilful use of this water through elaborate irrigation systems the people of the oases had made themselves agriculturally self-sufficient. If, for whatever reason, this irrigation was neglected or interrupted for any length of time then the desert, ever waiting its chance, would take over. The oasis would be abandoned and before long all signs of human habitation would vanish beneath the sands. The town of Niya 'died' in this way at the end of the third century AD, when the Chinese temporarily lost control of the Silk Road. It was soon swallowed up by the Taklamakan.

But however wisely the inhabitants conserved and controlled their water supplies, the processes of geography were working remorselessly against them. High above them in the mountains, the glaciers which fed the streams bringing them life were shrinking. This process, which had begun at the end of the Ice Age, resulted in a steadily diminishing flow of water throughout the Tarim basin. Lou-lan, near Lop-nor, was once the terminal oasis of the Konche river, which was still flowing at the beginning of the fourth century. By the end of the third century, however, the oasis ceased to be occupied as the river gradually receded. Rivers also sometimes changed course or silted up, and sites had to be abandoned. One such oasis was Yotkan, the original site of ancient Khotan, which today lies buried under alluvium.

But the ultimate reasons for the disappearance of the Buddhist civilisation from the Silk Road were the decline and eventual collapse of the T'ang Dynasty, the victories of the Arabs to the west and the final conversion of the whole Taklamakan region to Islam. The advance of this new religion along the Silk Road spelled the death of figurative art – the portrayal of the human form – for this was anathema to Moslems. Many statues and wall-paintings were damaged or destroyed by these iconoclasts, while temples and stupas were left to crumble and vanish beneath the sand. By the fifteenth century, Islam had become the religion of the entire Taklamakan region. Under the Ming Dynasty (1368–1644) the Silk Road was finally abandoned when China shut herself off from all contact with the West, and this led to the further isolation and decline of the area.

In face of all this, only the strongest and best-watered of the oases survived, and they with a new religion possessing its own art and architecture. The others, with their rich and forgotten secrets, lay buried beneath the sands of the Taklamakan, where they were to remain undisturbed for so many centuries.

2. Lost Cities of the Taklamakan

Among the oasis dwellers of the Taklamakan, strange legends of ancient towns lying buried beneath the sands had been passed down from grandfather to grandson for as long as anyone could remember. Hoards of gold, silver and other treasures, it was said, lay among the dunes ready for the taking by anyone with nerve enough to face the natural and super- natural terrors of the desert. In 1875, a Kirghiz tribesman who had once been a shepherd near the salt marshes around Lop- nor left a vivid account of one such lost city which he claimed to have seen from a distance.

The walls are seen rising above the reeds in which the city is concealed [he recounted]. I have not been inside the city but I have seen its walls distinctly from the sandy ridges in the vicinity. I was afraid to go amongst the ruins because of the bogs around and the venomous insects and snakes in the reeds.... Besides, it is a notorious fact that people who do go among the ruins almost always die, because they cannot resist the temptation to steal the gold and precious things stored there.... You may doubt it, but everybody here knows what I say is true, and there are hundreds of Kalmaks who have gone to the temple in the midst of these ruins to worship the god there.... Ranged on shelves all around the figure are precious stones and pearls of great size and brilliancy, and innumerable *yambs*, or ingots of gold and silver. Nobody has the power to take away any- thing from here. This is all well known to the people of Lop.

His account, published in an official Indian Government report, goes on to recount what befell one Kalmak tribesman who visited the city to worship but succumbed to temptation, secreting two gold ingots in his clothing. He had not gone far when he was suddenly overcome by great weariness and fell asleep. When he awoke the treasures were missing. Returning to the temple for more, he found to his amazement that the ingots he had taken were back in their place. He was so frightened, the tale goes, that he prostrated himself before the god and begged forgiveness. To his relief the figure smiled, but warned him against such sacrilege in future.

Other legends tell how these cities came to perish in the first place, usually as a punishment for the sins of their inhabitants. The sixteenth-century Moslem historian Mirza Haidar relates how such a fate befell the town of Katak, near Lopnor, when only the mullah and muezzin were allowed, thanks to their piety, to escape the engulfing sands. While the muezzin was calling prayers for the last time it started to rain sand, and before long the entire town, except for the mosque, slowly vanished from sight. The terrified muezzin, looking down from the top of his minaret, noticed that the ground around was rapidly rising towards him. Hurriedly completing his prayers, he leapt the few remaining feet onto the sand. Then he and the mullah took to their heels, agreeing that it was wise 'to keep at a distance from the wrath of God'. The city of Katak 'is to this day buried in sand', Mirza Haidar adds.

Some of these Sodom and Gomorrah stories date from much earlier times, when Buddhism was still flourishing along the Silk Road. In the seventh century the great Buddhist pilgrim-explorer Hsuan-tsang, later to be adopted by Sir Aurel Stein as his patron saint, told of another town which several centuries before had been buried in a sandstorm because its inhabitants had apparently neglected their religious duties. Hsuan-tsang relates that a great wind arose. 'Then on the seventh day in the evening, just after the division of the night, it rained sand and earth.' Before long the entire town, which he called Ho-lo-lo Kia, lay beneath a huge mound of sand. Hsuan-tsang goes on: 'The kings of neighbouring countries, and persons in power from distant spots, have many times wished to excavate the mound and take away the precious things buried there. But as soon as they have arrived at the borders of the place, a furious wind has sprung up, dark clouds have gathered together from the four quarters of heaven, and they have become lost.' Altogether, it was said, some three hundred towns lay buried beneath the barren sands of the Taklamakan.

But one neighbouring king was not to be deterred by Hsuan-tsang's 'furious wind', or any other of the desert's terrors, in his determination to get at the treasures of these lost cities. Ney Elias, the great Asiatic scholar and traveller, writing in 1895, refers to what he describes as 'perhaps the only systematic exploitation of the ancient sites ever undertaken'. This was carried out with slave labour by the Amir of Kashgar, the tyrannical Mirza Aba Bakr (who did in fact come to a bad end – he was beheaded in his sleep). A vivid account of the Amir's treasure-hunting in the Khotan region is given us by Mirza Haidar, who lived about the same time. Elias, in his introduction to a translation of this work, concludes: 'We may infer that nearly everything of intrinsic value was brought to light, while much that was of antiquarian interest was destroyed, so that when, at some future time, civilised explorers come to investigate the ruins and find little to reward their labours, they may feel indebted to the cupidity of Mirza Aba Bakr for their disappointment.'

That was written only five years before Stein set out across the snowy Karakoram on the first of his three great raids into the Taklamakan – expeditions destined to disprove dramatically that prediction. Elias was never to know this, for he died in 1897 while Stein was still planning his first journey.

Although in Ney Elias's day no European traveller had yet excavated any of these lost cities, for some years scholars in the West had been aware of their probable existence. The first real evidence, as opposed to mere legend, had been produced in 1865 by a native traveller. He was a 'moonshee', or Indian clerk, named Mohamed-i-Hameed, who had been sent by the British on a secret mission across the Karakoram to explore the oases of the Taklamakan, a region then virtually unknown. For the powers-that-be in Calcutta and London considered it too hazardous, both politically and personally, to dispatch British officers, even in disguise, into this unpoliced Chinese backwater between the frontiers of Russia and India. On the other hand, ever concerned about the threat posed to India by Tsarist Russia, they were anxious to possess accurate surveys of the routes likely to be taken across this no-man's-land by an invading army.

In the 1860s, Captain T. G. Montgomerie of the Survey of India, the body responsible for mapping the whole of British India and beyond, had hit upon a brilliant solution – the use of 'moonshees'. He explained the idea in a paper read to the Royal Geographical Society in London on May 14, 1866. 'While I was in Ladakh,' he told his audience, 'I noticed that natives of India passed freely backwards and forwards between Ladakh and Yarkand, and it consequently occurred to me that it might be possible to make the exploration by their means. If a sharp enough man could be found he would have no difficulty in carrying a few small instruments amongst his merchandise and with their aid I thought good service might be rendered to geography.'

The Lieutenant-Governor of the Punjab agreed to finance a one-man, native expedition into Chinese Central Asia, and Mohamed-i-Hameed, who already had some experience of route surveying, was chosen. He was given further training, issued with clandestine surveying instruments specially designed for the purpose, and dispatched to Yarkand. In place of the usual stand for his prismatic compass he was provided with an ordinary spiked staff like those often carried by Himalayan travellers. The head, however, was made rather larger than usual and cut off flat so that his compass could be placed on top of it. 'By this means,' Montgomerie explained, 'a steady observation could be readily secured without much trouble and in a way little likely to excite suspicion.' The moonshee's other instruments, which included a small tin lantern for reading the sextant at night and a copper jug and oil lamp for boiling a thermometer (to calculate altitudes), were all of the smallest size procurable. Detection, as both the moonshee and his spy-masters knew only too well, would mean almost certain death at the hands of what Montgomerie called 'the Khirgiz hordes who infest that road'. By 'that road' he meant the grim, skeleton-strewn trail from Ladakh, across the Karakoram to Yarkand in Chinese Turkestan.

Mohamed-i-Hameed left Kashmir for Ladakh, the last outpost of British influence, on June 12, 1863, proceeding thence by caravan across what Montgomerie described as 'the most elevated country in the world' to Yarkand, which he reached some three and a half months later. He lived there for six months, all the time making secret observations with his instruments for Montgomerie and noting down everything he saw and heard. Then, towards the end of March 1864, he was warned by a Moslem friend that Chinese officials had become suspicious of his activities and were making enquiries about him. Sending his incriminating equipment on ahead of him, the moonshee then slipped away from Yarkand without detection and headed back through the Karakoram passes to Ladakh.

Perhaps as a result of hardships suffered on this journey, the moonshee fell ill, together with a travelling companion. Both men died, almost within sight of home. It was thought at first that they had been murdered, possibly by Chinese agents, but investigations by one of Montgomerie's colleagues, Civil-Assistant William Johnson, who happened to be surveying in this region at the time, finally ruled this suspicion out. Although some of the moonshee's more saleable possessions were found to have disappeared, the precious notes he had kept so carefully and conscientiously throughout his secret mission were recovered by Johnson and passed to Montgomerie.

The Survey of India was principally concerned with the topographical intelligence contained in the moonshee's notes, as well as with his observations on the movements of the Russians in the area. However, Montgomerie also came upon an intriguing note which provided the first confirmation from a reliable source of what had previously been regarded as nothing more than fanciful legend.

Admittedly the details are rather scanty, but then the moonshee's business was not archaeology. 'Khotan, the old capital of the province, was long ago swallowed up by the sand,' reported Montgomerie, quoting from the moonshee's notebook. According to the local inhabitants, however, after sandstorms some of the ancient houses were uncovered and 'they often succeed in digging out various articles that have been buried'. The moonshee deduced from this that 'it would appear as if the city had been buried suddenly before the inhabitants had time to remove their property....' Devoid of the usual embellishments – divine retribution, priceless treasures, protecting spirits and the like – the moonshee's account, albeit hearsay, somehow rang true.

The first European explorer to run the gauntlet of the murderous Khirgiz and to reach the Taklamakan from Indian territory was the surveyor William Johnson who had investigated Mohamed-i-Hameed's death just one year before. Moreover, he actually visited a sand-entombed city near Khotan, if only briefly, and returned to India convinced of the existence of others. His chance to cross into Chinese Turkestan came unexpectedly one day when he was busy mapping the western end of the Kun Lun mountains, the range forming the northern bastion of Tibet. Trying to get a glimpse of the mysterious Taklamakan Desert, Johnson, a formidable mountaineer, had scaled three high peaks, known to the Indian Survey simply as E 57, E 58 and E 61. 'But I could not get a view of any of the important towns of Khotan which

I was so anxious to see,' he recounted later in a paper addressed to the Royal Geographical Society in London. Disappointed, he returned to Leh, the capital of Ladakh. However, there a surprise was in store for him. 'A native of Central Asia presented me with a letter from the Khan Badsha of Khotan inviting me to enter his territory,' he related. Its bearer explained to him that the Khan, having learned of his presence in the region the previous season, had sent runners to invite him to visit Khotan, but they had failed to find him.

Johnson knew full well that to make such a politically sensitive journey beyond India's frontiers required approval at the very highest level in Calcutta. He also knew that it would take weeks to obtain a reply to such a request, and that the answer would almost certainly be no. The Khan, in his note, gave an assurance that the Englishman would be allowed to return to Ladakh as soon as he wished, and local traders who knew the country and its ruler were reassuring on this point. Justifying his decision afterwards, Johnson said that he saw the Khan's invitation as an opportunity to gather valuable intelligence on this *terra incognita*, and particularly on the activities of the Russians in the area.

Crossing the Kun Lun by a previously unknown pass shown him by his Khotanese escort, he reached Khotan in safety, where he was comfortably housed in an old Chinese fort in which the Khan himself also lived. There he had almost daily audiences with the eighty-year-old ruler, of whom he declared: 'He is reported to be very ill-tempered and very strict in his government. I must however admit that he showed me much kindness while in his country and kept all his promises, with the exception of not allowing me to leave after a stay of four days, as had been agreed upon.' The reason behind this apparent duplicity, it transpired, was rather pathetic. The Khan was planning to hold him hostage, albeit in comfort, in an attempt to force the British Government to send him troops and arms with which to hold back the Russians, whom he greatly feared, and who, according to Johnson, 'are daily approaching towards Yarkand and Khotan'.

During his stay in Khotan Johnson managed to gather a great deal of political and military intelligence. But he was also able to add considerably to the information about sand-buried cities that the luckless Mohamed-i-Hameed had obtained. Johnson reported: 'At a distance of six miles to the north-east of Ilchi is the great desert of Taklamakan which, with its shifting sands that move along in vast billows over-powering everything, is said to have buried 360 cities in the space of 24 hours.' While he was in the Khotan area quantities of tea bricks, 'believed by the natives to be of great age', were dug from one of the sand-entombed cities, and he managed to obtain one of these. This tea, despite its age, was in great demand among local people, particularly as supplies from China had dried up. Johnson also heard that gold coins 'weighing four pounds', as well as other precious objects, had been dug from the ruins. Johnson reported that the location of the buried cities was known 'only to a few persons who keep it secret in order to enrich themselves'. He tells us, how-ever – though only in passing – that he was able to visit 'the site of an old city near Urankash, from which brick tea is exhumed'. But Johnson was a professional surveyor not an antiquarian and, tantalisingly, this is the only information he gives us.

He was finally allowed by the Khan to leave Khotan and return home. But although his journey was hailed by the Royal Geographical Society as a triumph, all he received from the Survey of India was an official rebuke for crossing into Khotan without permission from his superiors. Affronted, Johnson resigned from the Survey and accepted the governor-ship of Ladakh at three times his previous salary. Not many years later he was the victim of an assassin's knife.

Despite growing evidence that more than a grain of truth might now lie behind the legends of fabulous cities buried under the Taklamakan, antiquarians had still not begun to

show any serious interest in this region. What scientific interest there was confined itself to the geographical, geological
and strategical aspects of this Central Asian backwater. For
one thing European archaeologists were fully occupied with
Greece, Palestine, Mesopotamia and Egypt, where spectacular discoveries were being made. For another, no one dreamed
that a lost Buddhist world might lie in that waterless tract
beyond the Karakoram. If anything, any ruins there would
be Islamic. Lastly, as has been seen, access to the region was
fraught with difficulties and perils. Already several European
travellers had met with violent ends in the lonely passes leading to it.

One man, however, was fascinated by the thought of what
might lie hidden beneath the sands of the Taklamakan. He
was a senior Punjab civil servant and authority on Central
Asia, Sir Douglas Forsyth. In 1870, only five years after Johnson's trail-blazing journey, Forsyth led a mission to Yarkand
aimed at establishing friendly relations with Yakub Beg, a remarkable oriental adventurer who by 1866 had seized control
of much of Chinese Turkestan, and whom some saw as the
man to stem the tide of Russian expansion. The mission
proved a failure as Yakub Beg was away from his capital and
showed no sign of returning. Three years later Forsyth was
once again sent to try to make contact with him, this time
with a far larger expedition and rather more success. He was
fortunate in having the assistance of his old friend Johnson,
the surveyor-turned-Governor, to see his caravan safely
across the perilous Karakoram. Forsyth's paper, addressed to
the Royal Geographical Society in London on his return,
bears witness to his close interest in the dead cities of the Taklamakan. It was entitled 'On the Buried Cities in the Shifting
Sands of the Great Desert of Gobi'. (At that time, as few
people had ever heard of the Taklamakan, the name *Gobi* was
frequently used to describe both deserts.)

'Among the many objects of interest which attracted our
attention during the late mission to Kashgar,' he wrote, 'not

the least interesting was an inquiry regarding the shifting sands of the Great Desert of Gobi and the reported existence of ancient cities which had been buried in the sands ages ago, and which are now gradually coming to light.' Forsyth continued: 'On the occasion of my first mission to Yarkand in 1870 we were unable to gather much information. . . . On my second visit in 1873 I determined to make more searching inquiries, and for this purpose I endeavoured to collate all the information obtainable from published works.'

While there he noticed, as Johnson had seven years earlier, the 'black bricks of tea, old and musty, exposed for sale in the bazaar', which he was told had been dug up near Khotan. Forsyth was determined to locate one of these mysterious cities himself and see what he could find there. As he was unable to obtain permission from the local Moslem authorities to visit Khotan, he decided to take a leaf from Montgomerie's book and dispatch two of the native 'pundits' accompanying his mission with instructions to discover what they could about the entombed cities around Khotan. The first returned with two figurines from a buried city near Keriya, to the east of Khotan. One of these Forsyth recognised as depicting Buddha, while the other was a clay figure of Hunooman, the monkey-god. Forsyth tells us: 'These had only just been found, and it was fortunate that they soon fell into my pundit's hands, for the pious zeal of a Mahommedan iconoclast would have consigned them to speedy destruction.' The second man brought back 'some gold finger rings and nose rings . . . also some coins, of which the most remarkable is an iron one, apparently of Hermaeus, the last Greek king of Bactria in the first century BC, and several gold coins of the reign of Constans II and Pognatus, Justinus, Antimachus and Theodosius.' Forsyth adds in a footnote to his paper that scholars had since dated the figure of Buddha to around the tenth century, suggesting that the site had been engulfed by the desert some eight hundred years before.

His two 'pundits' reported to him that other ancient finds

had come to light in the Khotan region, including a gold orna-
ment representing a cow, and a gold vase weighing some sixteen pounds. This was only hearsay, but the figure of Buddha,
the monkey-god and the coins were real enough and appear
to be the first antiquities from the lost world of the Taklamakan to fall into European hands. As such, they represent a
small milestone in Central Asian studies.

Within a year or two, Russian travellers thrusting down
from the north also began to report finding abandoned cities
on the fringes of the Taklamakan. However, being botanists,
zoologists, cartographers and geologists with more urgent
tasks in mind, none stopped to dig. One of them, Colonel
Nikolai Prejevalsky, Russia's greatest Central Asian explorer,
stumbled upon various sand-buried or long-abandoned sites
during his Lop-nor expedition of 1876–7 and on his subsequent travels in the region. In 1879, after dodging Chinese
frontier guards, the Russian botanist Albert Regel discovered
a huge walled city near Turfan whose ruins were later identified as those of the ancient Uighur capital of Karakhoja. He
reported finding 'Buddhist idols', but he had no time to
explore further as the Chinese hustled him back to Russia.
That same year a Hungarian geological expedition entered the
great Buddhist cave temples at Tun-huang but, not being
antiquarians, went on their way.

Perhaps the first visitor to Chinese Turkestan to whom the
idea of digging occurred, although he did not attempt it himself, was Sir Francis (then Captain) Younghusband. In his
book *The Heart of a Continent*, an account of his race across
China with Colonel Bell in 1887, he tells how he engaged a
Pathan named Rahmat-ula-Khan whose life's ambition it was
to visit England. To achieve this he was proposing to lead
a string of rare white camels to London. Having visited the
Calcutta zoo, and noted the interest displayed in unfamiliar
animals, he was convinced that his camels would cause a
sensation in London. However, Younghusband suggested
another idea.

'I told him that if he would search about among the old ruined cities of this country and those buried by the sand, he might find old ornaments and books for which large sums of money would be given him in England.' Before they parted, Younghusband wrote letters of introduction on his behalf to the directors of the British Museum and those at Calcutta and Bombay.

Although archaeologists today would deplore such advice, nonetheless Younghusband showed remarkable far-sightedness in making this suggestion, particularly with his mention of old books. Indeed it is mystifying where he obtained the idea. For this was three full years before the discovery of the famous Bower manuscript which was to send a shock-wave through the world of Indian scholarship, pointing to the existence of a forgotten Buddhist civilisation awaiting excavation in China's back of beyond.

3. The Great Manuscript Race

Rahmat-ula-Khan, Younghusband's Pathan guide, appears either to have ignored his advice or to have dug in the wrong places. For nowhere in the record of early archaeological discoveries in the Taklamakan is there any reference to him, although other native treasure-hunters are named as the sources of particular finds. Writing some fifty years after their journey, Younghusband, by then a celebrated figure, notes that his letters of introduction were never used. It is possible that in a region where life was so cheap, the Pathan did not live long enough to make use of them. Anyway, within a year or two, others were busy with their spades and very soon a series of remarkable finds, including manuscripts written in previously unknown languages, began to emerge from the barren desert.

The first of these early discoveries (and the most important as it turned out) was made inadvertently in 1889 by a party of native treasure-hunters who decided to tunnel their way into a mysterious, dome-like tower near Kucha, south of the T'ien Shan on the northern arm of the old Silk Road. For it was believed locally that the ruined building contained treasure.

Once inside the tower (probably an old Buddhist stupa, or tomb) the intruders found themselves in a large room in the centre of which were heaped quantities of old papers. As their eyes became accustomed to the dark they also found themselves gazing on the mummified corpses of several animals, including a cow, propped up as though on guard. When touched these crumbled to dust. Written on one wall in characters they had never seen before was a mysterious inscription. Although disappointed at not finding the treasure they had hoped for, they carried the papers to the house of the local Qazi, or Moslem judge, in a basket. There, two days later, they were examined by a Haji (one who has been to Mecca) named Ghulam Qadir. Despite not being able to read a word of any of them, he decided to purchase several.

At the same time, combing the region for the murderer of a young Scottish traveller was an Indian army intelligence officer, Lieutenant (later Major-General Sir Hamilton) Bower. The dead man was Andrew Dalgleish, who had already made a name for himself as a Central Asian explorer. For no apparent reason he had been treacherously shot and then hacked to death on a lonely pass by a huge Afghan called Daud Mohammed from Yarkand. Lieutenant Bower (who died only in 1940) happened to be in the region at the time, apparently conducting a clandestine survey under cover of a shooting expedition. Receiving orders from the Indian Government to track down the killer and bring him to justice, Bower set about organising a private intelligence service with tentacles reaching into Afghanistan, China and Russia. (Eventually two of his agents tracked down Daud Mohammed in Samarkand, coming face to face with him in the bazaar.) Meanwhile Bower himself had taken up the murder trail along the old Silk Road. In pursuit of his quarry he eventually reached the oasis of Kucha, which lies to the south of the T'ien Shan. There he heard of the manuscripts in the possession of Haji Ghulam Qadir. One of these, consisting of fifty-one birch-bark leaves, he bought and dispatched to Calcutta to the Asiatic Society of Bengal. At first the pages were judged to be unintelligible. However, they were finally deciphered by an Anglo-German orientalist, Dr Augustus Rudolf Hoernle. Consisting of seven distinct but incomplete texts, and written in Sanskrit using the Brahmi alphabet, the manuscript dealt largely with medicine and necromancy. Dating from around the fifth century, and probably written by Indian Buddhist monks, it proved to be one of the oldest written works to survive anywhere, older than anything that had come to light in India. It was only because of the extreme dryness of the Taklamakan region, whose climate can be likened to that of Egypt, that it had survived.

The importance of the find is best summed up by Hoernle himself, who declared that 'the discovery of the Bower manuscript and its publication in Calcutta started the whole modern movement of the archaeological exploration of Eastern Turkestan'. Another scholar, writing in the *Journal of the Royal Asiatic Society*, declared, with some exaggeration, that as a consequence of Lieutenant Bower's find and Hoernle's publication: 'All scientific Europe set forth on the quest for further antiquities in this region.'

Meanwhile, the rest of the Kucha manuscripts acquired from the treasure-hunters by Haji Ghulam Qadir were beginning to find their way by tortuous routes into Hoernle's hands. After Bower's purchase, the Haji had sent all those he had left to his younger brother in Yarkand, who took them the following year across the Karakoram to Leh. There some of them were acquired by a Moravian missionary named Weber who passed them to Hoernle. The rest then continued on their way to India with the Haji's brother, who left them there with a friend for four years. On his next visit he collected them and brought them back to Kashgar where he presented them to George Macartney, the British representative. In his turn, Macartney dispatched them back across the Karakoram – their third such crossing – to Simla, from where they too were forwarded to Hoernle in Calcutta. Thus in 1896, some seven years after their discovery in the ruined stupa, all three portions of the Haji's collection – now known to scholars as the Bower, Weber and Macartney manuscripts – were reunited.

But that still left those found in the stupa which had not been bought by the Haji. What had happened to them? Ever on the lookout for antiquities, the Russian consul in Kashgar, Nikolai Petrovsky, acquired these over the next few years. He was to keep scholars in St Petersburg supplied with a constant flow of manuscripts and other antiquities from the Silk Road until his retirement in 1903, some of which can be seen today in the Hermitage.

Aware of Petrovsky's successful antiquarian activities, pursued entirely through native dealers, Hoernle pressed the Government of India to give active support to the purchase of antiquities by its own representatives in Central Asia. As a result, the political agents in Srinagar, Gilgit, Chitral, Leh, Khorassan and Meshed – not forgetting Macartney in Kashgar – were alerted in August 1893 to look out for and acquire suitable items which were to be forwarded to Hoernle in Calcutta. Before long Hoernle was able to report: 'In response to these instructions a large number of Central Asian antiquities have already been secured, forming a very respectable British Collection, to which additions are still being made.' He could not restrain himself from adding: 'To me personally it is a source of much satisfaction to have thus been the means of initiating the movement.' It was a satisfaction which was to prove short-lived.

But competition for the manuscripts and antiquities of Central Asia was not limited to the British and Russians. In 1890, the year that the Bower manuscript reached Hoernle, two Frenchmen – a cartographer named Dutreuil de Rhins, and an orientalist called Fernand Grenard – set out on a French Government mission to Chinese Turkestan and Tibet. It was destined to last three years, involve them in appalling hardship, and to end in tragedy for Dutreuil de Rhins. While mainly concerned with map-making and other scientific work, the two explorers managed also to acquire a collection of antiquities. These included the terracotta figures of a Bactrian camel and a man's moustached head – and at least one important manuscript. This, written in ancient Indian characters on birch-bark, was only slightly later in date than the Bower manuscript, although Grenard claimed it to be much earlier. It was identified by scholars in Paris as part of the Dhammapada, a Buddhist sacred text.

This manuscript, together with all their other finds, had

nearly been lost when, in June 1893, the party was ambushed in Tibet by hostile tribesmen. In the ensuing gun battle Dutreuil de Rhins was mortally wounded in the stomach. While Grenard was trying to improvise a litter for his wounded leader, their attackers carried off the dying man and threw him into a river some seven miles away. They also plundered the expedition's baggage, dividing the loot and throwing away all field notes, films, instruments and antiquities. Grenard, who later had to face accusations that the tragedy was the result of their antagonising the local inhabitants, managed to escape with his life and eventually recovered some of their possessions, including the manuscript. On being examined in Paris, this was found to be incomplete. Soon after, however, other fragments of the same manuscript turned up in St Petersburg. These had been obtained by Petrovsky, though exactly how and from whom is not clear.

★   ★   ★

By the year 1899, the British Collection in Calcutta had reached sufficient size for Dr Hoernle to feel justified in issuing a report on its progress. The first part of the report entitled 'A Collection of Antiquities from Central Asia', was published as an extra number of the *Journal of the Asiatic Society of Bengal*. In it Hoernle listed with meticulous care, and in order of their acquisition, each consignment of manuscripts and other antiquities to reach him following the arrival of the Bower Manuscript nine years earlier.

Some of the manuscripts and block-printed books in Hoernle's possession were written in previously unknown languages but in known scripts. These were gradually deciphered by Hoernle and other philologists, and added to the canon of extinct languages. Others, however, were a puzzle to scholars as even the scripts in which they were written were unknown. Much time was spent by Hoernle and other orientalists in trying to analyse these, but without success.

Meanwhile, from Kashgar, Leh, Srinagar and elsewhere

Hoernle's men were enthusiastically dispatching to him their latest purchases as the dealers and treasure-hunters kept them supplied. A typical entry from the list of acquisitions in the Hoernle report reads: 'From Mr. G. Macartney, a collection of miscellaneous antiquities procured from Khotan and the Taklamakan consisting of (a) thirteen books, (b) pottery, (c) coins, (d) sundry objects. Seven books and the antiques were purchased by Mr. Macartney in Khotan for Rs. 95; the remaining six books were purchased by him from Badrudin [a native dealer]. The total cost was Rs. 150. The collection was received by me early in November 1897.' He singles out Macartney in Kashgar for particular praise among his suppliers, explaining that due to his close proximity to the Silk Road sites he had proved 'the most successful in his contributions to the collection'. Hoernle adds, with a pride understandable in a government employee, that the objects in the collection had been obtained for 'often trifling amounts of money'.

Most of the finds, Hoernle reported, came from sand-buried sites around Khotan. Fifteen such sites, he said, were believed to exist at various distances from Khotan, ranging from five to one hundred and fifty miles, although the existence of only two had been verified by European visitors. 'For the remainder,' Hoernle added, 'we have only the information given by native treasure-seekers.' Principal among these, he noted, was a certain Islam Akhun of Khotan. It was a name that Hoernle would have good cause to remember.

Islam Akhun's often highly coloured accounts of his forays into the Taklamakan in search of antiquities were faithfully taken down from him by Macartney and passed to Hoernle together with the finds. This enterprising native treasure-hunter had other customers as well, and numbers of his discoveries found their way between 1895 and 1898 into the great public collections in London, Paris and St Petersburg, where scholars scratched their heads over those in 'unknown characters'.

A typical account of one of Islam Akhun's finds published by Hoernle relates how the treasure-seeker came upon an old house half buried in the sand. 'As the door was not visible,' Hoernle tells us, 'a hole was made in one of the exposed sides. This done, Takhdash, one of Islam Akhun's companions, crept in and found himself in a small room of about three yards square. This room was considerably filled with sand, so much so that it was impossible for a person to stand up in it without his head touching the ceiling. Takhdash found the books while digging in the sand. There were many other books, but these were in such a dilapidated condition that they crumbled to pieces on being handled.' Perhaps in answer to a question from Macartney which he found too searching for comfort, Islam Akhun explained that he had been 'too frightened to inspect the interior of the house himself'.

To this Hoernle appended a warning which he would have done well to heed himself. 'This account, of course, must be taken *quantum valeat*,' he wrote, adding: 'But there is nothing intrinsically improbable in the local descriptions, and the distances fairly agree with those given of the same places at other times.' Hoernle explained away one discrepancy involving distances which he had spotted by observing that: 'Natives of Turkestan, as Mr. Backlund [a Swedish missionary in Kashgar] informs me, are very untrustworthy in their estimates of distances.'

Other sites which Akhun told Macartney he had found in the Taklamakan, and from which he had acquired manuscripts and block-printed books, included Quarā Qöl Mazār where he stumbled on 'an immense graveyard in ruins, about 10 miles long' which Hoernle helpfully suggested might well be Buddhist. Then there was Yābū Qūm, where he had found manuscripts among the bones in an old coffin, and whose name (it means 'load-ponies sands') Backlund speculated to Hoernle might mark the place where a caravan had once perished. A third site reported by Akhun was at a place he called Qarā Yāntāq where he said he had found a human skull using a bag containing a manuscript as a 'pillow'.

While pointing out that these sites might not be the real sources of Islam Akhun's finds (Hoernle suspected that somewhere the treasure-hunters had stumbled on an ancient library they wished to keep secret), he was nonetheless ready to believe in their great age. Observing that the dry Taklamakan sand was a natural preservative, he added: 'There is, therefore, nothing intrinsically improbable in the claim of the manuscripts and xylographs contained in the British Collection to be of very great antiquity.'

Hoernle, it must be said in fairness, did not duck the possibility of there being forgeries among the manuscripts and block-printed books in the British Collection. In fact, he recounted in his report an amazingly cautionary tale, but then doggedly rejected it. In a section of the report headed 'The Question of Genuineness', Hoernle observed: 'Considering the abundance of the block-prints and the mystery of their scripts, it is not surprising that the suspicion of forgery should suggest itself. It suggested itself to me at an early stage of my acquaintance with the Khotanese books, and I am informed that it has also suggested itself to some of the British Museum authorities and others.' He went on to quote a letter he had received from the Swedish missionary Backlund shortly before writing his report.

Backlund related how after purchasing three old books from Islam Akhun, who said he had dug them up from beneath a hollow tree, one of his own servants had approached him. 'Sahib,' the native had begun, 'I want to tell you that these books are not so old as they are pretended to be. As I know how they are prepared, I wish to inform you of it. When I lived in Khotan I wished very much to enter into the business, but was always shut out and could even get no information about the books. At last I consulted my mother about it and she advised me to try to find out from a boy with whom I was on very intimate terms, and who was the son of the headman of the business. So one day I asked him how they got these books, and he plainly told me that his father had the blocks prepared by a cotton printer.'

As though anticipating Hoernle's thought, Backlund added: 'Now it is evident that the servant might have said all this from jealousy only, but I am determined to examine the books with more critical eyes than before.' He then drew attention to several points which struck him as suspicious. He noticed, for example, that the books he had just bought from Akhun had a certain crispness or freshness and bore none of the signs of wear and tear normally associated with everyday use. He also noticed that the paper on which they were printed was 'exactly of the same kind as prepared in Khotan in the present day', and 'though very ill-treated (burnt and smoky) is still strong, almost as if it were new'. He further pointed out that the corners of the books 'are quite square (not round as they usually are in old books) and the edges recently cut, though in such a manner as to make them look old'.

But Hoernle painstakingly refuted all Backlund's points – to his own satisfaction at least – after weighing up the evidence on both sides. Reading his report today, it is hard to escape the conclusion that his wish to believe in the authenticity of these particular books and manuscripts had overriden his critical judgement. Again and again he comes down firmly on the wrong side of the fence. The worst that he seems willing to believe is that a supply of genuine old wood-blocks had been discovered by the treasure-hunters and that these were occasionally used to produce 'reprints' of old books.

His verdict was quite categoric: 'To sum up,' he wrote, 'the conclusion to which with the present information I have come to is that the scripts are genuine, and that most, if not all, of the block-prints in the Collection also are genuine antiquities; and that if any are forgeries they can only be duplicates of others which are genuine....'

Meanwhile, other important discoveries (about which there could be no such doubts) were beginning to come to light in the Gobi–Taklamakan region. Among the most significant were those of a Russian scholar, Dmitri Klementz. In 1898 he was sent by the Academy of Sciences in St Petersburg with the specific aim of investigating some ancient and mysterious ruins which Russian travellers had reported seeing around the oasis of Turfan, on the edge of the Gobi. It was the first ever purely archaeological expedition to visit Chinese Central Asia. In addition to confirming the existence of the ruins, some of which he photographed, Klementz brought back manuscripts and also fragments of Buddhist wall-paintings. His discoveries, as we shall see, were within a few years to lead to a flurry of archaeological activity in this region and, inadvertently, to one of the great tragedies of art history.

But, important as his finds were to prove, Klementz was not destined to be the first to uncover the long-lost secrets of the Silk Road. For, travelling eastwards across the Pamir, a new and remarkable figure had already entered the Central Asian arena, determined to discover the truth about the cities filled with treasure said to lie far out in the Taklamakan.

4. Sven Hedin – the Pathfinder

This brilliant figure, who was to shoot like a meteorite across the Central Asian scene, was a young and virtually unknown Swede called Sven Hedin. Bookish, bespectacled (at times he was threatened with almost total blindness) and small in stature, he was nonetheless destined to become one of the world's great explorers. His mild appearance concealed a man of extraordinary determination, physical strength and ambition, not to say occasional recklessness. A ruthless leader, he drove both himself and his men – a number to their death – without mercy. Yet he had a horror of killing animals, 'of extinguishing a flame I could not light again', as he put it. For his achievements during half a century of Central Asiatic travel he was festooned with honours by many governments, received by kings and dictators, and lionised by the great. In Britain he was awarded a knighthood, honorary doctorates by both Oxford and Cambridge, and two of the Royal Geographical Society's coveted gold medals. His published works – some popular, others scholarly – ran to nearly fifty volumes and were translated into thirty languages. His personal friends included the Tsar, the Kaiser, the King of Sweden, Hindenburg, Kitchener and Lord Curzon. Schoolboys, as well as readers of *The Times*, thrilled to his adventures. Other travellers were awed by his feats of endurance, and geographers by his professional achievements. And yet, when he died at the age of eighty-seven in 1952, he was a forgotten man. The meteorite, after a long trail of glory, had disappeared virtually without trace. He died, moreover, reviled by many of those who once had honoured him.

Few people today can probably recall what caused this abrupt reversal in Hedin's fortunes. Briefly, he made the fatal mistake – at least in the eyes of many of his former friends – of twice becoming involved in power politics, each time moreover on the losing side. A man of passionate beliefs, Hedin was prepared to sacrifice universal esteem during World War I, and again in World War II, by taking an uncompromising pro-German stand, a puzzling decision in view of his part-Jewish ancestry. Entire books were written aimed at denigrating him. One, published in 1916, was a satire purportedly by 'Hun Swedin'. Another, which appeared in Britain the next year, ended: 'You have denied humanity, Sven Hedin, and in return you are denied today by the Swedish people. We do not know you. What do your discoveries mean to us? What does it interest us whether you have discovered both Tibet and China?'

However, Hedin's accomplishments as an explorer are beyond question. Judged merely by his maps he was brilliant, as today's satellite surveys of Central Asia have shown. Sir Francis Younghusband, who met him at Kashgar in 1890 when he was still unknown, was much struck by him. 'He impressed me as being of the true stamp for exploration – physically robust, genial, even tempered, cool and persevering ... I envied him his linguistic ability [Hedin was fluent in seven languages], his knowledge of scientific subjects, and his artistic accomplishments. He seemed to possess every qualification of a scientific traveller, added to the quiet, self-reliant character of his northern ancestors.' On this first visit to Kashgar, Hedin also made valuable friendships with Petrovsky and Macartney, and met Father Hendricks, a remarkable Dutch priest much beloved by all travellers in the region.

The visit was merely a reconnaissance, and four years later, aged twenty-nine, he was back there again to begin a series of historic and often perilous journeys across Central Asia and Tibet which would span some forty years. This time he reached Kashgar by crossing the Pamir. He had ignored warnings of the dangers of attempting a winter crossing of the grim pass over the lofty *Taghdumbash*. The conditions had been appalling, with the mercury freezing in his thermometer and the temperature falling one night to minus thirty-seven degrees. Not only did he suffer from mountain sickness but due to the extreme cold, temporarily lost his sight, and had to be led blindfolded on the descent to Kashgar.

Hedin, as Younghusband had pointed out, was highly qualified for his role as a scientific explorer. When only twenty-one, after youthful journeys through Persia and Russian Central Asia, he had returned to Sweden determined to acquire the skills he felt he needed for what he saw as his life's work. He enrolled at the University of Stockholm where for two years he studied geology, physics and zoology. After graduating he enrolled at Berlin University, studying physical geography under the great Baron von Richthofen – himself a celebrated Asiatic explorer – as well as historical geography and palaeontology under other leading professors. He broke off his studies in 1890 to make his first journey to Kashgar, where he met Younghusband, returning for a further year's tuition under von Richthofen.

Then followed his nightmarish crossing of the Pamir and three expeditions across Chinese Central Asia. The first, in February 1895, was to prove to those who followed him – notably Sir Aurel Stein – that travel into the interior of the Taklamakan desert, and not merely around it, was possible, albeit extremely dangerous. His subsequent two Taklamakan expeditions, in December 1895 and September 1899, were to yield discoveries of enormous archaeological importance.

Like all visitors to the region, Hedin had listened to endless tales of lost cities, strewn with ancient treasures, lying deep in the Taklamakan. Many men, it was said, had ventured in search of them, hoping to make their fortunes. The few who had returned to tell the story spoke fearfully of how the guarding spirits had foiled them in their attempts to remove the treasure. One man from Khotan, Hedin was told, was luckier. He had fallen into debt and went into the desert hoping to die. Instead he had stumbled on a hoard of gold and silver and was now a rich man.

Hedin was fascinated by these legends, and was convinced that behind them must lie some grain of truth. He determined, in the course of his more serious task of mapping and exploring this *terra incognita*, to find one such city. To him the call of this ocean of sand was irresistible. 'Over there, on the verge of the horizon, were the noble, rounded forms of sand-dunes which I never grew tired of watching,' he wrote. 'Beyond them, amid the grave-like silence, stretched the unknown ... the land that I was going to be the first to tread.'

Hedin's first venture into the Taklamakan was very nearly his last. He left Kashgar on February 17, 1895, his thirtieth birthday, and proceeded to Merket on the Yarkand-daria, or River Yarkand. Here his caravan leader bought camels and provisions for a month's travelling in the Taklamakan, and Hedin hired three other men, one of whom claimed to know the region well. They set off on April 10 with eight camels, two guard dogs and a mobile 'larder' of three sheep, ten hens and a cock. Their journey, Hedin wrote afterwards, 'proved to be one of the most difficult I ever undertook in Asia'. His objective was to cross the Taklamakan, mapping its southwestern corner between the Yarkand and Khotan rivers, and then push on to Tibet. As the small party left Merket and headed into the desert the villagers shook their heads and prophesied that they would never return.

Fifteen days later there came a grim warning of trouble. Hedin discovered to his horror that they had only enough drinking water left for another two days. At the last well his men had been told to fill the tanks which the camels were carrying with enough water for ten days, to allow an ample supply until they reached the Khotan-daria. Hedin cursed himself for not personally supervising this. The guide swore they would reach the river in two days, but Hedin was far from convinced. Afterwards, with hindsight, he admitted that he should have turned back. Had he stopped to weigh the risks, he wrote, 'the caravan would have been saved and no life would have been lost'. Instead, after drastically reducing the party's water ration, with none at all for the camels, he decided to press on.

That night they dug in vain for water, working frenziedly for several hours by candle-light but finding nothing. Next day Hedin decided to abandon two ailing camels and all superfluous baggage. Rain clouds gathered briefly, greatly raising their hopes, but then dispersed. A sandstorm next struck the exhausted caravan, forcing them to steer by compass alone. Another camel had to be left behind to die. Then Hedin's men discovered that Yolchi, the guide, had been stealing their precious water. There was now none left. But for Hedin's intervention the others would have killed him for his treachery. Hedin now made what he feared would be the last entry in his travel diary. He wrote: 'All, men as well as camels, are extremely weak. God help us!' Five full days had now passed since their discovery that they only had enough water left for two.

On May 1, after being without water for an entire day, in desperation Hedin tried quenching his thirst with the spirit brought for the primus stove. Soon he found himself unable to move. His only hope was for the rest of the party to reach the river and then come back for him, so they pressed grimly on without him. After a while, however, his strength returned and he crawled on, following their trail across the sand and catching them up where they had been forced to halt. No one now had the strength to move. That moment, Hedin wrote afterwards, 'was the unhappiest I lived through in all my wanderings in Asia'.

By now one of his four men was unconscious. The others killed the rooster they still had with them and drank its blood. Next came the turn of the sheep, but Hedin found himself unable to swallow its coagulating blood. Two of his men tried drinking camel's urine, only to be violently sick.

Tormented by the thought of the grief his disappearance would cause to his family, Hedin made one last resolution to keep going. Discarding even his small medicine chest, but keeping his pocket Bible, he set off at sunset with two men and the five surviving camels in a desperate attempt to reach the river. Behind them they left their two dying companions, including Yolchi the water thief. His last words to Hedin were: 'Water, sir! Only a drop of water!' But there was none. During the night another camel died. Then one of Hedin's two companions – Islam Bai, the caravan leader – announced he could go no further. Again there was no choice, and he was left behind, this time with the remaining camels and equipment. Hedin and Kasim – the last of his men – crawled on at night, digging themselves into the sand during the day.

On May 4, their fifth day without water, they were amazed to see footprints. At last, they believed, they must be near the Khotan-daria, and life-giving water. But almost immediately they realised that these were simply their own tracks. They had been travelling in a circle. The next morning, Hedin recalled, 'Kasim looked terrible. His tongue was white and swollen, his lips blue, his cheeks were hollow, and his eyes had a dying, glassy lustre.' But then, as the sun rose, they saw with incredulity a dark green line on the horizon.

'The forest!' yelled Hedin. 'The Khotan-daria! Water!' By 5.30 a.m. they had reached the shade of the trees, but three hours later had still not come upon the river. Both men collapsed once again from exhaustion and dehydration. By the evening Hedin had recovered a little and was able to crawl on alone through the trees. But when he finally reached the river he found it completely dry. A terrible desire to sleep came over him, but he knew that he would die if he were to lose consciousness, so he forced himself to crawl for another mile along the river bed.

Suddenly, ahead of him, there was a splash as a water-bird rose. 'The next moment,' Hedin writes in *Through Asia*, 'I stood on the brink of a little pool filled with fresh, cool water – beautiful water!' He thanked God for his miraculous deliverance, then began to drink feverishly, scooping up the water in a tin. 'I drank, drank, drank, time after time.... Every blood-vessel and tissue of my body sucked up the life-giving liquid like a sponge.' His pulse, which had dropped to only forty-nine, began to beat normally again. 'My hands, which had been dry, parched, and as hard as wood, swelled out again. My skin, which had been like parchment, turned moist and elastic....'

His thoughts then flew to the dying Kasim, lying somewhere back by the dry river bed. Filling his leather boots with water, Hedin staggered back in the moonlight to look for him, occasionally calling out his name. At dawn he came upon him, lying just as he had left him. Kasim whispered: 'I'm dying.' Hedin held one of the boots filled with water to his lips. Kasim gulped it down, followed by the contents of the other. Later, after being helped by passing shepherds, they discovered with joy that Islam Bai too had survived and had also been found by shepherds. He threw himself at Hedin's feet, weeping. 'He had thought we would never meet again,' wrote Hedin. One of the camels – the one carrying Hedin's diaries, maps, money and two rifles – had also survived. Everything else, including the surveying instruments, had been lost. Of the two other men nothing more was ever heard, and eventually their widows were compensated by Hedin. There was now no choice but for the three survivors to return to Kashgar, which they finally reached on June 21. Hedin had failed to find his lost city. He had, moreover, learned a bitter lesson. But it had in no way lessened his determination to unravel the secrets of the Taklamakan. He immediately sent a messenger to the nearest telegraph station on the Russian border to signal for a new set of surveying instruments to be dispatched to him as soon as possible.

*   *   *

More determined than ever to be the first European to explore one of the lost cities of the Taklamakan, Hedin set out from Kashgar again on December 14, 1895. He took with him the faithful Islam Bai (the other survivor, Kasim, had meanwhile become a watchman at the Russian consulate) and three new men. Skirting the western edge of the desert via the old Silk Road, they covered the three hundred miles to Khotan in twenty-one days. Here, Hedin knew, small antiquities could be obtained from local treasure-hunters. He had learned this from Petrovsky, who used to buy them from merchants arriving in Kashgar from Khotan. Every summer when the snows melted in the mountains, causing flooding in the area, artefacts were washed out of the loess (the red soil of the region) and picked up by the natives.

'To the inhabitants these things, unless they are made of gold or silver, are valueless, and they give them to their children to play with,' Hedin wrote. He was taken to the spot from where they were obtained, an ancient village called Borasan, to the west of Khotan. Being January, however, 'the season's harvest of antiquities had been already gathered in ...' Hedin explained, 'for they never fail to make their annual search for gold and other treasures'. Nonetheless, he managed to turn up a few small objects himself, and to acquire from local treasure-seekers some five hundred assorted antiquities as well as manuscripts and coins. Although not an archaeologist, these modest discoveries were to give him a lifelong interest in such relics and to form the basis of the large collection of Central Asian antiquities now belonging to the Sven Hedin Foundation in Stockholm. The treasures he brought back from Borasan (later identified as Yotkan, the region's ancient capital) included terracotta images of Buddha, figurines of men, women and camels, and also a number of relics pointing to the presence of early settlers or visitors from the West, most notably a copper cross. Here indeed were the remains of a lost city, albeit only on the fringe of the desert and now obliterated by centuries of flooding and looting.

Hedin had heard, however, that in the heart of the desert to the north-east lay another mysterious city, almost totally buried in the sand, which the oasis-dwellers called simply

'Taklamakan'. Accompanied by local guides who said they knew the way, he set out in the direction of the Keriya river. After travelling for ten days in sub-zero temperatures – for it was now mid-winter – they came at last upon the fabled ruins. At first all they could see was the occasional wooden post or section of wall protruding from the sand dunes. Then to his excitement, on one of the walls Hedin spotted several stucco figures clearly depicting Buddha and Buddhist deities. He realised at once that, in this desolate spot, he had stumbled on the remains of the long-lost Buddhist civilisation so vividly described by Fa-hsien and other early Chinese travellers on the Silk Road. Not only did this vindicate them, but also the modern oasis-dwellers with their tales of lost cities far out in the Taklamakan.

As he scanned the bleak ruins around him – 'this second Sodom' he calls it in *Through Asia* – he realised the enormous importance of what he had found, even if he did not yet know its identity. However, he was only too aware that he had neither the knowledge, the time nor the equipment to conduct a proper scientific excavation, although he stayed there long enough to explore several of the sand-filled buildings. In *My Life as an Explorer*, written many years afterwards, Hedin explains: 'The scientific research I willingly left to the specialists. In a few years they too would be sinking their spades into the loose sand. For me it was sufficient to have made the important discovery and to have won in the heart of the desert a new field for archaeology.'

His own digging revealed not only ancient houses but traces of gardens and avenues of poplars. He also found the remains of plum and apricot trees. In some of the houses his men unearthed strange gypsum figures, eight inches high, and flat at the back indicating that they had served as wall decorations. They also found a life-size human foot, again in gypsum. In one building, which his men said was a temple, they came upon a number of wall-paintings representing female figures 'somewhat airily clad' and executed in 'masterly manner'. Hedin noted: 'Their hair was twisted in a black knot on the top of the head, and the eyebrows were traced in a *continuous* line, with a mark above the root of the nose, after the custom among the Hindus of the present day.'

Considering he was neither art historian nor archaeologist, Hedin's observations on the iconography of his finds were surprisingly perceptive. He noted, for example, Indian, Greek, Persian and Gandharan influences. Serindian art – a term invented later by Sir Aurel Stein – was at that time still unknown. After removing what he could carry and remarking on the difficulty of digging in the dry sand ('as fast as you dig it out, it runs in again and fills up the hole') Hedin pushed on eastwards towards the Keriya river which he proposed to map and follow northwards into the desert.

On reaching the river he learned of another sand-buried city nearby called by the natives Karadong, or 'black hill'. This proved to be smaller than the first. Hedin noted that the architecture was similar, as were the ancient materials used. He also found wall-paintings executed in a similar style to those in the other city. After spending two days there, Hedin continued northwards along the Keriya river to the point where its waters finally vanished beneath the sand. From there he and his men completed a perilous northwards crossing of the Taklamakan before eventually returning to Khotan, having also made numerous important geographical and zoological discoveries. From Khotan, where he spent a month working on his maps and notes, Hedin embarked on another major journey, this time to explore parts of Tibet, the mysterious land he had failed to reach on his ill-fated expedition the previous year. From Tibet he finally returned to Sweden via Peking and the Trans-Siberian railway, to discover that he was already famous.

*　　　*　　　*

It was on his next expedition into the Taklamakan in September 1899 that the indefatigable Swede scored his greatest archaeological triumph, the discovery of the ancient Chinese garrison town of Lou-lan. His subsequent removal of scores of important manuscripts from its ruins, some dating from the third century, is something Chinese scholars find hard to forgive. Had it not been for a lost spade, moreover, he might never have stumbled upon it, and the site – so important to Chinese historians – might have been left intact for their own archaeologists to discover and excavate.

Financed this time by King Oscar of Sweden and the millionaire Emmanuel Nobel, Hedin left Europe once again for Kashgar where he had a happy reunion with his old friends Petrovsky, Macartney and Father Hendricks. On September 5, together with Islam Bai – now proudly wearing the gold medal of the King of Sweden – he set out for the village of Lailik on the Yarkand river. This was to be the starting point of a remarkable venture – an expedition through the Taklamakan by boat. Hedin's aim was to survey and map first the Yarkand river and then its continuation, the Tarim. His ultimate destination was Lop-nor, the salt lake in the heart of the desert into which the Tarim emptied, and which appeared to have shifted dramatically over the years. Hedin, primarily a geographer, was determined to solve this riddle (it would take him thirty-five years to do so conclusively).

First he bought a locally made boat, on which he and his men were to live for the next eighty days. Then they built a smaller craft for exploring narrow or shallow parts of the river and also to serve as the expedition's larder with its cargo of live chickens and vegetables. Finally, after signing up a crew of five, the expedition set sail.

Apart from the hazards posed by *burans*, rapids, shallows and the occasional fallen tree blocking the river, Hedin found it an idyllic way of travelling through the grim landscape. At times, where the river flowed swiftly, the current carried the two boats downstream at breakneck speed, the crew staving them off with long poles when they got too close to the banks. At other times they had to hoist a sail to move at all. Sometimes, by way of relaxation, Hedin would switch on his musical box and the strains of *Carmen* or the Swedish national anthem echoed out over the desert. Nothing like this had ever been seen – or heard – in the Taklamakan before, and they received astonished looks from the occasional shepherd or passing caravan.

During the day Hedin worked non-stop on his survey, for there could be no gaps in the chart which would eventually fill one hundred sheets. At night the vessels were tethered to the bank. As winter deepened, Hedin's one fear was that the river would freeze over, forcing him to abandon his task until spring. Finally, on December 7, it happened, nearly three months after their departure from Lailik and some one hundred and forty miles short of their destination. There was no way of going on, and Hedin decided to occupy himself, until the river unfroze, by undertaking a number of exploratory overland journeys in the area. He had no tent, although nocturnal temperatures sometimes fell to minus twenty-two degrees and it snowed incessantly. Their drinking water was carried in the form of blocks of ice and at times it was so cold that the ink froze solid in Hedin's fountain pen, forcing him to abandon it for a pencil.

After a twenty-day desert crossing they reached the southern Silk Road oasis of Cherchen, then turned north-east and headed towards the Lop desert at the extreme eastern end of the Taklamakan. After travelling for a further twenty-two days they came suddenly on a curious sight – several very ancient wooden houses, each perched on a hillock eight or nine feet high, in the middle of nowhere. These had apparently been stranded there, high and dry, as centuries of erosion had eaten away at the loess around them. A hasty search revealed several ancient Chinese coins, a few iron axes and some wooden carvings depicting men. These were loaded onto two camels and sent back with one of the men to the expedition's base camp on the Tarim. That might well have been the end of it, had it not been for one man's forgetfulness. For Hedin was anxious not to linger, intending to complete the final stage of the Tarim survey and then strike southwards into Tibet again, this time with the aim of reaching Lhasa. Moreover, the hot season was not far off and their water was beginning to run low.

After travelling for some hours they decided to dig for water in a promising looking spot. It was then found that their only spade was missing. One of the men confessed to having left it by mistake beside the ancient houses, and Hedin sent him back on his own horse to find it. When the man returned with the spade he said he had lost his way in a sandstorm but had stumbled on some ruins they had missed before. Sticking out of the sand, he said, were some beautiful wooden carvings. Hedin immediately sent him back again, this time with other men, to collect these. When he saw the carvings Hedin felt 'dizzy' with excitement. He wrote: 'I wanted to go back. But what folly! We had water for only two days.' He resolved instead to return the following winter and excavate the site more thoroughly.

When the river survey was completed the party struck south once more across the desert, making their way through the grim mountain passes into Tibet and again briefly out of this narrative. After losing one of his men, ten horses and three camels (another man lost both his feet through frostbite), Hedin decided to leave Tibet and return to the mysterious ruins in the Lop desert. On arrival, he drew a careful plan of the site and then began to excavate, offering a reward to the first of his men to find 'human writing in any form'. Before long one of them came forward with a piece of wood bearing an Indian inscription. Excavation of each house continued, and soon one of the men found a piece of paper with Chinese characters on it. After this more and more scraps of ancient paper bearing Chinese writing were discovered – thirty-six in all. In addition, one hundred and twenty wooden documents were found, together with a fragment of an ancient rug, its colours still quite bright, and bearing a swastika design.

These manuscripts, one of which identified the site as that of Lou-lan, were to provide scholars with an amazingly intimate and rounded picture of life in this Chinese garrison town. Originally founded to safeguard China's western frontier and the vital traffic along the Silk Road, it had finally fallen to the barbarians at the beginning of the fourth century. Once a large and flourishing community, with civil service, post office, hospital and schools, it had already lain beneath the sands of Marco Polo's ghoul-infested Desert of Lop for close on a thousand years when he passed that way in 1224.

From the mass of wooden slips and scraps of (the then newly invented) paper unearthed by Hedin, the minutiae of its citizens' day-to-day lives have been pieced together to reveal a people very like ourselves. The discoveries include everything from records of punishments meted out to tax-evaders to the scribblings of children faced by such familiar problems as to what nine-times-nine makes. One of the houses they emptied of sand was found with its door wide open – 'just as it must have been left by the last inhabitant of this ancient city more than 1,500 years ago', Hedin observed. Together with his earlier discovery of mysterious 'Taklamakan', the finding of Lou-lan made a remarkable double for the indefatigable Swede. In all, he spent seven days excavating there before heading south once more in another attempt to reach Lhasa, this time disguised as a Buddhist pilgrim.

Meanwhile, at the other end of the Taklamakan another European traveller, Marc Aurel Stein, had already started on the first of three great archaeological raids on the Silk Road. A man every bit as determined as Hedin, his expeditions – spread over sixteen years – were to result in the removal of enough works of art and manuscripts from Chinese Central Asia to fill a museum. They were also to earn him the bitter opprobrium of the Chinese who, to this day, regard him as foremost among those foreigners who robbed them of the bones of their history.

5. Aurel Stein –
Treasure-Seeker Extraordinary

Sir Aurel Stein's expeditions, which were to carry him some twenty-five thousand miles through Chinese Turkestan, have been described by another famous excavator, Sir Leonard Woolley, as 'the most daring and adventurous raid upon the ancient world that any archaeologist has attempted'. Professor Owen Lattimore, himself an eminent Central Asian traveller and historian, has called Stein 'the most prodigious combination of scholar, explorer, archaeologist and geographer of his generation'.

Such appraisals by fellow professionals can be substantiated by the facts, but superlatives must be used carefully. One writer, for instance, has described Stein as 'the greatest explorer of Asia since Marco Polo'. This is to detract from the achievements of Sven Hedin, only some of whose travels – those concerned with archaeology – were chronicled in the previous chapter. Indeed, taking into account his Tibetan expeditions, Hedin was arguably the greater explorer, geographically speaking. Besides considerable mutual respect, mixed with a disdain for those who operated only on the fringes of the Taklamakan, the two men had much in common. Like Hedin, Stein was knighted by the British Government for his contribution to Central Asian studies, received honorary doctorates from Oxford and Cambridge, and won the gold medal of the Royal Geographical Society, to name just a few of a lifetime's honours. Both men were small and compact (Stein was a mere five feet four inches in height), both were bachelors, both wrote voluminously of their travels, and both lived into their eighties. They were born, more-

1 Sven Hedin

2 Sir Aurel Stein

3 Albert von
Le Coq
(*seated left*)
and Theodor
Bartus
(*seated
right*)

over, within three years of one another, Stein being the elder.

There was, however, one fundamental difference between them. Stein was a brilliant orientalist who turned to exploration to confirm certain theories he had about what lay buried in China's back of beyond. He was, in his own words, 'an archaeological explorer'. Hedin, a highly trained geographer and cartographer, was an explorer pure and simple and in that respect had more in common with the great Russian Asiatic traveller Prejevalsky. Nonetheless, as an explorer of history, Stein's discoveries put him head and shoulders above his rivals. He is, indeed, the giant of Central Asian archaeology.

Born of Jewish parents in Budapest in 1862, he was baptised a Christian because they believed that, in the climate of those times, he would fare better. To quote Jeannette Mirsky, his biographer: 'Baptism, as the elder Steins saw it, was the key that unlocked the ghetto and proffered ... access to the riches of the world outside.' Nor was he to disappoint them, although they did not live to see his unique contribution to those riches. His adopted faith was to remain with him all his life. When in 1943 he was dying in Afghanistan (from where, at the age of eighty-one, he was planning one last great Central Asian journey) he asked on his death-bed for a Church of England burial service.

From his schooldays to his grave Stein was fascinated by the campaigns and travels of Alexander the Great. He was to spend much of his life trying to retrace the routes and pin-point the battlefields which carried the Greeks, together with their art and learning, into Central Asia. Their art he was to pursue further, across the passes of the Karakoram and east-wards along the ancient Silk Road. Perhaps too, like the Hungarian orientalists Csoma de Koros and Arminius Vambery before him, he was attracted subconsciously to Central Asia by the ancient belief that the Hungarians are descended from the Huns. Certainly he was influenced and inspired by these two great travellers.

After studying oriental languages at the universities of Vienna and Leipzig, and receiving his Ph.D. from Tübingen at the age of twenty-one, he came to Britain, which was eventually to become his adopted country. He spent three years at Oxford and at the British Museum studying classical and oriental archaeology and languages, but omitted Chinese – a gap in his linguistic armoury which was to cost him dear some twenty years later at the Caves of the Thousand Buddhas near Tun-huang. His studies in Britain were interrupted, most fortuitously as it happened, by a year's conscript service in the Hungarian army where he was trained in field surveying, a skill which would prove invaluable in the unmapped regions of Central Asia where he was to make his name.

When his parents died (his mother was already forty-five when he was born) he turned his back on Hungary for good, moving to India where in 1888 at the age of twenty-six he joined the education service at Lahore. There he became a friend of Rudyard Kipling's father who was curator of the 'wonder house', the museum of Gandhara and other Indian art immortalised in the novel *Kim*. From him Stein learned much about the iconography of India as well as all that was known at that time of the art of Buddhist Central Asia. From Lahore he made the first of his many forays into areas where no European had set foot before – a rapid archaeological survey of mysterious Buner while accompanying a punitive expedition to the north-west frontier region of India.

Despite the solitary life he was to lead, sometimes not seeing another European for a year or more at a time, Stein enjoyed warm friendships. These, of necessity, had to be maintained over enormous distances by correspondence usually written at night in his tent by candlelight and conveyed across desert and mountain range by native mail carrier. Nonetheless his work always came first, whether he was writing up his field notes at the end of a long day's work in the desert, or later preparing the monumental accounts of his expeditions at his isolated tented home in Kashmir.

However, it was not until May 1900, at the age of thirty-seven, that he set out on the first of his great expeditions across the Karakoram mountains into the Taklamakan desert. On this initial journey, which was to last almost a year, Stein was officially stateless, for although he had surrendered his Hungarian nationality he had not yet obtained his British passport. (His new citizenship finally came through in 1904.) He would have liked to have set out earlier, having heard rumours that Russian and German expeditions were being planned and that Hedin was about to return to the region, but he first had to obtain permission from the Indian Government to cross into this politically sensitive area. The Chinese, moreover, had to be persuaded to agree to the expedition. Finally he had to obtain leave of absence from his job and raise the money to finance the venture.

In a carefully argued application to the Government of India he presented his case. 'It is well known from historical records,' he wrote, 'that the territory of the present Khotan has been an ancient centre of Buddhist culture ... distinctly Indian in origin and character.' He listed some of the manuscripts and other antiquities that had emerged from the Taklamakan desert, pointing out that if 'the casual search of native treasure-seekers' had yielded these, then systematic exploration of the Silk Road sites by a European archaeologist might be expected to produce finds of the greatest importance.

Stein's expedition had the enthusiastic support of Dr Rudolf Hoernle, a powerful ally in Calcutta's corridors of power. In a letter supporting the venture he argued strongly that the southern part of Chinese Turkestan belonged by rights to the British sphere of influence, adding that 'we should not allow others to secure the credit which ought to belong to ourselves'. Had he foreseen one result that the journey would yield he might have felt less jingoistic.

In addition to Hoernle's backing, Stein had the unexpected good fortune of gaining as an ally the most powerful man in India, the new Viceroy. In April 1899, when Lord Curzon was visiting the Punjab, Stein was asked to conduct him around the Lahore Museum. In the course of their tour Stein explained to him the significance of Gandhara art, simultaneously seizing the opportunity to tell him of his plan to solve the mysteries of what lay beyond the Karakoram. Curzon, still only forty, had himself written a book on Central Asia, albeit on Russian ambitions there, and was keenly interested in what Stein had to say. He instructed the British Minister in Peking to seek from the Chinese authorities a passport allowing Stein to enter Chinese Turkestan via the Karakoram route. In due course this arrived, together with authorisation from the Indian Government for the expedition to proceed. The Chinese document ordered the local ambans, or chief magistrates, to protect Stein and, perhaps more important, in no way to hinder him.

Meanwhile, Stein had been making careful preparations for his journey. He had obtained much valuable knowledge about the peculiar problems facing travellers in the Taklamakan from *Through Asia*, Sven Hedin's two-volume account of his discoveries there, which had just been published. He had learned from Hedin's near fatal encounter with the Taklamakan that the only possible time to explore and excavate the sites far out in the desert would be during the winter months. It would thus be arctic conditions and not the appalling heat of summer that he would have to prepare himself for. First he purchased a Stormont-Murphy arctic explorer's stove with which to heat his tiny tent. The latter, furthermore, he had fitted with an additional lining of thick serge. (Despite this, the ink was at times to freeze in his pen, as Hedin's had.) He also took thick furs for travelling and sleeping in. But water was his biggest problem in a desert where it rained on average only once in ten years. He ordered some specially made galvanised iron water tanks, each designed to take seventeen gallons, the maximum a Bactrian camel could carry in the desert. This would be supplemented with blocks of ice once the temperatures fell below zero.

Stein next travelled up to Srinagar, in Kashmir, where he set up camp on Mohand Marg, a grassy meadow ten thousand feet above sea level, which was to be his home on and off for many years, and the launching point of all his expeditions. He was joined there by the four men who were to accompany him. They were Ram Singh, a Gurkha surveyor seconded by the Survey of India to help him with the important mapping programme; Mirza Alim and Sadak Akhun, Stein's servant and cook; and Jasvant Singh who was to perform similar duties for Ram Singh. The final member of the expedition was a small terrier called Dash, the first of a succession bearing that name which he took with him on his four Central Asian journeys.

A month later, on May 31, 1900, the party left Srinagar at the start of a rugged but uneventful eight-week trek across the Karakoram to Kashgar. There Stein spent the remainder of the summer at Chini-Bagh, the comfortable official residence of George Macartney and his wife. Macartney was a man of unusual background, being the son of a Scottish father, Sir Halliday Macartney, and a Chinese mother (of whom he never spoke, even to his own children, and to whom there was no reference in his obituary in *The Times* when he died in 1945). He was to serve for twenty-eight years as Britain's representative in this remote Central Asian listening post, claimed by geographers to be further from the sea than any town on earth. He and Stein, who shared many common interests, struck up a close friendship and Stein was to stay with the Macartneys on further expeditions. Their hospitality was legendary. 'Every traveller in Central Asia knows (and blesses) the British Consulate-General at Kashgar, for it is a haven of comfort and a centre of hospitality to the European who elects to try his luck in Chinese Turkestan.' So wrote Colonel Reginald Schomberg in 1933 of the tradition established by the Macartneys at Chini-Bagh and continued by their successors until that small corner of Britain in remotest Asia was finally handed back to the Chinese Government in the late 1940s.

Despite the Chinese passport obtained for him by Lord Curzon, Stein's presence in this politically sensitive area where three empires met was not made any easier by the activities of Petrovsky, the Russian consul-general and Macartney's arch rival (for antiquities as well as political intelligence). Petrovsky did his best to persuade the local Chinese authorities, who were in considerable awe of him, that Stein was really a British spy travelling in the guise of an archaeologist. Despite this, once the heat of the Taklamakan summer began to wane Stein and his party left Kashgar for Khotan, the first of the old Silk Road oases he intended to investigate. For Khotan was the town from where Islam Akhun, chief supplier of 'old books' to the British Collection (and simultaneously, as it turned out, to St Petersburg), claimed to have made his forays into the surrounding desert. Despite the conviction of his friend Hoernle that these were genuine, Stein had serious doubts. One of his main purposes in visiting Chinese Turkestan was to check the treasure-hunter's story by sending out local scouts to try to find further examples of Akhun's unknown scripts and also by examining personally some of the sites described by Akhun to Macartney and subsequently incorporated in Hoernle's report.

He also aimed to visit 'Taklamakan' that mysterious city of Hedin's north-east of Khotan, and conduct more thorough excavations there. He hoped, moreover, that by making enquiries in the oasis towns, he would discover new sites for himself. In addition, he and Ram Singh, with plane-table and theodolite, hoped to fill in many of the blank spaces on the map. Finally, by following in the footsteps of the seventh-century pilgrim Hsuan-tsang (spelled Hiuen-Tsiang by Stein), who returned home from India along the southern arm of the Silk Road, he hoped to identify some of the sacred Buddhist sites described by the traveller, who had been another of his heroes since undergraduate days.

Shortly after setting out from Kashgar, Stein gained his

first brief taste of the Taklamakan. After villagers had
reported to him the existence of a *kone-shahr*, or ruined town,
in the desert to the east he turned hopefully off the main
caravan trail, sending the rest of the party ahead. But failing
to find the site, whose location his informants had been extremely vague about, Stein abandoned the search and set off
in pursuit of the others.

In *Sand-Buried Ruins of Khotan*, his account of this expedition, he describes this first brief encounter with the great
Chinese desert with which he was to become so familiar over
the next thirty years. 'Far away to the south stretched a sea
of sand curiously resembling the ocean with its wave-like
dunes.... The sand-dunes to be crossed steadily increased in
height, and the going became more difficult.... The ponies'
feet sank deeply into the loose sand, and each ascent of thirty
to forty feet was thus a tiring performance.' After five miles
of struggling across the dunes they met up with the main party
at a well which someone had protected from the advancing
sandhills by erecting a crude wooden shed over it. The water,
lying six feet below the desert surface, was so brackish, however, as to be undrinkable.

On reaching Yarkand, where the caravan trails to India and
Afghanistan once branched away from the main Silk Road,
Stein discovered to his annoyance that two of his camels and
two ponies had developed sores. Also money which should
have been awaiting him there had failed to materialise. This
meant sending a messenger all the way back to Kashgar to
collect the money, a journey totalling some two hundred and
forty miles. It also meant halting a week in Yarkand while
the animals' sores healed. Stein was particularly annoyed
because he suspected that their condition had been carefully
kept from him, with the result that their sores had become
steadily worse. 'The experience was not thrown away on me,'
he wrote drily. 'Thereafter inspections of the animals were
held almost daily, and those responsible for their loading
learned to understand that the hire of transport in place of

animals rendered temporarily unfit would be recovered from their own pay.'

The Chinese amban, or chief magistrate of Yarkand, received Stein warmly and they soon discovered that they had a shared interest in Hsuan-tsang. The amban threw a banquet for his new friend consisting of sixteen courses and lasting three hours. Not being used to 'eating sticks', Stein was provided with a rather grubby fork. In the course of the meal he was asked for news of the Boxer uprising which had broken out some two thousand miles away in Peking. He told the amban and the other guests that he knew nothing beyond the fact that the foreign legations were safe. It was clear to Stein that they did not believe him, but attributed his reticence to his wishing – in the oriental manner – to hold back unpleasant tidings. It was equally clear to him that it was apprehension 'about their own individual fortunes, not those of the nation' which secretly troubled them.

His camels and ponies now having recovered, Stein's party continued eastwards along the Silk Road. Apart from the fertile and cultivated regions around the oases, with their snow- and glacier-fed water supplies from the mountains, most of the going now was across totally barren desert. On one stretch they found the route marked by wooden posts placed there to prevent travellers from straying away from the caravan trail at night or during a sandstorm as so many unfortunates had done over the centuries. To their left, in the dust haze, stretched the Taklamakan, while on the right, in the far distance, rose the mighty snow-capped ranges which form Tibet's northern bastion. The heat and glare of the sun and the ankle-deep dust of the road were made less disagreeable for Stein, however, by his awareness of history and of those who had preceded him.

'Walking and riding along the track marked here and there by the parched carcases and bleached bones of animals that had died on it, I thought of travellers in times gone by who must have marched through this same waterless, uninhabited waste', he wrote. 'Hiuen-Tsiang, who travelled here on his way back to China, has well described the route. After him it had seen Marco Polo and many a less-known medieval traveller to distant Cathay. Practically nothing has changed here in respect of the methods and means of travel. . . .'

After passing through tiny Siligh Langar ('a collection of wretched mud-hovels') and Hajib Langar ('another uninviting wayside station'), they found themselves once again amidst the fertile gardens and fields of another river-fed oasis, this time Guma. Somewhere in the desert between Guma and Khotan, one hundred miles to the east, lay the mysterious sites where Islam Akhun claimed to have found many of his books and manuscripts. Here was Stein's chance to discover the truth, to see who was right, himself or Hoernle. 'It was at Guma', he wrote afterwards, 'that I first touched the ground where it was possible to test the treasure-seeker's statements by direct local inquiries.' It was to take him just one day.

He started by asking the elders and officials whether they knew of the discovery of any old books in the desert around Guma. Nobody had. Of the list of sites which Islam Akhun had included in his itinerary published by Hoernle, only two were known to them. As both lay close to Guma, Stein rode out to inspect them. 'Riding to the north-east with a lively following of Begs [local officials] and their attendants, I soon reached the area of moving sand-dunes 20 to 30 feet high which encircle Guma from the north.' Three miles further on he came upon Qarā Qöl Mazār (to use Hoernle's spelling), where Islam Akhun claimed to have discovered an immense ruined graveyard some ten miles long. The name of this spot translates as 'shrine of the black lake'. All that Stein could find was a small reed-covered saline pond and a sandhill from which protruded some poles hung with votive rags, indicating the supposed resting place of a saint. 'Of the vast cemetery round the shrine where Islam Akhun alleged that he had made finds of ancient block-prints, I could discover no sign,' Stein recorded. Three miles further on they came to the oasis of

Karatagh-aghzi surrounding which, Islam Akhun claimed, were ruined sites from which he had removed old books and other curious finds. The inhabitants, when closely questioned, knew nothing of such sites and still less of such discoveries. This was no proof, of course, that the books were forgeries. It proved, however, that the Khotan-based treasure-hunter was a liar, though it was still possible that he had invented these sites to protect the real source of his finds. Hoernle himself had suggested that Akhun might have stumbled upon an ancient library, whose whereabouts he wished to keep secret.

His enquiries momentarily over, Stein left Guma the following morning for Khotan, five days' march to the east. Several times he turned away from the trail to investigate ruins which he heard of from various sources. All proved disappointing. Apart from fragments of pottery, all traces of these once flourishing settlements had been wiped out by the corrosive effects of winds and sandstorms over the centuries. One or two of the sites he examined were on Islam Akhun's 'itinerary'. But Stein decided that the physical conditions absolutely ruled out any possibility of manuscripts or books surviving there. He noted: 'There was a weird fascination in the almost complete decay and utter desolation of the scanty remains that marked once thickly inhabited settlements.'

As Stein finally approached the oasis of Khotan, celebrated throughout Central Asia for its jade and rugs, he remembered a curious legend related by Hsuan-tsang. About thirty miles to the west of the town, the seventh-century traveller had noticed 'a succession of small hills' which the local people assured him had been formed by the burrowing of sacred rats. These creatures, led by a rat-king, were protected and fed by the locals because, it was said, they had saved the Buddhist inhabitants of Khotan from a great army of Huns by consuming their leather harness and armour. Of the rodents Stein saw no sign, though, interestingly, he found modern Moslem wayfarers piously feeding other sacred creatures – thousands of pigeons maintained in a kind of bird monastery. 'I too', Stein confessed, 'bought some bags of Indian corn from the store of the shrine and scattered their contents to the fluttering swarms.'

After crossing the dry river bed of the Kara-kash, or 'Black Jade River', some three-quarters of a mile in width, Stein and his caravan entered the town of Khotan. He had carefully avoided alerting the local treasure-hunters of his approach lest inadvertently he set the forgers to work on his behalf. However, on his arrival he at once arranged for small prospecting parties from the town's 'fraternity of quasi-professional treasure-seekers' to act as scouts for him. To scour the area thoroughly, he was told, would take some time, so in the meantime he and Ram Singh set out on ponies with their surveying instruments with the aim of mapping unexplored regions of the Kun Lun and fixing, for the first time, the exact position of Khotan.

One night, from their camp on the mountainside, Stein looked down upon the moonlit Taklamakan, thousands of feet below. He described lyrically what he saw: 'It seemed as if I were looking at the lights of a vast city lying below me in the endless plains. Could it really be that terrible desert where there was no life and no hope of human existence? I knew that I should never see it again in this alluring splendour. Its appearance haunted me as I sat shivering in my tent, busy with a long-delayed mail that was to carry to distant friends my Christmas greetings.' After a modest meal and 'a last look at the magic city below' Stein turned in for the night.

His survey work in the Kun Lun ('Mountains of Darkness') finished, Stein descended from their inhospitable heights where, he declared, 'the utter barrenness of Nature had given no chance for history to leave its traces'. Awaiting him in Khotan with their various finds were the prospectors who had been scouring the desert during his month's absence. One man who had not approached him, Stein noted wryly, was Khotan's most famous treasure-seeker, Islam Akhun. Indeed, he appeared to have left town rather hurriedly. However, one old book which had reportedly passed through his hands was offered to Stein. When this was subjected to the 'water test', the mere touch of his wet finger was sufficient to wipe away the 'unknown characters'. To Stein's highly trained eye, moreover, it looked suspiciously like certain of the books in Hoernle's collection in Calcutta.

The treasure-seeker whose discoveries most excited Stein was an old Taklamakan hand called Turdi, who had been digging up ruins in search of gold for thirty years, and his father before him. He produced several pieces of fresco bearing Indian Brahmi characters, fragments of stucco reliefs clearly Buddhist in origin, and an ancient piece of paper with cursive Brahmi of a Central Asian variety on it. Carefully questioned by Stein about the location of the site from where he had obtained his 'samples', Turdi indicated that it lay some nine or ten marches north-east of Khotan, far out in the Taklamakan.

Although the old treasure-seeker called it Dandan-uilik, or 'place of houses with ivory', from his description Stein believed that this must be Hedin's 'Taklamakan'. He knew, moreover, that in one brief day's digging there Hedin had stumbled upon remarkable traces of the lost Buddhist civilisation that he himself had come to find. How much more might he, an archaeologist, bring to light in a serious and unhurried excavation? Mysterious Dandan-uilik, Stein decided, would be the target of his first sortie into this wasteland which had swallowed up an entire chapter of China's imperial history. He immediately set about preparing for a winter in the Taklamakan.

6. Stein Strikes it Rich

Dandan-uilik, with its 'ghostly wrecks of houses', was reached after a journey of eleven days, the last six across the frozen Taklamakan. During the day the temperature never rose above zero, and at night sometimes fell to ten degrees below. Even in his heated tent, Stein found it impossible to work when the mercury dropped below six degrees. Sleeping, too, had its problems. 'It was uncomfortable', he wrote, 'to wake up with one's moustache hard frozen with the respiration that had passed over it.' Ultimately he had to adopt the device of pulling his fur coat over his head and breathing through the sleeve.

At the village of Atbashi, the last oasis on the edge of the Taklamakan, he had recruited thirty labourers, each with his own *ketman*, or native hoe. The men, understandably enough, had been reluctant to venture into the desert, fearing, among other things, the *jins*, or demons. However, pressure from their headman, the attractive rates of pay, and reassurance about the desert from Turdi and two other veterans Stein took with him changed their minds. But before they set out Stein had everybody provided with the thickest winter clothing available locally.

As the caravan pressed further and further into the desert, the feet of both men and camels sank into the soft sand, making the going slow and exhausting and holding the progress of the heavily laden party down to a mere one and a half miles an hour. The day's march, consequently, rarely exceeded ten miles. They finally reached Dandan-uilik, 'amid its strange surroundings, pregnant with death and solitude', a week before Christmas. At a glance Stein could see that treasure-seekers had already been there, for there was much visible damage. (Perhaps he counted Hedin among them, although tactfully he does not say so.) Turdi himself admitted to a number of visits, though he had yet to find what he was really hoping for – gold. But this did not deter Stein in the least. He knew that these small raiding parties did not have the resources to stay in such a god-forsaken area for more than a day or two at a time. They had dug freely into the visible structures, but left alone those which had been swallowed up by the dunes. Here Turdi's familiarity with the site was to prove invaluable since he was able to point out to Stein the buildings which had not been looted.

Stein's most immediate problem was to keep his men from freezing to death at night in the sub-zero temperatures, despite their thick clothing. He somewhere had to find a source of fuel for fires. Fortunately it lay close at hand – centuries-old timber from the orchards which had once blossomed in this city of the dead. Having pitched his camp, he dispatched the camels to the Keriya-daria, three days' journey to the east, where they would find fodder and gain strength for the marches that lay ahead.

Excavations began next morning, for every minute was precious. It was the moment for which Stein had been waiting and planning for years. His theories, knowledge and skills would be tested here at Dandan-uilik, his first Taklamakan site. He started work on the remains of a small square building immediately to the south of his camp. It had long before been dug into by Turdi, who told him it was a *but-khana*, or 'house of idols'. However, Stein was less concerned with finding antiquities in this first building than with familiarising himself with the lay-out and construction of such shrines.

Jeannette Mirsky, his biographer, explains: 'Dandan-uilik was the classroom where Stein learned the grammar of the ancient sand-buried shrines and houses: their typical ground plans, construction, and ornamentation, their art, and something of their cultic practices. He also used it as a laboratory in which to find the techniques best suited to excavating ruins covered by sands as fluid as water, which, like water trickled in almost as fast as the diggers bailed it out. He had no precedents to guide him, no labour force already trained in the cautions, objectives and methods of archaeology. . . . He felt his way from what was easy to what was difficult, from what he knew he would find to discoveries he had not dared to anticipate. His approach was both cautious and experimental.'

Despite his caution, and the fact that the temple had already been plundered, the first day's digging yielded a steady stream of ancient Buddhist frescoes and stucco reliefs. Each was carefully photographed *in situ* before removal and labelled with the details of where it had been found. In all, one hundred and fifty finds were thus prepared for their long and perilous journey to the British Museum. Next day Stein switched his operations to a small cluster of buildings buried under some eight feet of sand. Here, too, he found frescoes, though mostly too fragile to move. But so far, apart from one small scrap of paper, no manuscripts had come to light. Yet it was precisely these, with their revealing data, that Stein most wanted to find. He decided, therefore, like Hedin, to offer a cash reward, in silver, to the first man to uncover one. Within less than an hour there was an excited shout of 'khat!' – the Turki word for 'writing'.

The find was an oblong-shaped leaf of ancient paper bearing words in a non-Indian language. It proved to be a single leaf from a *pothi*, a characteristic Indian manuscript form in which a number of leaves are placed together, perforated with a circular hole and tied together with string. From then on manuscripts turned up in quick succession, all Sanskrit texts of the Buddhist canon. Some of them appeared to date back to the fifth and sixth centuries. Stein quickly realised that the building they were clearing must harbour an entire library, probably that of a Buddhist monastery.

What was puzzling, though, was how these manuscripts came to lie in a room which other relics showed to have been a kitchen. Moreover, they were found embedded in loose sand several feet *above* the original floor. There was only one possible explanation. They must have fallen from an upper room – the library of a small monastery – into the kitchen below, all traces of the upper structure having long before been reduced to dust by wind and sand.

On Christmas Day 1900, he began work on a group of sand-filled buildings apparently a temple complex, lying half a mile to the north-east of his camp. Although these showed the usual signs of having been ravaged by treasure-seekers, intuition told him that careful excavation might still yield important discoveries, as indeed it did. He first came upon two paintings on wood. The larger of these, when the encrusted sand was carefully removed months later at the British Museum, was seen to depict a human figure, but with the head of a rat wearing a diadem and seated between two attendants. It was clearly meant to represent the king of the sacred rats which had saved Khotan.

The next finds to turn up were two scraps of paper bearing characters which Stein at once recognised as belonging to a 'peculiar cursive form of Brahmi' already familiar to him from Dr Hoernle's collection. Soon other similar scraps emerged from the dry sand. With fingers numbed by the cold, Stein opened these crumpled documents. Cursory examination – later confirmed by Dr Hoernle – suggested an obvious connection between them and the similar ones in the Calcutta collection. Stein thought it highly probable that the latter represented finds made by Turdi during his earlier visits to Dandan-uilik. Detailed examination of the faded and flimsy sheets subsequently showed them to be records of official and private transactions, including deeds of loan and requisition orders, dating from the eighth century.

Christmas Day still had some surprises in store, including the discovery of documents in Chinese. One of these, when translated later by Macartney, proved to be a petition for the recovery of a donkey. It had been hired out to two men who,

4 Professor Paul Pelliot

5 Count Kozui Otani

6 Professor Langdon Warner

7 Islam Akhun, from a photograph by Sir Aurel Stein

after ten months, had still not returned it, and indeed had apparently disappeared themselves. But more important, it bore a precise date – the sixth day of the second month of the sixteenth year of the Ta-li period, which corresponds to the year 781 of the Christian calendar. The place referred to in the petition could be variously read as Li-sieh, Lieh-sieh or Li-tsa. This almost certainly was the original name of Dan-dan-uilik. Other like documents also bearing this name had already found their way to Calcutta. Very possibly these too had originally been dug up by Turdi, for he well remembered finding similar-looking ones in Chinese characters here some years previously which he had sold to a dealer in Khotan.

Stein's last adventure that Christmas Day was one which, but for Turdi, might have ended in tragedy. Walking back to camp with his men as evening approached, Stein picked up a Chinese coin at the foot of a sand dune. Its date showed it to be some twelve hundred years old, and he lingered there looking for more while his men went on ahead. He later recounted what followed. 'When after a while I set about to return in the twilight I mistook the track, and then after tramping through the low dunes for about a mile vainly attempted to locate my camp. There was no sound nor any other indication to guide me.' Realising the danger he now faced of getting completely lost in the dark and freezing to death during the night he at once started to retrace his footsteps while he could still see them. Suddenly he recognised, protruding from the sand, the remains of some ancient walls which he had noticed some days before at a considerable distance to the south-east of his camp. 'Trusting to my recollection of their relative position,' he wrote, 'I turned off to my right and, keeping along the crest-line of the dunes which I knew to be running mainly from north-west to south-east, made my way slowly onwards until I heard my shouts answered by some of my men.' Turdi, growing uneasy at his absence, had sent the men out in couples in search of him. 'The shelter of my tent and the hot tea that awaited me were doubly welcome after this little incident,' wrote the relieved and grateful Stein with much understatement.

Next day he began to excavate the ruined structures that had helped to save his life the previous night. The first building to be cleared of sand, a small Buddhist temple, yielded a number of interesting frescoes and painted panels, as well as fragments of further manuscripts. More important, however, were the finds which came to light in the ground-floor rooms of the next building they tackled. Here they extracted from the dry sand a small cache of neatly rolled documents in Chinese. Some of these were badly decayed due to the damp which many years earlier, before the town's water resources finally dried up, must have seeped up through the mud floor. Others, fortunately, were in a good state of preservation. These were later translated by two of the leading sinologists of the day, Edouard Chavannes and Sir Robert Douglas. Two transpired to be bonds for small personal loans – one money, the other grain – made by one Chien-ying, described as a priest of the Hu-kuo monastery. The names of the borrowers, together with those of their guarantors, are also appended as pledging the whole of their household goods and cattle as surety. Both documents bear the date of the same year: 782.

As Stein points out, the Chinese designation of the monastery (Hu-kuo, literally 'country protecting') and the Chinese names of the superintending priests recorded in a third document 'leave little doubt as to the nationality of the monkish establishment', adding: 'That the population which supported it was not Chinese is plainly indicated by the ... names of the borrowers and their sureties.' To Stein the value of these finds lay in their very triviality. He explains: 'Unimportant in character and insignificant in size and material, it is highly improbable that these documents should date back to a period preceding by any great length of time the final abandonment of the building.' All bore dates ranging from 782 to 787, thus suggesting that Dandan-uilik was deserted around the end of the eighth century.

In the same building that yielded the cache of rolled-up documents, Stein also found three finely painted wooden panels, one of which depicted a man riding a horse and another astride a two-humped Bactrian camel. Its art-historical significance was at once recognised by Stein as he brushed the sand off it. Here indeed was the clearest proof he had yet found that his theories were correct. Not only did the drawing and composition demonstrate the high standard which Silk Road artists of the seventh century had already achieved, but its unmistakable 'mix' of Indian, Persian and Chinese influences provided a text-book example of how Serindian art had evolved during its slow passage eastwards.

Stein describes this exquisite little painting thus: 'The rider of the horse, whose handsome, youthful face shows an interesting combination of Indian and Chinese features, wears his long black hair tied in a loose knot at the crown.... The feet are cased in high black boots with felt soles, very much like those still worn by men of means in Chinese Turkestan, and are placed in stirrups.... From a girdle hangs a long sword, nearly straight, and of a pattern that appears early in Persia and other Muhammadan countries of the East.' Referring to the harness and trappings, he adds: 'We could not have wished for a more accurate picture of that horse millinery which in the eighth century flourished throughout Turkestan as much as it does nowadays.'

In all Stein excavated a total of fourteen buildings during nearly three weeks at Dandan-uilik. He also made a detailed survey of the site, noting its ghostly orchards and avenues of poplars, their gaunt, splintered trunks half buried in the sand. Here and there he found traces of old irrigation channels 'evidently constructed after the fashion that still prevails in the country'. He concluded that Dandan-uilik was not abandoned because of any sudden catastrophe, and suggested two possible explanations. Either political troubles had led to neglect of the community's irrigation system – without which life could not be sustained – or the streams supplying that system had dried up over the years, giving the inhabitants no choice but to leave. All the archaeological evidence, he argued, pointed to a gradual abandonment and nothing had been found to support suggestions, contained in local legends, that this once-flourishing caravan city had met with a Sodom and Gomorrah style fate.

On January 6, 1901, after paying off his labourers, Stein set off eastwards across the desert with his treasure-laden caravan towards the Keriya river, intending to follow it upstream to the oasis of Keriya. Of Dandan-uilik, which had so triumphantly confirmed what he had long believed about the Taklamakan, he wrote: 'It was with mixed feelings that I said farewell to the silent sand-dunes amidst which I had worked for the last three weeks. They had yielded up enough to answer most of the questions which arise about the strange ruins they have helped to preserve, and on my many walks across these swelling waves of sand I had grown almost fond of their simple scenery. Dandan-uilik was to lapse once more into that solitude which for a thousand years had probably never been disturbed so long as during my visit.' To reach the river they had to cross a succession of *dawans*, or sandhills, some rising as high as a hundred and fifty feet. Finally they reached the river with its 'glittering ice', and turned south-wards towards the relatively modern oasis of Keriya, where Stein hoped to learn of other ruins in the neighbourhood.

To the modern archaeologist, who is prepared to devote years of his life to one site, Stein's rapid progression from one excavation to another would be unthinkable. But in his day, it has to be remembered, scientific archaeology was still in its infancy. Moreover, in this inhospitable region excavations could never be more than lightning raids, their duration limited by the supplies that could be carried. Added to this, Stein was no Schliemann, backed by a huge personal fortune. He had had to wring the small budget required for his expedition from reluctant bureaucrats, and would have to justify himself to them when he got back. He was, furthermore, a civil servant himself, with a job to return to within a stated period, so time was all important. Only by covering as much ground as possible and showing that spectacular finds were to be made in the Taklamakan, could he hope to obtain support for future expeditions.

The caravan halted for five days at Keriya where Dash, Stein's terrier, managed to make enemies of the local dog population. 'We had no little trouble', wrote Stein, 'in protecting him from the large village dogs which he persisted in provoking by his self-assertive behaviour.' The day after their arrival, as the result of local enquiries, Stein heard stories of another ruined city in the desert north of Niya, the next major oasis eastwards along the old Silk Road. This was confirmed by an old man who said that he himself had seen these ancient ruins, some ten years before, half buried in the sand.

On January 18, Stein set out for Niya. 'Scarcely two miles beyond the town we were again in barren sands, the outskirts of the great desert northwards,' he wrote. In Niya, itself an ancient oasis, he received unexpected confirmation of the great antiquity of the site they were proposing to investigate some seventy miles to the north. One of his men fell into conversation with a villager who owned two inscribed wooden tablets which he said had come from this *kone-shahr*, or 'old town'. On examination these proved to be written in Kharoshthi, an ancient script used in India's extreme northwest a few centuries before and after the beginning of the Christian era. Further enquiries produced the man who had actually found them in a ruined house there the previous year while digging for treasure. He had come across several, thrown some away, including the two brought to Stein for examination, and given the rest to his children to play with. Stein generously rewarded the man who had rescued the two from the roadside – much to the chagrin of the original finder, a man called Ibrahim. However, he signed on Ibrahim as their guide, with promises of rich rewards if he could lead them to the ruined houses where he had found the panels. But he issued instructions to his men to watch Ibrahim closely lest he change his mind and slip away, preferring perhaps to keep this potential goldmine to himself. 'It had been impossible', explained Stein, 'to hide from him the value which I attached to these tablets, and . . . he subsequently seemed to regret not having himself made a haul of them.'

After travelling down the frozen Niya river for five days, with the snow-capped Kun Lun sparkling in the distance behind them, the party sighted the first two ruined houses, looking not unlike the ghostly structures of Dandan-uilik. But Stein soon realised that this site (which has come to be known as Niya, although far to the north of the present town of that name) was a good deal older, judging from the style of some finely carved pieces of wood he came upon in one house in which an early Gandhara influence was clearly visible.

By the end of the first day, it was evident to Stein that Ibrahim had brought them to the right spot. Eighty-five inscribed tablets were found in one room alone, with many more emerging from rooms subsequently cleared of sand, most of them excellently preserved. All, significantly, were wooden, for at that time paper had yet to reach Turkestan from China, where it had been invented in AD 105. The tablets were mostly in wedge-shaped pairs, from seven to fifteen inches long, and held together with string. Where the pairs had remained together, with their Kharoshthi texts facing inwards, the black ink looked as fresh as if it had just been applied. Rather like a modern envelope, the outside surface carried only a brief text, suggesting an addressee. A number of the tablets bore clay seals, the secrets of which were to emerge later. After examining a number of the mysterious documents in his tent that night, Stein decided that they probably represented official orders or letters written in an early Indian Prakrit language, but using the Kharoshthi script.

Stein now turned his attention to the first two houses they had passed on their arrival. During the next few days his men, reinforced by labour from the nearest village to the south, unearthed from these a number of interesting relics, including a beautifully carved stool, which today can be seen in the British Museum. Other finds in these and other houses included an ancient mousetrap, a boot last, a stout walking-stick, part of a guitar, a bow still in working order, another carved stool, a piece of a rug designed in elaborate geometric patterns and dyed in harmoniously blended colours, as well as many other everyday household objects. However, as at Dandan-uilik, Stein came upon little of intrinsic – as against historical – value. This site too, it appeared, had been evacuated gradually, rather than as the result of some catastrophe, giving the inhabitants time to remove their valuables. This possibility apparently never occurred to the native treasure-seekers, who remained ever hopeful of finding hastily abandoned gold or other valuables at these ruined sites.

While excavating the two isolated houses, Stein suddenly realised that he was standing in the middle of an ancient *bostan*, or garden. The trunks of poplars, dead for many centuries, could still be seen rising eight to ten feet above the sand and forming avenues and little squares. 'It was with a strange feeling, obliterating almost all sense of time,' he wrote, 'that I walked between two parallel rush fences that still form a little country lane just as they did nearly seventeen centuries ago.' Beneath the sand, beside the boles of the white poplars, his diggers found the remains of fruit trees, including apple, plum, peach, apricot and mulberry, the wood of which they recognised from their own village.

Stein next moved his operations to an area two miles north of his camp. For there he had spotted half a dozen more groups of ruined buildings scattered over an area several miles square. Spread on the sand around one crumbling ruin he came upon a number of wooden tablets, their inscriptions bleached off by the sun. He decided to dig here, and soon turned up a narrow slip of wood bearing Chinese characters. Before long he realised what he had unearthed – an ancient rubbish heap. 'For three long working days,' Stein wrote afterwards, 'I had to inhale its odours, still pungent after so many centuries, and to swallow in liberal doses antique microbes luckily now dead.' For embedded in an ancient morass of broken pottery, rags, straw, bits of leather 'and other less savoury refuse', he came upon layer after layer of inscribed wooden tablets.

Despite his cold-benumbed fingers and the stench raised by the fresh breeze, Stein kept a careful record of the stratification of each piece – some two hundred in all. Although disagreeable, this was essential to enable those whose task it would be to translate their texts to establish their chronology. In addition to the wooden tablets, he extracted two dozen Kharoshthi documents on leather, each neatly folded. These, he could see, were official documents of some kind. Most were dated, but frustratingly, only by the month and day.

A number of the wooden tablets, like some of those he had found the first day, bore clay seals. On cleaning the first of these Stein was astonished to recognise the figure of Pallas Athene, with aegis and thunderbolt. Other seals also depicted Greek deities, including a standing and a seated Eros, Heracles and another Athene. A number bore portrait heads of men and women with barbarian features but executed in classical style. Here was powerful evidence of how western iconography, travelling eastwards along the Silk Road, had penetrated far into this remote corner of Central Asia. As if to symbolise this fusion of East and West, one wooden 'envelope' bore two seals. One of these, according to its Chinese inscription, belonged to the Chinese political officer in charge of the Lop district far to the east. The other, showing a portrait head, was clearly cut in classical western style.

This rich hoard of documents, which is still being studied by scholars today, proved to consist of reports and orders to local officials and police: complaints, summonses, orders for safe conduct or arrest, lists of labourers, accounts, and other everyday matters in this long-dead community. The language used throughout was, as Stein had surmised, an early Indian

Prakrit written in Kharoshthi script. No documents of such early date concerned with day-to-day life have yet come to light in India. Their discovery adds some credence perhaps to a local tradition, recorded by Hsuan-tsang and also found in ancient Tibetan texts, that the Khotan region was conquered and colonised by Indians from Taxila (today in Pakistan) about two centuries before the birth of Christ. Numerous coins they found dating from the later Han dynasty – which collapsed in AD 220 – and a document bearing a precise date corresponding to the year 269, when the Emperor Wu-ti II ruled the 'western regions', led Stein to conclude that the site was abandoned not long after this. 'Great political and economic disturbances must have accompanied the withdrawal of Chinese authority from these parts,' he wrote, 'and with them one feels tempted to connect directly or indirectly the final abandonment of the site.'

Although there were many ruined buildings still to yield their secrets, Stein and his men were utterly exhausted after sixteen days of continuous digging in the bitter Taklamakan winter. It was no surprise to him therefore when men sent out to spot undiscovered buildings lurking behind sand dunes failed – 'for obvious reasons of their own' – to find any. But, with the season of sandstorms about to begin, he knew it was time to move on again, for he had heard in Niya of yet another site, further still along the Silk Road, which he wished to explore before finally starting home with his many treasures.

Leaving the Niya site on February 13, he struck eastwards across the desert towards the Endere, yet another of the snow-fed rivers which debouched into the thirsty Taklamakan. For it was on the far side of this river that the new site was said to lie. A week later, after reaching and crossing the frozen river, Stein came upon what was now becoming a familiar sight – rows of ancient wooden posts thrusting out of the sand, indicating that a once-thriving community had existed in this desolate spot. In addition, surrounding some of the ruined structures, was a huge clay rampart some seventeen feet high and thirty feet wide at the bottom. This was topped by a parapet of brick, adding a further five feet to its height. Obviously it had been built for protection, but against whom? While Stein was pondering this his labourers arrived from Niya, some one hundred and twenty miles away. As usual, his meticulous planning had paid off and he was able to commence work at once. During the next seven days, intensive excavations were carried out from early morning until, by the light of bonfires, late evening.

It took nearly two days to clear the remains of what was once a Buddhist temple standing within the ancient ramparts. Here, among the crumbling remains of life-sized stucco figures, Stein found what scholars later established to be the oldest known specimens of Tibetan writing. Written on tough, yellow paper they proved, on subsequent examination in London, to be sacred Buddhist texts. Scratched on nearby walls he also found graffiti in Tibetan which he carefully photographed.

Another inscription, this time in Chinese, presented something of a puzzle. It recorded the visit, in 719, of a Chinese administrator. And yet when the Buddhist traveller Hsuan-tsang passed that way some seventy years earlier he reported seeing no inhabited place during his ten-day march. However, at the precise spot where Stein was now excavating (today known as Endere), Hsuan-tsang mentions that there was an abandoned settlement. Stein was to clear up the mystery on a subsequent visit to the site. Evidence he discovered in an ancient rubbish dump showed that, after being abandoned to the desert for several centuries, Endere was then reoccupied by the Chinese, but some time after Hsuan-tsang's visit. The circular rampart had clearly been built to try to keep the warlike Tibetans at bay. The Tibetan graffiti found within the rampart bear witness to what is already known from the Chinese annals – that at the end of the eighth century the fierce Tibetans finally drove the Chinese from the area.

At Endere Stein had reached the easternmost point of his first Silk Road journey. Delighted with all he had found and learned, he knew it was time to start the homeward journey. But he was in no hurry, and there were still several sites which he intended to visit *en route*. In Keriya he heard that wild rumours were already circulating among the oases about what he had found in the lost desert cities he had visited. His camels, it was said, were returning heavily laden with gold and other valuables. Luckily Stein was able to convince the local amban that his 'treasures' were of quite a different variety by showing him some of the Kharoshthi documents.

His next target was the ruined town of Karadong. This lay far out in the Taklamakan at the 'mouth' of the Keriya-daria, and Stein had learned of it too from Hedin's book *Through Asia*. They reached it after a particularly unpleasant journey, for the season of sandstorms had now begun with a vengeance. Even goggles, Stein found, offered little protection from the dust and sand which got into everything. Forced to shelter when he could no longer see the route, he sent his locally employed guides ahead to find the ruins. Soon one returned with a piece of old pottery, saying that the site lay some three miles to the west. But Karadong was a disappointment, and represents one of Stein's rare failures. Although he and his men dug continuously for two days, they came upon nothing of consequence except for small quantities of ancient wheat, rice, oats and a kind of local porridge which Stein found useful for gluing envelopes. Most of the buildings had been totally obliterated by what he calls 'the full force of erosion', long before being swallowed up by the protective desert.

In *Sand-Buried Ruins of Khotan*, his account of this first expedition along the Silk Road, Stein observes that to describe Karadong as an ancient city 'would imply more imagination than an archaeologist need care to take credit for'. This appears to be a gentle dig at Hedin for sending him on a totally wasted journey, and an unpleasant one at that. Considering how much he owed Hedin (Dandan-uilik for a start), the remark seems somewhat uncharitable as well as uncharacteristic of Stein. His ill-humour was soon to evaporate, however, for his next site, the spectacular Rawak, would make up for everything.

It was on leaving Karadong that Stein received by runner from Macartney a message informing him briefly of the death of Queen Victoria. Although not yet officially British, he was already a true servant of the Empire. He calls Queen Victoria 'our Queen-Empress . . . the greatest ruler England has known since her expansion over the seas began'. Stein adds: 'I could see that my two Indian followers, to whom I communicated the news, understood, and in their own way shared the deep emotion which filled me.'

Rawak, which lies in the desert north of Khotan, means 'high mansion'. His guide had spoken simply of 'an old house' lying half-buried in the sand. However, Stein's first glimpse revealed a large stupa standing alone among the sand dunes. It was by far the most imposing structure he had yet seen. Much of it lay buried beneath some twenty-five feet of sand, but other parts were exposed to view. To his amazement Stein saw, scattered about on the ground, the shattered heads of colossal stucco figures which had obviously been cast aside by native treasure-seekers looking for hidden gold. Realising that he had found a site of major importance, he immediately sent a message to the nearest village, a day's march away, asking for labourers to be sent post-haste.

During the next nine days Stein and his men uncovered row upon row of huge statues representing Buddha and Bodhisattvas. In all, they retrieved from the dunes ninety-one of these, as well as many smaller figures of attendant deities and saints, and a number of small frescoes. Stein realised regretfully that, because of their size and condition, none of the larger-than-lifesize statues could be removed. Even if he had known what he was going to find here, and come provided with specially made crates, it would have been impossible to transport safely these massive but delicate sculptures all the way to India or Europe. He had to content himself with photographing them and recording their precise position, noting as he did so their very close affinity to early Gandhara works.

Conscientiously Stein replaced the sand he had so painstakingly removed from around the statues. 'It was a melancholy duty to perform,' he wrote, 'strangely reminding me of a true burial, and it almost cost me an effort to watch the images I had brought to light vanishing again, one after the other, under the pall of sand which had hidden them for so many centuries.' As it turned out, his efforts to safeguard these astonishing works of art, which had survived some fifteen hundred years in this utterly barren region, proved to be in vain. It had been Stein's hope that one day Khotan would have its own museum into whose protective care the sculptures could be placed. But on returning to Rawak some five years later he found to his dismay that a party of Chinese tomb-robbers had visited the stupa and smashed all the sculptures in the belief that they might conceal treasure.

Stein's first expedition to Chinese Turkestan was now finally over. Although it was only April, the heat of the desert was such as to make further work there impossible. But before setting out for home, his camels and ponies laden with works of art and documents, he had one more task to perform. The results of it were to cause a stir among orientalists, and a great deal of embarrassment to one in particular. Stein headed south, through the blazing desert heat and suffocating dust-storms, to Khotan.

7. The Unmasking of a Forger

Before starting the long journey which would take him and his treasures back to London, Stein was determined, once and for all, to discover the truth about Islam Akhun. Although he now had sufficient evidence to brand the Khotan treasure-hunter a liar, and furthermore had, in his own excavations, failed to find any trace of writing in Akhun's 'unknown characters', this did not prove conclusively that his 'old books' were all forgeries or that he was a forger. There was only one way to determine this. Stein had to confront the man 'whose productions', as he put it, 'had engaged so much learned attention in Europe'. He first took Pan-darin, the friendly and scholarly Chinese amban of Khotan, into his confidence. 'As an attempt on the part of Islam Akhun to abscond was by no means improbable,' Stein wrote, 'and as time was getting short, I took care to impress the learned Mandarin with the necessity of prompt and discreet action.'

On the morning of April 25, 1901, Akhun was produced by the amban's men from a nearby village where he had spent the winter practising as a *hakim*, or native doctor. Caught completely off his guard, he was marched before Stein accompanied by 'a motley collection of papers' which had been found in his possession and at his Khotan home. It was no surprise to Stein to recognise, among these, pieces of artificially discoloured paper bearing the now familiar unknown characters. Despite this damning evidence, Akhun protested total innocence. 'The examination of this versatile individual proved a protracted affair,' wrote Stein, 'and through two long days I felt as if breathing the atmosphere of an Indian judicial court.' Akhun's defence was that he had merely sold the manuscripts to Macartney and others in Kashgar for certain persons at Khotan, since dead or absconded, who, rightly or wrongly, told him that they had discovered them in the desert. On realising how eagerly these books were sought by Europeans, he had simply asked those persons to find him more. 'Now, he lamented, he was left alone to bear the onus of the fraud – if such it was,' Stein adds.

Akhun named the individuals responsible for landing him in this embarrassing situation as Muhammed Tari and Muhammed Siddiq, who had fled to Yarkand and Aksu respectively, while a third man had conveniently died. Stein observes: 'It was a cleverly devised line of defence, and Islam Akhun clung to it with great consistency and with the wariness of a man who has had unpleasant experience of the ways of the law' – as indeed he had. For posing once as Macartney's agent and blackmailing villagers, Akhun had been flogged and imprisoned. Again, for forging another sahib's handwriting to obtain money he had been forced to wear the huge and dreaded Chinese punishment collar of heavy wood, designed to prevent a prisoner from feeding himself.

Before beginning what Stein calls his 'curious semi-antiquarian, semi-judicial inquiry', he gave Akhun his personal assurance that he had no intention of pursuing the matter in the amban's court, '... for I was aware that such a step, in accordance with Chinese procedure, was likely to lead to the application of some effective means of persuasion, i.e. torture.' Stein added: 'This, of course, I would not countenance; nor could a confession as its eventual result be to me of any value.' How then was he to obtain the confession that he needed? Stein had one trump card still to play – the Hoernle report itself.

In the course of his protestations, Akhun had denied ever having been to any of the places from which the books were said to have come, claiming that only his three suppliers had been there. He had merely passed details of these sites, together with the finds, to the eventual purchasers. What he did not know, or perhaps had forgotten, was that Macartney had meticulously taken down his often graphic descriptions of his personal role in these treasure-seeking expeditions. Indeed, these had gone verbatim into Hoernle's report, which Stein now produced. When he began to read aloud from it, Akhun was visibly taken aback. It had never occurred to him that the stories he had told years before would even be remembered, let alone recorded permanently in an official document which would be quoted against him.

Akhun's defence now began to crumble fast. His first line of retreat was to admit that he had seen old books being manufactured at a deserted shrine by three men for whom he had eventually sold them. But then, realising that he stood before Stein convicted by his own past lies, he confessed to more and more. Finally he admitted everything. Until 1894, he told Stein, he had only dealt in coins, seals and other such antiquities which he acquired from villages around Khotan. But then he had heard from Afghan merchants of the high prices being paid by sahibs for the old books that Turdi and others had unearthed at Dandan-uilik. He determined to get in on this act. 'But the idea of visiting such dreary desert sites, with the certainty of great hardships and only a limited chance of finds,' Stein wrote, 'had no attraction for a person of such wits as Islam Akhun.' So it was that he hit upon the idea of writing his own ancient manuscripts.

Before long, he and at least one other partner were producing from their small factory a steady stream of such manuscripts. Their best customers were the two rivals, Macartney and Petrovsky, both of whom were eager to buy – Macartney especially so following Calcutta's instruction to its Central Asian representatives to try to obtain antiquities. So, while Islam Akhun cultivated the Englishman, one of his partners, Ibrahim Mullah, supplied the Russian. Ibrahim possessed a smattering of Russian, signs of which could be detected (in hindsight) in the shapes of some of the unknown characters produced by this unholy alliance. Indeed, scholars had noticed these, but had assumed that the Cyrillic-looking

8 Edge of Taklamakan desert, from a photograph by Sir Aurel Stein

9 The Bazaar, Yarkand

10 Abbot Wang, self-appointed guardian of Tun-huang,
from a photograph by Sir Aurel Stein

characters were of ancient Greek origin. Stein would have liked to have interrogated Ibrahim Mullah together with Akhun, but the former had judiciously vanished from Khotan the moment he heard of Akhun's arrest.

The forger's first handwritten manuscript was produced and sold in 1895. At first, Akhun told Stein, he had attempted to imitate the cursive Brahmi characters found in genuine manuscripts from Dandan-uilik. Indeed, in this he and his partners were entirely successful, for many of these had found their way into major museum collections in Europe where scholars continued to scratch their heads over them. The factory prospered and the partners gained confidence. Stein writes in *Sand-Buried Ruins of Khotan*: 'As Islam Akhun quickly perceived that his "books" were readily paid for, though none of the Europeans who bought them could read their characters or distinguish them from ancient scripts, it became unnecessary to trouble about imitating the characters of genuine fragments.' Each of the partners, therefore, was allowed to invent his own 'unknown characters'. Stein adds: 'This explains the striking diversity of these queer scripts, of which the analysis of the texts contained in the British collection at one time revealed at least a dozen – not exactly to the assurance of the Oriental scholars who were to help in their decipherment.'

Akhun and his partners soon found that they could not keep up with the demand, since it took time and care to prepare these forgeries. They therefore decided to step up production by means of the only technology at hand – block printing. In 1896 they produced their first block-printed books. So successful were they, however, that forty-five of these were fully described and illustrated by Dr Hoernle in his scholarly report of 1899. 'These too', Stein writes, 'showed an extraordinary variety of scripts in their ever-recurring formulas, and were often of quite imposing dimensions in size and bulk.'

Once his defence had collapsed, Islam Akhun told Stein

everything he wanted to know about the operations of the strange little factory in this remote corner of China which had for so long deceived Hoernle and other scholars. 'In fact,' writes Stein, 'he seemed rather to relish the interest I showed in them.' The paper they used, he told Stein, was bought locally. This was then stained yellow or light brown with *toghruga*, a dye obtained from a local tree. Once the writing had been added, either by hand or by block printing, the pages were hung over a fire 'so as to receive by smoke the proper hue of antiquity'. This was sometimes done with insufficient care, for Stein notes that some of the books in the Calcutta collection showed scorch marks. However, even these had failed to put Hoernle on his guard. Next the pages were bound up. The way this was done should have added the final nail in their coffin, so far as authenticity was concerned. For they were bound in crude imitation of European volumes, particularly the later 'discoveries'. In the event, even this anomaly failed to persuade Macartney, Petrovsky, Hoernle and others that they were being hoodwinked. Last of all, before being taken to Kashgar and offered to their unsuspecting purchasers, the forgeries were thoroughly encrusted with the fine sand of the Taklamakan as they would have been had they come from a sand-buried site. 'I well remember', Stein recounts, 'how, in the spring of 1898, I had to apply a clothes brush before I could examine one of these forged "block prints" that had reached a collector in Kashmir.'

Stein had decided not to ask for any charges to be brought against Akhun, and had already given him such an assurance in order to obtain a frank confession. He felt anyway that every bit as much to blame as these semi-literate counterfeiters were those who had unwittingly encouraged them by snapping up their forgeries so eagerly and undiscriminatingly. In *Sand-Buried Ruins of Khotan*, Stein omits any names, though he clearly indicts his friend Macartney and the Russian Petrovsky. Nevertheless, when he reflected on the valuable time wasted by Hoernle and other scholars on these worthless works, he felt quite glad that Akhun had been punished by the Chinese authorities, albeit for other villainies.

All the same, Stein was clearly intrigued by this remarkable and enterprising scoundrel. He was, Stein wrote, 'a man of exceptional intelligence for those parts, and also possessed of a quick wit and humour'. He found himself wondering whether Akhun could be of Kashmiri descent, which would explain this wiliness. Stein added: 'He greatly amused me by his witty repartee to honest old Turdi, whom with humorous impudence he adduced as a living demonstration of the fact that "there was nothing to be got out of the desert"....' Akhun, Stein relates, was greatly impressed at seeing his own handiwork so perfectly reproduced in the photogravure plates of the Hoernle report, and was keen to learn how this was done. 'I had no doubt', Stein adds, 'he was fully alive to the splendid opportunities for fresh frauds which this "Wilayeti" [town] art might provide. How much more proud would he have felt if he could but have seen, as I did a few months later, the fine morocco bindings with which a number of his block-printed Codices had been honoured in a great European library!'

Stein was anxious to obtain some of the wood blocks used by the forgers to produce their books, since this would provide irrefutable corroboration of Akhun's story, especially if one of them could be matched up with an actual page from one of the counterfeits. Akhun, who had been held between sessions of Stein's cross-examination in the amban's lock-up, was released so that he could go and find some. But the next morning he produced one only, and that from his own house. Word of his disgrace had quickly spread through the bazaars of Khotan and he now found all doors barred against him – especially those of his former associates. In the course of the two-day 'trial' Stein had flippantly told Akhun that he was far too clever to waste his life among the ignorant townsfolk of Khotan. This had been intended as no more than a joke, but Akhun evidently took it seriously. On the eve of Stein's departure from Khotan, Akhun turned up and begged to be allowed to travel to Europe with him, an idea prompted, Stein reflected, by the thought that there might be wider opportunities there for his special talents than in Chinese Turkestan.

It was now time for Stein to leave Khotan and to say his farewells to those who had served him so faithfully during that harsh winter in the desert. Stein's most regretful parting was from Turdi, who travelled with him as far as Zawa, the last village of the Khotan region. Turdi's experience and local knowledge had been invaluable to the success of the expedition. He had, at Dandan-uilik, probably saved Stein's life. Stein rewarded him with more 'treasure', as he put it, than the old treasure-seeker had brought back from all his own humble expeditions into the desert put together. He had also secured a steady local job for Turdi, who felt he was getting too old to wander around the Taklamakan any more in search of gold. Their farewell was a touching one, for Turdi, whom Stein was never to meet again, began to weep. 'I could see how genuine the tears were that at our parting trickled over the weather-beaten face of the old treasure-seeker,' Stein wrote later. He, too, was clearly much affected by this leave-taking. However, before long he was approaching the shrine of the sacred pigeons which he had passed seven months before, and his thoughts turned to a more cheerful theme – 'the results I was bringing back from Khotan'. His expedition had been more successful than he had ever dreamed, and this was merely the first. Stein halted briefly at the shrine, offering to the birds 'a liberal treat of maize and corn as my grateful *ex-voto* on leaving Khotan'.

Twelve days after bidding farewell to Turdi, Stein was back in Kashgar enjoying the hospitality of the Macartneys. He had not seen another European for eight months and was worried lest he should exhaust his hosts 'by a pent-up torrent of talk'. The next two weeks were spent disbanding his caravan, selling off his camels and ponies, and repacking his treasures for transportation to London via the Russian railhead at Andijan, the eastern terminus of the Trans-Caspian Railway. His ponies, he records proudly, were sold practically without loss, despite the fact that they had served him for eight wearying months, while the camels lost only a quarter of their original price. Had he been able to wait until the caravan season into Russia was once again in full swing, Stein writes, 'I should probably have recovered for the Government the whole of the original outlay on my Turkestan transport.'

Finally, exactly one year after first setting out from India, it was time for him to take leave of his hosts and depart with his twelve crates of treasures for London. On May 29, 1901, he left Kashgar for Osh, the nearest Russian town across the frontier, his antiquities and other baggage carried by eight ponies. Before departing, however, he had another painful leave-taking, this time from Dash, the little fox-terrier who had travelled so far with him. There could be no question of the dog accompanying him to England, and it was decided that he would return to India with Ram Singh. 'Equal as my little companion had proved to all the hardships of mountains and deserts,' Stein wrote, 'it would have been cruel to subject him to weeks of a wearisome journey by rail merely to leave him at the end to a confinement of quarantine on reaching England. Yet I confess I felt the separation from the devoted companion of all my travels until we joyfully met again one November night on a Punjab railway platform.' (The two-month trek from Kashgar, over the Karakoram, to India was to be the little dog's last great journey. For he died, apparently of a broken heart, when once again Stein had to leave India for London. He is buried in alpine Kashmir which, wrote Stein, 'he loved like his master'.)

*   *   *

Stein's first task on reaching England was one of the utmost delicacy. He had to go and see Hoernle, now living in Oxford, and break it to him that he had been made a fool of by a group of semi-literate villagers. Knowing that the great scholar was

already working on the promised second part of his report
on the Calcutta collection, due for publication that year, he
had written him a warning letter. But now he had the deeply
embarrassing task of telling him to his face. His embarrassment was heightened, moreover, by the fact that he had
good reason to be grateful to Hoernle, for it was this scholar
who, more than anyone else, had encouraged him in his
venture and given it his full official backing. Furthermore,
Hoernle was the leading scholar in Stein's own field – the linguistics of India and Central Asia – as well as being a personal
friend from Calcutta days. And now Stein's very triumph was
to result in Hoernle's humiliation. It certainly could not have
been with any feelings of pleasure that Stein caught the train
to Oxford that July morning.

⋆   ⋆   ⋆

Augustus Frederic Rudolf Hoernle, son of an Anglican missionary of German extraction, was born in India in 1841, making him Stein's senior by some twenty-one years. After graduating in Switzerland, he travelled to London where he
spent several years studying Sanskrit under the scholar Gold-
stucker. In 1865 he returned to India, initially to teach philo-
sophy at a college in Benares. From then on he devoted his
working life to the study of Indo-Aryan and other languages
and to the deciphering of ancient Indian manuscripts. (In all,
he published more than one hundred and fifteen books,
articles and papers, including his *Comparative Grammar of
the North Indian Vernaculars*, which took him five years to
compile.) Moving to Calcutta, then the capital of British India, he became a leading light in the Asiatic Society of Bengal,
over which he eventually presided, before finally retiring to
Oxford.

He had first found himself in the front rank of orientalists
in 1881 when confronted with fragments of a manuscript in
an archaic Indian script discovered in a north-west frontier
village. It had aroused considerable curiosity among In-

dologists, but no one succeeded in reading it until it was sent
to Hoernle. 'He attacked it at once and with striking success,'
wrote a contemporary. 'Although it had neither beginning nor
end, and consisted merely of disorganised fragments with not
a single leaf complete, he succeeded in deciphering the greater
part of it.' Hoernle proved it to be an ancient mathematical
treatise by an unknown author. Although its literary significance was not great, its decipherment marked out Hoernle
as a philologist of rare talent. Thus, exactly ten years later,
he was the natural choice for the task of deciphering the
famous, and immensely more important, Bower manuscript.
It was his brilliant work on this manuscript that resulted in
Hoernle being entrusted with the so-called British Collection
of Antiquities from Central Asia, and which indirectly led to
the international scramble for further manuscripts and antiquities from this region.

Precisely what passed between Stein and Hoernle no one
will ever know. Stein tactfully avoids any mention whatever
of this meeting in *Sand-Buried Ruins of Khotan*, his otherwise
detailed account of the expedition. Indeed, fellow scholars in
this field appear to have closed ranks in an effort to spare
Hoernle's feelings. Other than in the second part of Hoernle's
own report on the Calcutta collection, there appears to be no
mention of Stein's sensational and embarrassing discovery in
scholarly publications or newspapers of the time. When
Hoernle died in 1918, at the age of seventy-seven, his six-page
obituary in the *Journal of the Royal Asiatic Society* made no
mention of this humiliating episode.

The meeting between the two men was clearly friendly, for
Stein stayed with Hoernle and his family for several days.
However, the shock that Stein's revelations must have caused
the great Indologist is more than hinted at by Stein in a letter
to his brother Ernst, then living in Hungary. 'Understandably,' Stein reported, 'he is deeply disappointed by Islam
Akhun's forgeries, but to my satisfaction has recovered and I
am spared a painful discussion.' No doubt Stein's remarkable

linguistic finds offered some solace to Hoernle in his discomfiture, enabling him to turn his mind to something fresh. Indeed, his work on the Stein manuscripts was to lead, among other things, to the discovery of the long-lost language of Khotanese.

But a much more immediate problem faced Hoernle. In his 1899 report on the Calcutta collection he had discussed the possibility of the 'old books' being forgeries, but had firmly rejected it. How was he to extricate himself from this humiliating error of judgement? He confided to Stein that he wanted to have the report destroyed. That much we know from a second letter Stein wrote to his brother. However, the impossibility of this must have struck Hoernle almost at once. The report had been published as an extra number of the *Journal of the Asiatic Society of Bengal* and had been widely circulated. Suppression, therefore, was out of the question. There remained, moreover, the awkward matter of the promised second part. Hoernle had no choice but to go ahead with this. He had here two alternatives: either he could make a clean breast of his error, or he could gloss it over, hoping that his readers would not compare Parts 1 and 2 too closely. He was only human and chose the latter course.

So skilfully was it done that unless one turned back to the original report of 1899, or had read and remembered it at the time, one would have had the greatest difficulty in realising – from Part 2 – that he had ever been fooled at all. Far from admitting that he had originally come down on the side of the manuscripts and books in his care being authentic, he omits any reference to this now highly embarrassing verdict. He cleverly avoids having to do this by declaring – in Part 2 – that when he wrote the 1899 report 'the question of forgery was still an open one'. (This was only too obviously true, though anyone who had read Hoernle's original verdict might not have thought so.) He now put the record straight, albeit without conceding that it was he who put it wrong in the first place, by declaring that '... Dr. Stein has obtained definite proof that all "blockprints" and all the manuscripts in "unknown characters" procured from Khotan since 1895 are modern fabrications of Islam Akhun and a few others working with him'. He directs readers who might wish to see what these forgeries look like to a publication by the Russian scholar Dmitri Klementz (perhaps to show that the Russians were fooled too), as well as to an article, also containing plates, which he himself had contributed to the *Journal of the Asiatic Society of Bengal*. He carefully avoids drawing attention to the most obvious source of such illustrations – Part 1 of his own report – with its damning text. There he leaves the matter, for the bulk of the second part of his report was understandably concerned with genuine manuscripts, pottery and terracottas in the British Collection.

Hoernle, it might be added, was undoubtedly fortunate in the age in which he lived. Were such a distinguished scholar to be hoodwinked today by a semi-literate oasis-dweller living in Central Asia, next morning he would find half Fleet Street camped on his doorstep demanding a public explanation.

* * *

Meanwhile, Stein's discoveries from his first expedition had caused a sensation in antiquarian circles throughout Europe. Here was evidence of a previously unknown Buddhist civilisation going begging in one of the world's backyards, complete with its own remarkable art and literature. Hitherto, archaeologists had been concerned almost entirely with classical, ancient Egyptian and biblical sites. Central Asian archaeology was something new. When the 13th International Congress of Orientalists was held the following year in Hamburg, a special resolution was passed congratulating Stein on his amazing discoveries. This was to prove both an asset and a liability to him. While it undoubtedly helped him to obtain permission and funds from the Indian Government for a second expedition (albeit after much prevarication), it also attracted the interest of orientalists in Paris, Berlin and St

Petersburg to the region's possibilities. For some time, scholars there had been urging their governments to dispatch archaeological expeditions to this remote corner of China. Here was the spur they needed.

Curiously though, it was not an expedition from Europe which next chose to brave the hardships of the Taklamakan, but one from nearer the spot. Indeed, it was not a proper expedition at all, but a small and somewhat disorganised party of Buddhist monks from Japan which left for Central Asia in August 1902. Far more important, however, was the interest engendered in Germany by Stein's finds. For it was from the Ethnological Museum in Berlin that Stein's first serious rivals were to emerge. Just two months after the Hamburg conference a powerful German expedition, led by Professor Albert Grünwedel, set out to try its luck in Chinese Turkestan.

8. The Race Begins in Earnest

With the arrival of the Germans and the Japanese on the scene, in 1902, there now began what has been described as an 'international race' for the ancient Buddhist treasures of the Taklamakan and Gobi deserts. It was to last a quarter of a century and, by the time it was over, to have involved the archaeologists of seven nations. The vast quantities of antiquities which they removed were to end up in more than thirty museums and institutions spread across Europe, America, Russia and the Far East. On the whole, in public anyway, the rival expeditions were conducted in gentlemanly manner. Just occasionally, however, feelings ran high, and once, in a quarrel over who had the right to dig a particular site, the Germans and the Russians all but came to blows, the latter threatening angrily to expel the former by force of arms.

Stein, on the other hand, was content with the occasional scoff at his competitors, usually in private correspondence. The Germans, he wrote to a friend, 'always go out hunting in packs'. Considering the modest size of their expeditions (though not of their archaeological hauls) to call these 'packs' was patently absurd. But it indicates the irritation their presence caused him in a field which he felt he had pioneered, and would obviously have liked to have kept to himself for a few years longer. There was, in fact, ample room for all comers in this vast, archaeologically untouched region, with its multitude of sites. Yet it is clear that the rival groups spent much time looking over their shoulders.

The first of the four German expeditions which were to operate in Chinese Turkestan between 1902 and 1914 consisted of three Europeans, all on the staff of the Ethnological Museum in Berlin. It was led by Professor Albert Grünwedel, head of the museum's Indian section and author of a notable work on Buddhist art. His second-in-command was Dr George Huth, another art-historian, who was to die soon after their return from Central Asia, largely as a consequence of the hardships he suffered in the course of the expedition. Finally there was the colourful, ever-resourceful Theodor Bartus, the museum's handyman, who was to accompany all four expeditions.

For some time Grünwedel and his colleagues in the Indian section had had their eye on Chinese Turkestan and pondered on its archaeological potential. Like Stein, they had guessed from the clues that had begun to emerge from the region that this might prove to be an ancient meeting point between the art of classical Greece and that of Buddhist Asia. However, they were discouraged from venturing there by fear of the dangers and discomforts they were likely to encounter. But when the intrepid Hedin returned unharmed to tell his dramatic tale, followed soon afterwards by Stein with his impressive haul, the Germans decided it was time to join in the hunt.

They chose as their target the region around Turfan, on the northern arm of the Silk Road. Some five years earlier it had been visited by the Russian scholar Klementz, who had brought back frescoes, manuscripts and inscriptions to St Petersburg, and reported seeing at least one hundred and thirty Buddhist cave temples in the region, many containing well-preserved wall-paintings. Unlike Stein, whose first expedition was largely a gamble, the Germans knew that if Klementz was to be believed, then they were virtually guaranteed a rich harvest of treasures from around Turfan. Moreover, it was more accessible than Stein's far-flung sites along the southern caravan route, and its ruins apparently less plundered by native treasure-seekers.

The town of Turfan lies one hundred and fifty miles north of the top-secret site near Lou-lan where China tested her first generation of nuclear weapons. A green fertile oasis, it stands in a huge natural depression of some thirty thousand square miles, said by geographers to be the deepest anywhere on earth. Surrounding the town are earthquake-scarred hills, destitute of all life, and equally sterile deserts. To the north lies the snow-capped Bogdo-Ola ('Mountain of God'), higher than anything in Europe and forming the easternmost spur of the great T'ien Shan. Sir Eric Teichman, the British traveller, was reminded by the region's stark and dramatic scenery, of the Grand Canyon when he passed that way in the winter of 1935. So cold was it that his party had to light fires beneath the engines of their vehicles each morning to get them to start – 'a very dangerous procedure', he pointed out, but in that part of the world regarded as routine. By contrast, the heat in summer is so intense that the mercury often soars to 130 degrees Fahrenheit, driving even the residents underground into specially dug cellars. Yet scattered across this barren, rainless landscape are some of the most fertile oasis-villages anywhere in Chinese Turkestan. In the heyday of the Silk Road, wines, melons and fresh grapes were supplied from here to the imperial court at Ch'ang-an. The secret of this surprising lushness lies in an ingenious irrigation system, originally borrowed from Persia, which brings the melted snow from the mountains of the north via deep subterranean channels to these communities which could not otherwise exist.

Mildred Cable and Francesca French, those two intrepid missionaries who spent many months in the region during the 1920s and '30s, describe the oasis vividly in their book *The Gobi Desert*. '. . . Turfan lies like a green island in a sandy wilderness, its shores lapped by grit and gravel instead of ocean water, for the division between arid desert and fertile land is as definite as that between shore and ocean. Its fertility is amazing, and the effect on the traveller, when he steps from sterility and desiccation into the luxuriance of Turfan is overwhelming.' However, not all the oases in the Turfan region fared so well over the centuries, many of them having been abandoned. It was from among the scattered ruins of these that the Germans were to make a series of rich discoveries between 1902 and 1914, when the war brought their enterprise to a close.

The first expedition, led by Grünwedel, was away from Berlin for a year, but spent less than five months exploring and excavating in the Turfan region. The rest of the time was taken up in getting there and back. Financed largely by Friedrich Krupp, the arms' king, this first foray served primarily as a reconnaissance. However, Grünwedel's discoveries (forty-six cases of them), whilst modest compared with those of the three subsequent expeditions, caused a considerable stir among German Asiatic scholars, and even caught the imagination of the Kaiser himself. The finds included Buddhist frescoes, manuscripts and sculptures. As a result of the expedition's success, a committee was formed to organise a longer and more ambitious programme, and a fund was set up to equip it, both Krupp and the Kaiser contributing personally to this. But Huth's untimely death and Grünwedel's ill-health meant that an interim leader had to be found. The committee chose Albert von Le Coq, a man who was to prove as remarkable in his own way as either Hedin or Stein, and every bit as determined.

Born in Berlin on September 8, 1860, the son of a wealthy Huguenot wine merchant, it was assumed that he would follow in his father's footsteps. However, while still a schoolboy, he became involved in what his German obituarist describes as 'a forbidden alliance' but then dismisses as a 'harmless little peccadillo'. Whatever this was, it resulted in his being expelled. His father, who had been educated at an English public school, was furious, though we do not quite know what ensued. His obituarist skates over this period rather discreetly, picking up the thread again when he was twenty-one. By this time his relations with his father appear to have been restored, because he was sent first to London and then to America to train for the family business. While in the United States he also studied medicine. It was a skill which was to prove useful more than once, later on. At the age of twenty-seven he returned to Germany and joined the firm of A. Le Coq, wine merchants in the town of Darmstadt, which had been founded by his grandfather. His heart was not in it, however, and after thirteen years he sold the business and moved to Berlin. There he studied oriental languages for several years, including Arabic, Turkish and Persian at the School of Oriental Languages, and Sanskrit under the scholar Pischel. In 1902, at the age of forty-two, he joined – initially as an unpaid volunteer – the Indian section of the Ethnological Museum in Berlin, just as Grünwedel was mounting the first German expedition to Chinese Central Asia.

Now, only two years later, it was his turn. His expedition consisted of just himself and Theodor Bartus. They left Berlin in September 1904, first visiting St Petersburg to obtain the official passes necessary to see them across Siberia. They were also given letters of recommendation by savants at the Russian Academy of Sciences which, before very long, would be dispatching its own expeditions to the region. Their plan was to take the Trans-Siberian Express as far as Omsk, catch a boat there up the River Irtysh to Semipalatinsk, and then travel by horse-drawn *tarantass* to the frontier post at Bakhty from where they would continue to Urumchi and finally Turfan. But in Moscow they ran into difficulties. The station-master there objected to the amount of baggage (over a ton in weight) accompanying them, insisting that he would have to put on an extra luggage van to carry it all. In *Buried Treasures of Chinese Turkestan*, von Le Coq's account of the expedition, he describes with relish (for he had no time for the Russians) what followed. '... holding a 50-rouble note behind my back, I passed up and down before the Cerberus, gently waving the paper. When I had passed him three or four times the note disappeared and the station-master said: "Well, we'll manage." And sure enough they did manage....'

After travelling for five days in a train packed with Russian officers (only a few of whom 'came up to our idea of officers') bound for the Russo-Japanese War, they reached Omsk. The Irtysh steamer took them as far as Semipalatinsk ('an appalling hole') where they hired their *tarantass* to carry them across the melancholy Siberian landscape to the Chinese frontier. At Chuguchak, their first halt in Chinese territory, they were warned by the Russian consul that civil war was raging locally and that the country was unsafe. Von Le Coq, who was carrying twelve thousand roubles in gold, sat on top of it, rifle in hand, for the remainder of the journey to Urumchi, then the capital of Chinese Turkestan. Few European travellers have a good word to say for this seedy, flyblown town with its blood-stained past. Mildred Cable and Francesca French, who lived there for a time, recalled its 'jaded, unhealthy-looking people' and its 'sordid streets ... typical of its sordid civic life'. In their day it teemed with police informers. 'A secret report can always command a price,' they wrote in *The Gobi Desert*, 'and promotion often depends upon supplying it, therefore no man trusts his neighbour.' They added that 'no one enjoys life in Urumchi, no one leaves the town with regret, and it is full of people who are only there because they cannot get permission to leave....'

Urumchi's traditions of hospitality 'are all its own', observes Peter Fleming in *News from Tartary*, adding by way of explanation that 'the death rate at banquets is appalling'. This is a reference, not to food-poisoning, but to two notorious banquets, held there some twelve years apart, and both attended by the able but autocratic Governor, General Yang Tseng-hsin. To the first of these – in 1916 – he invited all those whom he suspected of plotting his overthrow. When his guests were well filled with drink, Yang brought in the executioner and, while the band played outside, had them beheaded one by one, before calmly continuing with his own meal. The second banquet took place in 1928. This time it was the General's turn to die – with other officials – in a hail of bullets, just as a toast was being drunk to the Soviet

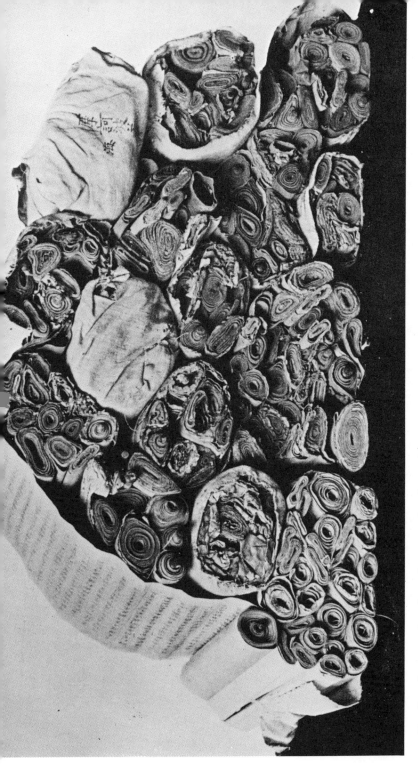

11 Bundles of manuscripts from the secret chamber at Tun-huang

12　Buddhist grottoes at Tun-huang

consul-general, who hastily sought refuge with his wife in a lavatory.

Despite the eighty-six-course banquet laid on for them by the Chinese (which happily everyone survived), the two Germans found Urumchi every bit as unsavoury as most other European travellers. One of the first things they witnessed on arrival was a particularly cruel form of execution in progress in the town's main street. The victim was incarcerated in a specially built cage known as a *kapas*. His head, firmly secured, stuck out of the top, while his feet rested on a board. The latter was gradually lowered, day by day, until on about the eighth day his neck finally broke. Von Le Coq took a photograph of the dying man in his cage which appears in *Buried Treasures of Chinese Turkestan*. 'The traffic', he wrote, 'went on as usual past this barbaric apparatus.' Beside it, the photograph shows, a melon dealer sits surrounded by his fruit, totally unperturbed by his neighbour's dying agonies. The sight, von Le Coq wrote, 'made a very unpleasant impression on me'. The two Germans were also horrified by the behaviour of the Russian consul. It was his custom to drive imperiously through the town in an open carriage, his escort of forty mounted Cossacks lashing across face or shoulders with their whips anyone who failed to jump aside. Von Le Coq protested to the consul about this but was told that this was the only way to treat such people.

The two Germans then continued their journey to Turfan, one hundred miles further into Chinese Turkestan, where they were soon introduced to the repulsive insect life. In addition to mosquitoes, fleas, sandflies, scorpions and lice there were two particularly unpleasant varieties of spider. There were the jumping kind, with bodies the size of pigeons' eggs, whose jaws produced a crunching sound and which were said to be poisonous. Then there were the smaller ones, black and hairy, which lived in holes in the ground. These were particularly feared for their bite, which, if not actually lethal, could be extremely dangerous. However, it was the huge Turfan cockroaches which the Germans found most repellent. 'It was enough to make a man uncontrollably sick to wake in the morning with such a creature sitting on his nose, its big eyes staring down at him and its long feelers trying to attack its victim's eyes,' von Le Coq wrote. 'We used to seize the insect in terror and crush it, when it gave off an extremely disagreeable smell.' A pleasant surprise, for a change, lay in the rapturous welcome received by Bartus, who was fondly remembered by the natives from Grünwedel's expedition of the previous year. At first the two Germans had been mistaken for Russians, who were greatly disliked locally. Then a butcher, an enormous Uighur, recognised Bartus and raised the cry of '*Batur! Batur!*', meaning 'Hero! Hero!', a pun on his name.

On November 18, 1904, the two men reached Karakhoja, an ancient ruined city built of mud lying in the desert to the east of Turfan, where they planned to spend some time excavating. It was to yield them rich finds. But as they stood there on that first day the prospects could hardly have looked very promising. Much of the old city had been levelled by local villagers so that the rich soil could be used for cultivation. Buildings had been demolished by farmers in search of frescoes whose bright pigments, it was believed, made a potent fertiliser. Quantities of ancient beams and other timber had been removed for use as building material or fuel. Where paintings depicting men and beasts had survived the fertiliser-seekers, the eyes and mouths had been picked out. 'For the belief still exists', von Le Coq wrote, 'that painted men and animals, unless their eyes and mouths at least had been destroyed, come to life at night, descend from their places, and do all sorts of mischief to men, beasts and harvests.' Even in the short time that had elapsed between Grünwedel's visit and their own much fresh damage appeared to have been done.

But this initial disappointment was not to last long. For in the heart of this great, mud-walled city of the dead, peasants led them to the remains of a six-foot-high fresco they had just found. An imposing male figure with a halo, and surrounded by acolytes of both sexes, dominated the painting. It proved to be an auspicious start to their expedition, for it almost certainly depicts Manes, the founder of the Manichaean faith. If so, it is the first portrayal of this mystical figure ever to come to light. Writing in 1926, four years before his death, and surrounded by the staggering wealth of art treasures he, Grünwedel and Bartus had removed from the Silk Road, von Le Coq still felt that this ninth-century wall-painting represented one of the most important of all their finds.

From the discoveries that followed, it is clear that around the middle of the eighth century Karakhoja (or Khocho, to use its ancient name) had nurtured a flourishing Manichaean community. This strange and ascetic faith had been founded in Persia some five centuries earlier by Manes. His heretical ideas provoked intense hostility among believers of rival faiths, including Christians, Moslems and Zoroastrians, and after being defeated in a debate with Zoroastrian priests, he was crucified as a heretic. In the Middle East and Balkans the faith suffered savage persecution, to the point of extermination, with the result that no traces of its written records or religious literature have survived there. To escape persecution, some five hundred Manichaeans fled eastwards to Samarkand, today in Soviet Central Asia, where they found refuge. From there their creed and art (Manes himself was a renowned artist) was gradually carried further eastwards along the Silk Road, absorbing Buddhist influences as it travelled, until it eventually reached Karakhoja. It is the dearth of evidence of the Manichaeans elsewhere that made von Le Coq's discoveries at Karakhoja so important.

The finds included beautifully and brilliantly illuminated manuscripts, frescoes, hanging paintings executed on cloth, and other textiles. All of these, as might be expected, showed strong Persian influences. The manuscripts – on silk, paper, parchment and leather, and displaying superb calligraphy – were to contribute much to scholars' meagre knowledge of this long-extinct faith. The contribution might have been far greater, von Le Coq argues, had the German expeditions reached Karakhoja earlier, in time to prevent the wholesale destruction of much of the old town. For it was here that he learned of the Manichaean library which a frightened peasant had tipped into the river. It was here also that he himself came upon another library, irretrievably damaged by muddy irrigation water, in a Manichaean shrine. 'The loess water had penetrated the papers,' he wrote, 'stuck everything together, and in the terrible heat of the usual summer . . . all these valuable books had turned into loess. I took specimens of them and dried them carefully in the hope of saving some of these manuscripts; but the separate pages crumbled off and dropped into small fragments, on which the remains of beautifully written lines, intermingled with traces of miniatures executed in gold, blue, red, green and yellow, were still to be seen.' He added sadly: 'An enormous treasure has been lost here.' Given the immense strides that modern technology has enabled conservationists to make in recent years, one suspects that nowadays something might have been retrieved from this mess. An Agatha Christie-like footnote to this find was the discovery of the dried-up corpse of a murdered Buddhist monk, still wrapped in his blood-stained robe, at the entrance to the library. For Buddhism appears to have coexisted with Manichaeism here.

Nor was he the only murder victim they were to stumble on at Karakhoja. 'In one of the southern domed buildings . . . we made a horrible discovery,' wrote von Le Coq. After breaking open the door they found the heaped-up corpses of at least a hundred Buddhist monks, many still showing horrifying wounds. One skull had been split from crown to upper jaw with a single savage blow. Von le Coq attributes this thousand-year-old massacre to religious persecution by the Chinese authorities.

In *Buried Treasures of Chinese Turkestan*, now long out of print, von Le Coq describes vividly the day-to-day discomforts he and Bartus suffered during their months at Karak-hoja. They began work at sunrise, sometimes at 4 a.m. or before, and worked on in the extremes of heat and cold until 7 p.m., when the workmen received their daily wage and the two Germans settled down to recording and packing the day's finds. One of the curses of excavating at Karakhoja was the dust which rose in suffocating clouds. 'In the evening,' von Le Coq complains, 'we often used to cough up solid streams of loess from our bronchial tubes.' Although this dust took some of the heat out of the cruel Turkestan sun, it also made photography difficult and all their early pictures were under-exposed. Meals were extremely monotonous – 'rice mixed with mutton-fat or . . . mutton-fat mixed with rice', von Le Coq records. In summer, moreover, the mutton-fat was invariably rancid. This unappetising diet was supplemented all the year round with grapes and fresh melon as well as dried fruits and the excellent bread baked by their landlady. Just occasionally the Germans allowed themselves to crack one of their precious bottles of Veuve Cliquot Ponsardin, which they first cooled Turkestan-style in a piece of wet felt. For a case of this had thoughtfully been provided by von Le Coq's sisters as a farewell gift.

Even when they had finished their day's work there was no respite for von Le Coq. The courtyard of the house in which they were staying would soon fill up with sick people, many of whom had travelled great distances and all of whom expected instant cures from the 'foreign gentleman'. As most of them were suffering from rheumatism or malaria, with the help of aspirin and quinine and the medical training he had received in America, von Le Coq soon acquired an unwanted reputation as a miracle healer and inevitably the number of his patients multiplied. One evening, by chance, he dis-covered an old woman at the gate in tears. She explained that she could not afford the 'fee' to see him. On further question-ing he discovered to his horror that his landlord Saut was mak-ing a profitable sideline by charging all the sick a fee before allowing them into the courtyard. Von Le Coq was so angry that he gave him a couple of lashes with a riding whip – 'the only time I had ever struck a native', he wrote. He also threatened to report the miscreant to the Wang of Lukchun, the local potentate, who, Saut knew, would punish him with the 'big stick', a heavy cane with an oar-shaped end. One stroke of this was sufficient to draw blood and twenty-five would kill a man. No sooner had the two Germans retired to bed that night than a loud wailing began outside. The wily Saut had sent his grandmother, mother, wife, beautiful daughter and all his other female relations to intercede on his behalf with sobs and gifts. Von Le Coq allowed himself to be persuaded on a promise of better behaviour in future.

One day, when the Germans had been working at Karakhoja for some time, two local dignitaries called on them saying: 'Sir, it is not good that you two should live alone. You must marry.' Von Le Coq explained that they already had wives, but this was brushed aside. The dignitaries' own daughters were ready to marry them, the Germans were told. 'This', wrote von Le Coq 'was an unpleasant revelation.' Anxious not to hurt local feelings, he thanked the men profusely, saying that in Berlin he and Bartus would receive twenty-five strokes with the big stick if they were discovered by the Kaiser to have taken second wives.

In spite of such distractions, work at Karakhoja continued steadily, yielding a rich flow of interesting, if not spectacular, finds. Apart from the remarkable wall-painting of Manes, the most impressive discovery was a beautiful, near life-size statue of Buddha in Gandhara style, unfortunately headless. It had once been embellished with brilliant colours, but these had mostly been washed away over the centuries by melting snow and the rare but torrential rainstorms. In describing it, von Le Coq betrays a strong bias towards classical as opposed to oriental art. He writes: 'The drapery falls in noble lines, not yet degraded by Eastern Asiatic misunderstanding of classic forms.' He was much puzzled by this classically influenced

Buddha and other Hellenistic sculptures found here and else-where. How was it, he wondered, that sculptures had managed to retain their Greek character while the wall-paint-ings had already absorbed Chinese influences? This mystery was to be solved months later when, at another site, Bartus stumbled upon an ancient workshop full of stucco moulds for mass-producing parts of large sculptures. Clearly these were intended to be used again and again, which accounted for the survival of an archaic sculptural style. Subsequent finds sug-gested that, around the ninth century, casts were redesigned to depict oriental features, including slanting eyes, shorter noses and straighter hair.

Another startling find at Karakhoja was a small Nestorian church which lay outside the walls of the old city. It contained the remains of a distinctly Byzantine-style mural showing a priest and people carrying branches – possibly intended to depict a Palm Sunday service. For the most part, however, the Karakhoja finds consisted of coins, fragments of silk and other woven fabrics, and many scraps of sacred texts, the latter apparently torn up deliberately, though by whom is not clear. Among the manuscripts they found which had escaped such vandalism, twenty-four different scripts were later identified.

By now they had been working continuously at Karakhoja for nearly four months. Although only the end of February, it was already getting hot in the Turfan depression. Feeling that they had more or less exhausted the site's possibilities, the two men decided to move north to a series of stupas perched above the grim Sangim gorges. Here, although cooler, they were imperilled by frequent avalanches of stones and mud unleashed by the melting mountain snows. But these risks were quickly to prove worth while, for the men soon brought to light two entire manuscript libraries in different stupas, one discovered by Bartus and the other by von Le Coq. One alone was large enough to fill 'several corn sacks', the latter records.

To the Germans' astonishment they realised one day that

they were not the only people excavating there. Across a stream they spotted two old women busily digging into a mound, clearly looking for treasures. Bartus and von Le Coq had found nothing that day. To their chagrin they observed that the two lady treasure-seekers opposite were enjoying considerable success, unearthing sculptured demons' heads and quantities of fine manuscripts. To add insult to injury, the crones turned out to be hard bargainers, forcing the Germans to pay extortionate prices for their booty.

Since their arrival at Karakhoja, von Le Coq had been making regular reports to Berlin on their progress. From letters he received in reply, he was disturbed to discover that the sponsoring committee seemed to have magnified the importance of the finds. Even the Kaiser was showing overmuch enthusiasm for relics that von Le Coq knew to be largely of academic interest. It must be remembered that, due to Grünwedel's ill-health, his own position as expedition leader was temporary. He knew that at any moment he might be replaced, and therefore had only limited time in which to make his name. He was hampered in this by Grünwedel's instructions to leave alone what, in effect, were the best sites. To add to von Le Coq's frustration, his superior's plans seemed to change with every post. When a letter now arrived saying that Grünwedel was still not coming to take over from him, von Le Coq decided to risk his displeasure and head for the nearby Buddhist cave complex of Bezeklik (meaning 'Place Where There Are Paintings') – despite instructions to the contrary. It was a gamble that paid off, for he and Bartus were soon to be rewarded by a series of dazzling finds.

9. Von Le Coq Spins a Coin

The Buddhist monks who a thousand years ago built the great monastery complex at Bezeklik chose its position with ingenuity. Even in von Le Coq's day a visitor to this remote and dramatically barren region could pass quite close to the site without realising it was there. Its hundred or so temples, mostly hewn out of the rock, occupied a long narrow terrace perched high on a cliff face. The only approach was by climbing a winding pathway leading to, and then along, the clifftop. From there a precipitous stairway descended to the monastery some thirty feet below. Only from one spot could it be seen, and to ensure both security and privacy the architects had built a wall to block this view from the eyes of passers-by. Today this vast honeycomb of temples still stands, leaving a profound impression on the visitor brave enough to face the rugged drive there. But the name of Albert von Le Coq is not one to conjure with locally.

On arrival, the two Germans set up their headquarters in an old temple building, at one time inhabited by goatherds, at the southern end of the monastery complex. The walls of this, and other temples around it, had once borne murals, but these had been ruined by smoke from the goatherds' fires. Von Le Coq and Bartus decided therefore to investigate those temples at the northern end of the terrace. For these had been protected from occupation by the sand which over the centuries had cascaded down from the hills above, filling them from floor to ceiling. Entering one of the largest, von Le Coq clambered unsteadily along the heap of sand piled high against the wall. Immediately, the movement of his feet started a small avalanche beneath him. 'Suddenly, as if by magic,' he wrote, 'I saw on the walls bared in this way, to my right and left, splendid paintings in colours as fresh as if the artist had only just finished them.' He shouted excitedly to Bartus to come and see this amazing chance discovery. After examining what could be seen of the frescoes, the two men solemnly shook hands, for here was something they knew was likely to prove momentous. 'If we could secure these pictures,' von Le Coq wrote in *Buried Treasures of Chinese Turkestan,* 'the success of the expedition was assured.'

After laboriously removing quantities of sand, they found themselves staring at six, larger-than-lifesize paintings of Buddhist monks, three on either side of the entrance. More followed as they dug further into the sand-filled temple. Some of the figures were distinctively Indian, wearing yellow robes, and with their names recorded in Central Asian Brahmi script beside them. Others, in violet robes, were clearly from Eastern Asia, their names being written in Uighur and Chinese. Von Le Coq observes in his book that these thousand-year-old portraits were not the usual stereotypes done with stencils, but were attempts at achieving real likenesses.

Continuing their advance along the corridor they next brought to light from beneath the sand fifteen giant-sized paintings of Buddhas of different periods. Other figures, shown kneeling before the Buddhas offering gifts, were of particular interest to von Le Coq since they depicted individuals in costumes of different nationalities. They included Indian princes, Brahmins, Persians – and one puzzling character with red hair, blue eyes and distinctly European features.

In the temple cella, or central shrine, they came upon frescoes of grotesque-looking Indian gods, six-handed demons, some human-headed birds which had seized a child and were being pursued by hunters, and a king on a hunting expedition accompanied by his attendants. In the cella's four corners, dressed in suits of armour, were the four legendary Guardians of the World. Other figures included the temple's human benefactors, the men on one side, women on the other, with faded names still inscribed beside some of them.

This was their most exciting coup so far, and von Le Coq was determined at all costs to remove every one of the paintings and transport them to Berlin. 'By dint of long and arduous work,' he wrote later, 'we succeeded in cutting away all these pictures. After twenty months of travelling they arrived safely at Berlin, where they fill an entire room of the museum.' He added, 'This is one of the few temples whose sum-total of paintings has been brought to Berlin.'

A Czechoslovak scholar, Professor Pavel Poucha, who in 1957 was allowed to travel through Chinese Turkestan, claims that the Germans used a sword to remove these delicate paintings. This is certainly not what we are told by von Le Coq. According to him each painting was first carefully cut around with a very sharp knife, the incision being deep enough to penetrate the clay, camel dung, chopped straw and stucco on which it was painted. Next a hole had to be made in the rock beside it with a pick-axe or hammer and chisel to allow a fox-tail saw to be inserted. 'When the surface-layer is in a very bad condition, men are sometimes employed to keep boards covered with felt pressed firmly against the painting that is to be removed,' von Le Coq explains. 'Then this painting is sawn out; and when this process is complete, the board is carefully moved away from the wall, the upper edge being first carried out and down, bearing the painting with it, until at last the latter lies quite horizontal on the board. . . .' He adds: 'The physical exertion connected with this work is exceptionally great.' The most exhausting task, as even Bartus – with his 'Herculean strength' – found, was using the fox-tail saw.

Each painting was then laid face downwards on a board which had first been covered with dry reeds, next with felt and finally cotton wool. Another layer of cotton wool was placed on the back of this painting, then a second fresco laid face upwards on top of this. Finally, more padding and a second protective board was placed on top of the uppermost painting, thus completing the 'sandwich'. The boards were cut large enough to overlap the paintings and so give them added protection. Straw flax was stuffed into the space thus left, and the whole package then bound with ropes. Up to half a dozen wall-paintings were sometimes secured thus between one pair of boards. The package was then placed in a crate lined with straw flax to prevent any movement during transportation home. 'We have never had the least breakage in cases packed in this way,' von Le Coq claimed with pride. Large paintings were first sawn into several pieces, care being taken to cut around faces and other features of aesthetic significance.

It is interesting to note the slightly different technique evolved by Sir Aurel Stein, after much experiment, during his three expeditions. Like the Germans, he also used a saw, carefully inserted behind the frescoes, to cut them down from the wall. They were then backed with stout canvas saturated with glue. The paintings, each of them on average between one-and-a-half and two inches thick, were next placed face to face, but with a cushion of cotton wool, a sheet of Khotan paper, and then another layer of cotton wool between them. When Stein's supplies of cotton wool ran out, he used raw sheep's wool. Each pair of paintings was then bound round with rushes before being clamped together between wooden battens and secured with ropes. Finally they were placed in wooden cases stuffed with more rushes. Like those of the Germans, Stein's larger paintings, some of which were up to ten feet tall, could not be transported in one piece and had first to be cut into pieces, later to be carefully reunited after their long and arduous journey home by camel, pony, yak or other means.

It was at Bezeklik, half a century later, that the British writer Basil Davidson was shown by aggrieved officials the excisions left by von Le Coq and Bartus when removing frescoes. Each time they halted opposite a gap which had once contained a painting, Davidson's escorts uttered just one word – 'Stolen!'

In *Buried Treasures of Chinese Turkestan*, von Le Coq describes vividly the austere beauty of the landscape around Bezeklik. 'In the death-like silence that always reigns there, the splashing of the rushing stream, as it fell over the rocks at the foot of the gorge in the mountainside, sounded like scornful laughter,' he wrote. Despite its beauty, the region possessed an atmosphere that at times made both Germans feel uneasy. There was something about it that struck them as 'weird and uncanny', and which perhaps had inspired the hideous-looking demons which glared down from so many of the temple walls.

One moonlit night at Bezeklik, 'when all was still as death, ghastly noises suddenly resounded as though a hundred devils had been let loose'. The two men leaped out of bed and, grabbing their rifles, rushed onto the terrace. Von Le Coq goes on: 'There, to our horror, we saw the whole horse-shoe gorge filled with wolves that, head in air, were baying at the moon with long-drawn-out howls.' However, he and Bartus were reassured by their men that the wolves of this region were harmless. 'After a few shots, one of which hit one of the visitors,' von Le Coq adds, 'the animals left us after they had eaten their dead comrade.' They heard of one instance only of wolves killing a human being. The victim was a pretty, twelve-year-old Karakhoja child, known to both the Germans, who was betrothed against her will to a man of sixty. She ran away across the desert in the direction of a neighbouring oasis. Exhausted, she evidently stopped beside a spring and fell asleep and here the wolves discovered her. "All that was found later were blood-stained fragments of her clothing and her long top-boots with her legs still inside,' von Le Coq relates.

After briefly exploring another Buddhist temple site nearby which yielded more frescoes, dating from the seventh century, as well as embroideries and manuscripts, they moved on to the village of Tuyoq, which means 'carved out'. This region, von Le Coq informs us, was famous for its oval-shaped, seedless grapes which were sold, as raisins, as far away as Peking, nearly four months' journey to the east. Upstream from the village they found scores of temples, but all of them in ruins. Also, clinging like 'a swallow's nest on to the almost perpendicular slope of the mountainside', they came upon a huge monastery. Eleven years later, in 1916, the entire monastery plunged into the gorge when a severe earthquake convulsed the area. In one cave temple in this winding valley von Le Coq found a monk's cell whose architectural plan showed distinct Iranian influences and which, when cleared, turned out to contain quantities of religious texts. An unsuccessful attempt had been made to burn these, and the Germans were able to rescue sufficient to fill two sacks. Many dated from the eighth and ninth centuries. They also found what von Le Coq described as 'wonderful embroideries'.

Moving on once again, von Le Coq sent Bartus to investigate some ruins lying to the north of Turfan at Shui-pang while he set out for Urumchi with the large consignment of packing cases containing their finds. There, with the help of the Russian consul, he hoped to hire a reliable man to escort the heavily laden wagons to the nearest railhead across the Russian frontier. He took with him 6,000 roubles (about £650) in gold which he proposed to convert into Chinese money. Wisely he slept with it under his pillow, for one night while staying at a *caravanserai* at Dabanching they were the victims of thieves who broke in by first wetting – thereby weakening – the mud wall and then cutting their way through it with a sword. Fortunately they were disturbed and only got away with saddles and clothes for which von Le Coq received compensation from the authorities in Urumchi.

On returning to Karakhoja, where he and Bartus had agreed to rendezvous, he found that his colleague had dug from the ruined walls of Shui-pang 'a marvellous booty' of early Christian manuscripts. These included a fifth-century psalter, fragments of St Matthew's Gospel and the Nicene Creed in Greek, and texts dealing with the finding of the True Cross by the Empress Helena, and the visit of the Three Kings to the infant Christ. So excited was Bartus by his find that he had heaped the manuscripts on to a *mappa*, the two-wheeled, springless cart of China, and ridden non-stop with them to Karakhoja.

By now it was the beginning of August, and the furnace heat of the Turfan depression had become unbearable. Both men were suffering from prickly heat, a skin condition affecting Europeans in hot climates which causes intense itching. To escape from it they decided to move camp to Hami, some two hundred miles to the east. Lying on the edge of the Gobi, but in the foothills of the T'ien Shan, it would at least be cooler than Turfan (although Colonel Bell reported in 1887 that summer temperatures there reached 122 degrees in the shade). It took them twelve days to reach this former capital of Genghis Khan, stopping each night in one of the bug-ridden wayside inns. Nobody has much to say for this particular stretch of the Gobi. To Mildred Cable and Francesca French, who were not given to overstatement, it was one of those regions 'which surpass all others in power to horrify'.

Eighteen years before von Le Coq's visit, Colonel Bell had been badly received at Hami by Chinese officials who, having penetrated his Chinese disguise, had denounced him (perhaps not unreasonably) as a 'foreign devil'. He explained away this ungentlemanly behaviour by dismissing them as 'the scum and overflow' from the frontier towns. But von Le Coq and Bartus had an altogether happier experience of Hami. On hearing that they were coming, the Khan had sent provisions, including eggs, meat and fruit, to all the inns they halted at on the way. This did much to alleviate the attentions of the bugs.

On arrival they had an audience with the Khan in his sumptuous palace, some rooms of which, von Le Coq tells us, 'were furnished with exceptional beauty'. He continues: 'We saw on all sides splendid, fast-dyed Chinese and Khotan carpets, beautiful silk embroideries, both in Chinese style and also in that practised in Bokhara; valuable jade carvings from Khotan, side by side with Chinese porcelain; French clocks for the mantelpiece and, O horrors! terribly ugly Russian paraffin lamps of the cheapest and commonest kind.' On one wall was a cuckoo-clock which, von Le Coq adds, 'delighted us with its homely note'.

The one-time wine-merchant from Darmstadt was astonished to find in the home of this Moslem ruler, in the very heart of Central Asia, a cellar filled with the best French champagnes and Russian liqueurs. With these the Khan liberally plied both himself and his guests, repeatedly toasting them, but afterwards showing no trace of ill-effects. The inhabitants of Hami had for centuries enjoyed a reputation for good living and hospitality. Marco Polo wrote of them: 'They live by the fruits of the earth which they have in plenty, and dispose of to travellers. They are a people who take things very easily for they mind nothing but playing, singing, dancing and enjoying themselves.' But within a year or two of von Le Coq's death this richly furnished palace would be razed to the ground and its treasures plundered. For this town of bon-viveurs was to suffer terrible punishment at the hands of the Chinese following an abortive uprising.

Von Le Coq's visit to Hami, although a pleasant diversion, was archaeologically disappointing. Although eighteen years earlier Younghusband had reported seeing more ruined buildings than occupied ones in the vicinity, most of these transpired to be of recent date (casualties of an earlier insurrection) and not relics of the region's Buddhist past. Even so, the Germans managed to discover, in the foothills to the north-east, two Buddhist temples. Alas, they arrived far too late. The sculptures and other works of art, whose remains could still be seen protruding from the sodden ground, had over the years been reduced to a shapeless mass by melting snow from the mountains above. But von Le Coq could hardly complain. Only a year previously he had been merely a volunteer in the Indian department of his museum. By an accident of pure fate – Huth's death and Grünwedel's illness – he had been chosen to lead this expedition to Chinese Central Asia.

The Kaiser, who had personally contributed to its cost, had already expressed satisfaction with the expedition's progress. Since then there had been the triumph of Bezeklik. The crates containing those spectacular frescoes were even now trundling across Siberia on their way to Berlin. Von Le Coq could feel confident that his reputation was made.

But there now began a series of events which were to rob him of the greatest of all the Silk Road prizes. While he and Bartus were in Hami they had heard from a Turkoman merchant a remarkable story about a discovery which had been made five years before at the oasis of Tun-huang, a town lying some two hundred miles due south across the Gobi. According to his version, a Chinese priest had stumbled upon a vast library of ancient books and manuscripts which had lain hidden for centuries there in a secret chamber. That Tun-huang had since earliest times been a centre of Buddhist worship and study was well known to von Le Coq, although only a handful of European travellers had ever been there. Unlike Karakhoja and Bezeklik, its decorated chapels were still regarded as sacred by the local people. To attempt to saw out its frescoes, therefore, was unthinkable. But the library, if it really existed, might be another matter. It was certainly worth looking into. While von Le Coq and Bartus were discussing it, an unwelcome telegram arrived from Berlin. Grünwedel was at last on his way. He expected to reach Kashgar in six weeks' time and asked them to rendezvous with him there. Von Le Coq now found himself in a quandary. To reach Tun-huang would take them seventeen days. Clearly they could not visit Tun-huang and still reach Kashgar – twelve hundred miles to the west – in time to keep their appointment with Grünwedel. But Grünwedel had been vacillating for months and might easily change his mind again. What were they to do? Von Le Coq decided to spin a coin. It was a Chinese silver dollar, and it came down tails. Bartus saddled the horses and they set out together for Kashgar.

10. 'The Finest Paintings in Turkestan...'

It took them one and a half months to reach Kashgar. Riding ahead, von Le Coq arrived first, followed several days later by Bartus with the caravan of slow-moving *mappas*. To their dismay there was no sign of Grünwedel, nor any news of him either. Two weeks later they received word from him that he had lost his luggage somewhere in Russia (he had obviously not bribed the station-master in Moscow) and would be delayed for an indeterminate period. Von Le Coq and Bartus were furious. Not only had they hurried the whole inhospitable length of Chinese Turkestan to be there on time, but they had thrown away the chance of visiting Tun-huang in quest of the secret library. They comforted themselves with the thought that there was probably no library there. Both men had burned their fingers before by listening to native tales. Von Le Coq had once made a long and time-wasting detour to inspect a mysterious 'inscription' which a villager had told him about only to discover that the scratches were the work of a glacier. Bartus, too, had once spent a week looking for a non-existent site near Turfan during which the guide's dog had died of thirst and fatigue and the men and horses had very nearly shared the same fate. Nonetheless Grünwedel's failure to make the rendezvous was to affect their relationship with him throughout the expedition.

As there was no German consul in Kashgar, von Le Coq and Bartus stayed with the Macartneys while waiting for Grünwedel to arrive. There were two reasons for their preferring the hospitality of the British to that of the Russians. In the first place von Le Coq spoke English, had lived in England

and spoke no Russian. Secondly, he did not like what he had heard of Petrovsky, and 'had no wish to put himself in the power of such a tyrannical ruler'. Grünwedel and the unfortunate Huth had made the mistake of staying with Petrovsky during the first German expedition two years before. This had proved a disaster. Huth was Jewish, and the arrogant Petrovsky had once threatened to have 'this Jew flogged' after a disagreement. There were no such scenes at Chini-Bagh, the Macartneys' official residence, and von Le Coq, like all other travellers, writes warmly of this remarkable couple who lived for so long in that remote spot. Having become accustomed to the Turkestan way of life, the Germans took a little time to adjust to the comforts provided by their hostess. 'When Lady Macartney had installed me on an English bed in a well-furnished room, I thought I was in Heaven,' von Le Coq wrote. 'But after a short time ... I felt as if I should suffocate; I got up, took my rug, spread it on the verandah, used my saddle as a pillow and, wrapped in a light fur, slept out in the open air. It was some time before I could get accustomed again to the narrow confines of a bedroom.'

While von Le Coq and Bartus await Grünwedel's arrival it is worth taking a brief look at the remarkable talents and character of Bartus. The son of a Pomeranian weaver, he had spent many years at sea on sailing vessels. For a time, too, he had been a squatter in the Australian outback, where he had learned to ride a horse well and also to endure discomfort. This, allied to a natural resourcefulness and to the many practical skills he had learned on a wind-jammer, made him the ideal man to accompany such an expedition as this. Furthermore he was an excellent companion, blessed with perpetual good humour, courage, enormous strength and enthusiasm. He had joined the Ethnological Museum as a handyman on discovering, during a visit to Germany, that he had lost his life's savings when an Australian bank collapsed. He was to accompany all four German expeditions to Chinese Turkestan, working from dawn to dusk for months on end with great zeal and ingenuity. Indeed, as we have seen, he became such an enthusiastic digger himself that von Le Coq occasionally entrusted him with minor excavations of his own.

At last, on December 6, Grünwedel arrived in Kashgar exactly fifty-two days late. He came 'on an old pony at walking pace', wrote von Le Coq, making little attempt to hide his impatience. Worse, however, Grünwedel was ill, and it was another three weeks before the expedition – officially called the Third German Expedition – could start. They finally left Chini-Bagh on Christmas Day 1905, after lunching with the Macartneys. Also invited to the lunch were the Russians who, for reasons of their own, 'refused to touch a single bite of the festive meal', von Le Coq recalls, explaining somewhat lamely to their hosts that they had already eaten.

Grünwedel was still far from well, but the four Germans (Grünwedel had brought a Chinese-speaking assistant with him) felt that they could not take advantage of the Macartneys' generosity any longer, and there was important work to be done. Moreover, with Stein preparing for a second expedition, the Russians doing likewise and rumours of a French expedition in the wind, there was no time to be lost if claims were to be staked for the most promising sites. Grünwedel therefore travelled lying on a mattress in a hay-filled cart, an awning strung overhead to shield him from the sun. Their target was the complex of rock temples at Kyzil, in the T'ien Shan foothills, some thirty miles short of Kucha, on the northern arm of the old Silk Road.

*   *   *

Meanwhile, waiting impatiently in India for official approval of his plans for his second great raid across the Karakoram, was Aurel Stein. Like the Germans held up in Kashgar, he was worried about the intentions of his rivals in a region which so far he had virtually had to himself. His friend Macartney had written informing him of the delay facing the German expedition and also referring to 'jealousies' between von Le

Coq and Grünwedel. In this Stein took Grünwedel's side, commenting to a friend that: 'Grünwedel is a slow-moving man who wants to do things thoroughly.' He added that he hoped that Grünwedel would manage to confine 'his young museum assistants' to Turfan. However, it was with relief that he heard finally from Macartney that the Germans proposed to stick to the Kucha region. Stein's own sights were set elsewhere, and now his worries switched to the French. 'The true race', he wrote, 'will be with the Frenchmen.' He had heard that the brilliant young French sinologist Paul Pelliot proposed to set out from France in the spring. Stein was 'wicked enough', he confessed to a friend, to hope that the route across Russia might be barred to Pelliot, forcing him to take the far slower route through India, thereby giving Stein a head's start. In the meantime, while bureaucrats in Calcutta and London pondered unhurriedly over his proposals, Stein worked feverishly on the proofs of his two-volume masterpiece *Ancient Khotan*, a massive and scholarly account of his first expedition aimed, unlike his earlier *Sand-Buried Ruins of Khotan*, at archaeologists and students of Central Asian history. As he fretted over the prospects of his rivals stealing a march on him (he had just heard that the Russians were planning an expedition), he lamented to a friend: '... if only this great Indian machine could move quicker'.

The Germans, after briefly examining Buddhist ruins at Tumchuq which they decided to leave until later (in the event the Pelliot expedition beat them there), pressed on to the Kyzil region, which they knew to be rich in sites. They had been told by one of their native attendants of a huge *ming-oi* (local term for a complex of cave temples) hidden in the mountains nearby, which some Japanese travellers had visited. After working there for three months in April 1903 the Japanese had apparently been driven away by a severe earthquake. Von Le Coq and Bartus rode off to examine the site. They came upon the *ming-oi* overlooking the cascading Muzart river – 'a marvellous settlement of many hundreds of temples in the steep cliffs of a mountain range ...' wrote von Le Coq. Knowing that other expeditions were on their way, von Le Coq hired the sole habitation in this remote and desolate spot, a miserable, two-roomed mud hovel erected by a local farmer. Having thus staked their claim to this site, the Germans continued to Kucha where they paid their respects to the Chinese governor. They then rode on to Kumtura where they explored another *ming-oi*, but found that it had already been stripped bare by treasure-seekers. Further along the river valley they discovered a number of individual temples with their murals still intact, as well as sculptures, manuscripts and other Buddhist relics. 'We worked here with zeal and delight,' wrote von Le Coq, 'for hardly a day passed without some new and exciting discovery.' Grünwedel, who had by now almost recovered, made careful sketches of the paintings *in situ* and prepared plans of the grottoes.

Von Le Coq made a number of prospecting trips to sites in the region, but found for the most part that these had been ruined by damp and were not worth excavating. In one village he was warmly received by a Chinese official who found him lodgings in a small inn. He had just got into bed, he tells, when 'there suddenly appeared a tall young woman in a little Chinese jacket and splendidly embroidered undergarments'. She was accompanied by two pretty young attendants playing stringed instruments. 'I found that the beautiful lady was a well-known demi-mondaine who was anxious to offer her services to the foreign gentleman.' Von Le Coq assures us hastily that he 'dismissed the somewhat offended beauty' after buying a pair of fine earrings from her.

By now, two Russian excavators – the Beresovsky brothers – whom they had been expecting, had arrived in the Kucha region. When they found the Germans there, it very nearly led to violence. There was a history to this. At the time of the first German expedition, Grünwedel had for some reason come to an arrangement with St Petersburg by which the Germans would confine themselves to the later sites around Turfan, while the Russians would work the earlier ones in the Kucha district. However, when von Le Coq and Bartus had called at the Russian consulate in Urumchi, Dr Kochanowky had been surprised to learn that they were on their way to Turfan. For he had received letters from St Petersburg requesting him, in von Le Coq's words, 'to visit the Turfan settlements with the greatest possible speed in order to secure for Russian science all that was to be found in the way of pictures, manuscripts, etc'. Indeed, he had already removed what he could from Karakhoja, although he was unable to take any wall-paintings.

Von Le Coq had been angry at discovering this double-dealing by St Petersburg when, he felt, the Russians had already got the best of the bargain. He had tried to explain to Kochanowky that Turfan was in the agreed German sphere of influence, but the Russian had replied that he knew of no such agreement and was merely concerned with obeying his instructions. Von Le Coq had decided then and there that these instructions rendered Grünwedel's agreement with St Petersburg null and void, and he now managed to persuade Grünwedel of this. Furthermore, he pointed out that Kumtura and Kyzil (which they had still to excavate) were technically outside the Kucha region 'and therefore could not be affected by the literal wording of the agreement'. But when the Russians eventually arrived they found von Le Coq and Grünwedel excavating at a temple-complex called Simsim which was, beyond any question, within the Kucha region. Furious at finding their rivals operating on what they regarded as their territory, the Russians denounced them angrily. Von Le Coq managed to placate them, but not before the elder of the two Russians had threatened to evict them by force of arms. Realising that the Russians represented no real threat, however, having neither the means nor the expertise to remove wall-paintings, the Germans gave way gracefully, moving on instead to the far richer prize of Kyzil.

The seventh-century Chinese traveller Hsuan-tsang, who

passed through this region on his celebrated pilgrimage to India, has left us a detailed account of life in the Kingdom of Kucha (which then included Kyzil) over a thousand years before Grünwedel and von Le Coq dug there. He told his faithful biographer Hui-li of the kingdom's great size (it measured more than three hundred miles from east to west, and two hundred from north to south) and also of the luxuriance of its well-watered oases where even corn and rice were grown. We also learn that K'iu-chi, as he called it, produced grapes, pomegranates, plums and other fruit. Hsuan-tsang reported: 'The ground is rich in minerals – gold, copper, iron, lead and tin. The air is soft and the people honest.... They excel other countries in playing the lute and pipe. They clothe themselves with ornamental garments of silk and embroidery [von Le Coq noted the excellence of the local embroidery he examined in one village]. In commerce they use gold, silver and copper coins,' the pilgrim added.

In his day, outside the western gate of Kucha there towered two ninety-foot-high figures of Buddha, one on each side of the road. Here, every year during the autumn equinox, priests from all over the kingdom assembled for a ceremony lasting ten days. 'The King and all his people, from the highest to the lowest, abstain on this occasion from public business, and observe a religious fast,' Hsuan-tsang records. On the fifteenth day of each month as well as on the last day the king and his ministers met to discuss affairs of state 'and after taking counsel of the chief priests, they publish their decrees', he added. He describes a number of monasteries, and it seems more than likely that during his stay he visited the one at Kyzil and admired the very paintings and sculptures that twelve hundred years later the Germans removed to Berlin. The wall-paintings from Kyzil are perhaps the richest haul (Bezeklik included) that the Germans made during their four expeditions. For art historians regard the Kyzil frescoes as one of the high points of all Central Asian art.

Von Le Coq himself writes of those from one temple: 'The

13 One of the large, ninth-century wall-paintings removed by
von Le Coq from Bezeklik, later destroyed in Berlin during
World War II. Note saw cuts. A typical example of Serindian style

14 Life-size Buddhist figures from Bezeklik, depicting
Chinese monks. Destroyed in World War II

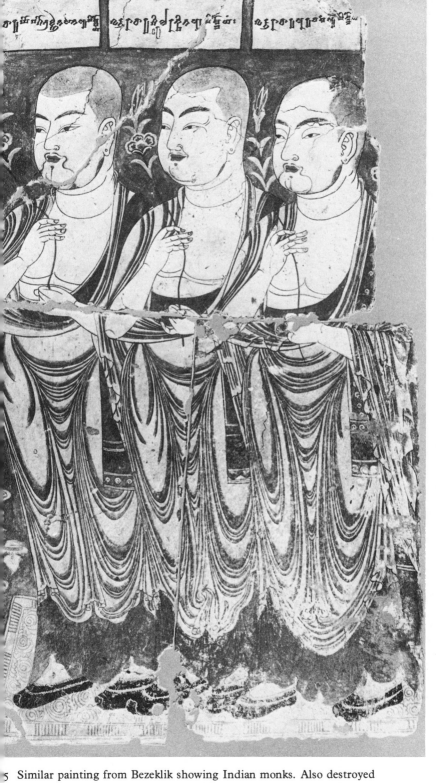

5 Similar painting from Bezeklik showing Indian monks. Also destroyed

16 Detail of another of the lost Bezeklik masterpieces, showing Persian
benefactors of the temple. Also destroyed

paintings were the finest that we found anywhere in Turkestan, consisting of scenes from the Buddha legend, almost
purely Hellenistic in character.' When the Germans first
entered this temple it appeared to be quite empty. However,
they soon found that the walls were coated with a one-inch-
thick layer of snow-white mould. Von Le Coq recounts: 'I
fetched Chinese brandy – no European can drink it – and
washed down all the walls with a sponge', thus revealing the
frescoes. That night he had an agonising headache and a temperature, presumably the effect of brandy fumes.

In another superbly painted temple nearby they were
dazzled by the extravagant use of brilliant blue pigment – the
precious ultramarine beloved by Renaissance artists, for
which they were prepared to pay twice its weight in gold. One
picture from here shows King Ajatashatru taking a ritual bath
in melted butter while an earringed courtier, who dare not
break to him the news of Buddha's death by word of mouth,
does so by means of a painting. Other beautifully preserved
works found here showed Buddha's temptation, scenes of him
preaching, the distribution of sacred relics and his cremation.

The breathtaking finds from the Kyzil sites 'far surpassed
any earlier achievements', von Le Coq declares. 'Everywhere
we found fresh, untouched temples, full of the most interesting and artistically perfect paintings, all of early date.' In none
of them was there yet any trace of Chinese influence, unlike
those from all the other sites they had excavated. This was
because, prior to AD 658 when it accepted Chinese rule, Kucha
had its own distinct school of painting, as well as its own language. In spite of more recent discoveries made there by
Chinese archaeologists, current knowledge of Kuchean painting is derived largely from the frescoes and manuscripts
brought back by the German expedition from Kyzil.

One day when all four men were working there in different
temples there was a noise like a clap of thunder and an avalanche of boulders suddenly cascaded down upon them. Von
Le Coq, Bartus and their labourers fled down the hillside

'pursued by great masses of rock, tearing past us with terrifying violence'. The river, von Le Coq could see, was 'in wild commotion – great waves beating against its banks'. Further up the river a huge pillar of dust rose heavenwards. 'At the same instant,' von Le Coq recounts, 'the earth trembled and a fresh roll, like pealing thunder, resounded through the cliffs. Then we knew it was an earthquake.' They watched the shock-wave as it continued to move violently down the valley, pillars of dust marking its progress. To their relief both Grünwedel, who had retreated with his sketchbook into a corner of his cave, and Herr Pohrt, his Chinese-speaking assistant, were unharmed. On another occasion, in a temple in which every blow of the pick dislodged a shower of pebbles and sand from the ceiling, von Le Coq again had a close shave. After examining the remains of some wooden figures he had found, he leaned against the cave wall, dislodging part of the facing. As he stepped back in surprise, a huge block of stone crashed down onto the spot where he had been standing. Others were less lucky. In another rock-fall one of the locally employed labourers was seriously injured and was paid compensation equivalent to £3. This, von Le Coq assures us, represented 'a considerable sum of money' in Chinese Turkestan where, he claims, a large family could live 'in comfort' for a month on twelve shillings. In another incident two men from a neighbouring town perished in a violent storm while on their way to seek work with the Germans.

Lesser storms too seem, from time to time, to have disturbed the tranquillity of the expedition. Men obliged to live in very close proximity, month in, month out, often under extremely disagreeable conditions, are bound at times to get on one another's nerves. Here there were additional sources of irritation. For a start, von Le Coq was obviously disappointed at having to surrender command of a highly successful expedition to Grünwedel, a man whose scholarship he respected but for whom he clearly had little time as an expedition leader. Grünwedel's late arrival, as we know, had also exasperated him. However, the main source of conflict between the two men arose over von Le Coq's penchant for the wholesale removal of temple contents, particularly wall-paintings. Grünwedel's approach is best summed up in an obituary of him written some thirty years later by a fellow-scholar. This declares: 'His expedition reports made it clear that he condemned, and himself avoided, the superficial examination of sites and the "grabbing" of conspicuous paintings and works of art. His aim was to approach each site scientifically, and study it in its entirety. Hence his procedure of making drawings and plans of all new finds. Otherwise, he felt, the removal of frescoes was nothing better than treasure-hunting and robbery.'

It was an approach for which von Le Coq and Bartus had little time, and it led to disagreements. When von Le Coq wanted to remove to Berlin the entire painted dome of one small temple, Grünwedel objected. He did this 'so energetically', wrote von Le Coq, 'that to have insisted on it would have meant the end of all friendly relations....' Grünwedel instead proposed that drawings and measurements should be taken so that a reconstruction could be made at the museum. He raised a similar objection over another painted dome. This von Le Coq was able to remove on the following expedition, which he led himself, though he remarks in his book that the paintings had greatly deteriorated in the intervening seven years. Another time, when Grünwedel objected to the removal of a statue which von Le Coq believed to be of considerable importance, the latter arranged for Bartus to pack it without the expedition leader's knowledge and smuggle it to Germany.

Only once did Grünwedel decide to conduct an excavation himself. With relish von Le Coq describes how his chief carefully picked himself a temple which seemed certain to yield rich finds. He goes on: 'There he began to work, but as he could not make the men understand, and the dust – which in such operations always rises in clouds and is very trying

– worried him too much he soon gave up in his attempt ...'
Bartus, von Le Coq tells us with ill-disguised pleasure, then
took over and – where Grünwedel had decided there was nothing to be found – 'soon brought to light whole layers of splendid big pages written in early Indian script'.

By now the chronic dysentery from which von Le Coq had
been suffering, and which perhaps helps to explain his anta-
gonism towards Grünwedel, was beginning to undermine his
health. Lest he fall seriously ill in this inhospitable region he
decided to leave at once for home. (Huth, it should be
remembered, largely through neglecting his health, had died
soon after returning from the first expedition.) Von Le Coq
collected together all the manuscripts they had found and prepared to leave for Kashgar – though not without one final prod
at the unfortunate Grünwedel. They had just heard that Stein
was proposing to visit Turfan. Von Le Coq therefore urged
his already flagging leader to press on quickly to Bezeklik –
some three hundred and fifty gruelling miles to the east – and
excavate its remaining temples before Stein did. After all,
Grünwedel had expressly asked that they leave these to him.
(Had he not, von Le Coq implied, then the contents of all
of them – and not just one – might now be safely in Berlin.)
With that he left, no doubt much to Grünwedel's relief.

11. Secrets of a Chinese Rubbish Dump

Apart from having to share a room with his horse (for fear of rustlers) and an anxious moment when the cart carrying the manuscripts nearly toppled into a raging torrent, von Le Coq reached Kashgar without incident, though much debilitated by his illness. As chance would have it, he just missed meeting his rival Stein, whose place – and bed no doubt – he took over in the ever-hospitable Macartney household. Stein had left Chini-Bagh for the south on July 23. Von Le Coq arrived there just a week later – a near miss in such a vast arena as Central Asia. He had been anxious to press on at once with his precious cargo, but the Macartneys insisted that he stayed for a while to recuperate and meanwhile arranged for a British officer, Captain J. D. Sherer, also *en route* for India, to accompany him over the Karakoram.

Their respective roles of invalid and escort were to be dramatically reversed before long when, on a nineteen-thousand-foot pass in the Karakoram, Sherer collapsed with enteric fever and pneumonia and could go no further. At the same time von Le Coq learned from his Turki servant that their caravan men were planning that night to steal their horses and slip away in the darkness. He sat up all night with a loaded rifle, threatening to shoot anyone who deserted. Next morning, leaving Sherer with the tent, the bulk of their provisions and his own loyal servants, von Le Coq set off along the skeleton-strewn trail to get help from Ladakh. Nine days later, after crossing three high and dangerous passes and living on nothing but flour-and-snow-water paste, he reached the nearest village, from where he sent back to Sherer fuel and provisions. Suffering badly from exhaustion himself, he swallowed nineteen raw eggs to restore his strength before dispatching a runner to the Moravian doctor at Leh with a description of Sherer's symptoms and an urgent request for medicines. He himself then set off back to where he had left Sherer, taking with him a hastily improvised stretcher on which the sick man, after a nightmare journey, was finally brought to Leh just before the snow closed the passes for the winter.

For this act of devotion and endurance von Le Coq was to receive the medal of the Order of the Hospital of St John of Jerusalem, struck for the first time in gold. The award was made on the recommendation of Sir Francis Younghusband, at that time British Resident in Kashmir, and a man with first-hand experience of the Karakoram passes himself. According to von Le Coq's obituary in *The Times*, written some twenty-four years later, Younghusband's commendation concluded: 'That Le Coq, a mere road acquaintance of Captain Sherer's and a man of different nationality, should cross the Sassar and Murghi passes three times in fourteen days, the third time in a blinding snow-storm, the first-named pass being 17,840 feet high and the summit consisting of some three miles of perpetual glacier, appears to be an act of self-sacrifice and devotion deserving of exceptional recognition.' Sherer (who was later to become a general) was so ill that he had to remain in the mission hospital at Leh for six months.

Von Le Coq finally reached Berlin with the manuscripts in January 1907 after being away for two and a half years. By the time Grünwedel, Bartus and Pohrt rejoined him at the Ethnological Museum later that year, after further fruitful excavations of their own – though not at Bezeklik – the total haul of the Third German Expedition amounted to one hundred and twenty-eight cases of treasures – twenty-five more than the previous expedition had yielded. With such a wealth of material to catalogue, conserve, publish and display, it was a further six years before the Germans, this time led by von Le Coq, were to return for more.

Meanwhile it was Stein's turn again, with the Frenchman Pelliot following close on his heels. As it happened, while Stein was staying with the Macartneys, Pelliot was temporarily stuck at Tashkent in Russian Turkestan, having, like Grünwedel, managed to lose his baggage. A brilliant linguist, the Frenchman filled in his time learning Turki, the principal language of Chinese Turkestan. Also in Central Asia at this time – in Ladakh – was the redoubtable Hedin. But he, for the moment anyway, was safely out of the running, his eyes being fixed single-mindedly on Tibet.

For his second expedition, Stein had taken a different route from India, travelling over the 'Pamir Knot' – grim meeting point of the Pamir, Karakoram and Hindu Kush – and cutting across the eastern corner of Afghanistan. This meant passing through 'badlands' where there was a serious risk of the party being attacked, particularly in view of Stein's now widespread reputation as a 'treasure-hunter'. As a precaution he took with him a modest armoury of rifles and revolvers. Also included in his small party were two old friends from his first expedition, Surveyor Ram Singh, seconded from the Survey of India, and Muhammadju, his old caravan man from Yarkand, who had braved the winter passes to join the expedition, narrowly surviving a terrifying brush with an avalanche which killed seven of his companions. Finally there was his fox-terrier Dash, whose predecessor had accompanied the first expedition. The new expedition, which was to last two years and seven months, was jointly sponsored by the British Museum in London and the Government of India. The museum's trustees had put up two-fifths of the cost and Calcutta the remainder. It was agreed that the material Stein brought back should be divided *pro rata* between the two sponsors. His principal target was Hedin's mysterious site of Lou-lan, discovered, it will be recalled, thanks to a forgotten spade. To reach it would mean crossing the dreaded Lop desert, but

Stein was determined to be the first archaeologist to reach it and to explore its secrets thoroughly.

Although he intended to travel eastwards along the southern arm of the old Silk Road, his first port of call lay to the north, at Kashgar. There he would renew his friendship with the Macartneys, catch up on the gossip of Central Asia and, by previous arrangement with George Macartney, take on his payroll a young Chinese called Chiang Ssu-yeh. Chiang's role was to teach Stein elementary conversational Chinese, act as interpreter with Chinese officials, and help him to evaluate any Chinese documents they might come across. The appointment was a great success, for Chiang proved a first-class companion, ever ready to face hardship and, moreover, taking a highly intelligent interest in the work. 'He took to archaeological work like a duck to water,' Stein was to write years later, '... How often have I longed ... for my ever-alert and devoted Chinese comrade, now, alas, long departed to his ancestors!'

The departure of their caravan from Kashgar was held up for a day by an event which much saddened the townspeople and in particular the small European community. This was the death of Father Hendricks, who had arrived in Kashgar in 1885 to open his one-man mission in a miserable mud-built hovel which served as both his bedroom and chapel. With his beard, dilapidated clerical hat and semi-Chinese costume he was a familiar and much-loved figure, although he made only one convert, an old Chinese shoemaker. His past was somewhat mysterious and in all his years in Kashgar he never received one letter from home. At first, his daily Masses were attended by a solitary Pole, who had found his way to Kashgar after exile in Siberia for taking part in the hanging of a Russian priest during a Polish uprising. One day, however, the two men fell out and the Pole was thereafter excluded from attending Mass. But undeterred, and unknown to the priest, he would crouch by the door with his ear to the keyhole, following the service.

When Macartney first arrived in Kashgar he and Hendricks became firm friends. Not only was the Dutchman highly intelligent and a brilliant linguist but he was also a first-class source of local intelligence – 'a living newspaper', Stein once called him. Macartney had found Hendricks subsisting on scraps given him as charity. He invited the Dutchman to share his own meals and eventually to live at Chini-Bagh. The old priest, however, insisted on moving out when, in 1898, Macartney returned from leave in England with a bride. Macartney eventually persuaded the local authorities to find Hendricks a house, but the Russian consul-general Petrovsky, who had a curious dislike of the priest, put pressure on the Chinese to withdraw the offer. This had resulted in popular demonstrations in support of Hendricks. Finally he was found a home in a squalid hovel in town.

It was here, on the morning that Stein was due to leave for the south, that Macartney found his old friend dead from cancer. 'Alone in his ramshackle house he had persistently rejected all offers of nursing and help,' wrote Stein in *Ruins of Desert Cathay*. 'So there was no one to witness the end. It was a pathetic close to a life which was strangely obscure even to the old Abbé's best friends.' Petrovsky, who had not spoken one word to Macartney between November 1899 and June 1902 – let alone to Father Hendricks – had now retired, and the new Russian consul-general, a more amiable man, undertook (for reasons that are not clear) to arrange the old priest's funeral for the next day. By the following morning the coffin was still far from ready so the Russian and several of his Cossack escort visited the carpenter's shop to hurry things along, first fortifying themselves with plenty of drink. When the coffin was finished, the body – 'terribly reduced by long sufferings', Stein recounts – was transferred reverently to it by the Cossacks who, bareheaded, carried it through the noon heat to the Russian cemetery.

That afternoon Stein and his party set off on the long journey along the southern arm of the old Silk Road. Because of the sweltering summer heat they soon began to find daytime travelling unbearable, and decided instead to move by night, lying up during the day. At first they tried sheltering in *kung-kuans*, the official Chinese rest-houses, in the villages where they halted. However, for ceremonial reasons these always faced south and thus absorbed the full heat of the midday sun. Moreover they were invariably filthy, so Stein and his men sought refuge instead in the homes of well-to-do villagers. During these brief halts Stein worked on the remaining page proofs of *Ancient Khotan*, the weighty, two-volume account of his first expedition, mailing them off in batches to Oxford, via Ferghana in Russian Central Asia.

Although Lou-lan was his principal target, Stein aimed first to excavate, or re-excavate, a number of other sites on the way, including Khadalik, Domoko, Rawak, Niya and Miran. There was little point, he knew, in hurrying. Lou-lan lay in the waterless and uninhabited heart of Marco Polo's 'Great Desert of Lop' and could only be reached and worked safely in winter. Moreover, thanks to George Macartney in Kashgar, Stein was kept fully briefed about the movements of his rivals via the native mail service. So it was that after five months of successful digging his heavily laden caravan finally reached the small and isolated oasis of Charkhlik, easternmost of the southern route towns. It was from here that Stein planned to launch his raid across the frozen sands to Lou-lan.

His caravan for the desert crossing consisted of his own small party, two local guides, fifty labourers, his seven baggage camels and eighteen locally hired ones. Each camel carried up to five hundred pounds' weight of ice, the expedition's sole source of water once they had crossed the Tarim. In addition, Stein hired thirty donkeys to ferry more ice in bags to a point two days beyond the last available water. There it was dumped, carefully stacked to face the sub-arctic winds which howled across the desert from Mongolia. Fa-hsien and Hsuan-tsang had both in their day crossed this desert, as also had Marco Polo, and all three were convinced that it was haunted. 'For this reason bands of travellers make a point of keeping very close together,' wrote the Venetian. But more recently – some five years before – Hedin had crossed it, and Stein had the benefit of his map.

Despite Macartney's reports on his rivals' movements, Stein was nonetheless apprehensive lest Pelliot had reached Lou-lan first. He wrote to a friend: 'It is an anxious thought, you can imagine, whether I shall find the French there already. . . . We shall then have to find a modus vivendi.' The slow journey, never more than fourteen miles a day, was a grim one for both men and camels. When the latter developed sore feet these were 're-soled' by the ancient but effective Taklamakan remedy of stitching pieces of leather to their skin. At times the desert air was so clear that Stein could see simultaneously the snow-capped peaks of the T'ien Shan, two-hundred miles to the north, and the Kun Lun slowly receding to the south.

On the eleventh day, when there was still no sign of Lou-lan, and the party's spirits seemed to be sinking, to boost morale Stein offered a generous prize in silver coins to the first man to sight one of the ruined structures. The pace of the caravan noticeably quickened, and before many hours had passed there was a shout from one of the camel men who had climbed to the top of a small feature. He pointed excitedly to a tiny blob on the horizon to the east. The prize was his, for Stein was able to confirm with the aid of binoculars that it was a ruined stupa. They had reached Lou-lan, remotest of all the desert sites. 'What a desolate wilderness, bearing everywhere the impress of death,' Stein wrote to a friend. As he and his party looked around them they found it hard to believe that this totally lifeless tract had once nurtured a large and thriving community. He need not have worried about Pelliot. The place was utterly deserted. No one had been near it since Hedin's visit in 1901.

Stein knew that Lou-lan, like Dandan-uilik, he owed to Hedin. Not only had the Swede discovered it, but it was the remarkable accuracy of his map which had got them there safely. Although they had approached it by different routes, Stein's own triangulation work and astronomical observations fixed Lou-lan in a position less than one mile in latitude, and a fraction more in longitude, from where Hedin showed it. It was, Stein wrote gratefully, 'a variance truly trifling on such ground'.

For the next eleven days he and his men dug among the sand-filled buildings, always in the teeth of icy gales, keeping themselves from dying of exposure by burning the bleached and desiccated trunks of centuries-dead trees. They were to discover no great fresco masterpieces, no colossal sculptures. Unlike Bezeklik and Kyzil, Karakhoja and Rawak – all of which were religious centres – Lou-lan was a garrison town. This much had already been shown by Hedin's fruitful if amateur probings. But Stein's more systematic excavations were to add graphically to the story. For they were to reveal a poignant sequel – that of a small imperial outpost totally cut off from the shrinking empire and left slowly to die.

During his excavations, of course, Stein was unaware of the message contained on the scraps of paper and wooden slips he discovered. He could not read Chinese, and he had left his Chinese assistant Chiang – protesting loudly – at the village of Abdal, fearing that the harsh desert crossing might prove too much for him. As it was, many of them were written in archaic Chinese, and it would take Chavannes and other scholars years of patient work to decipher all these fragments and piece together their meaning.

As we already know from Hedin's finds, Lou-lan had once been a flourishing military and mercantile community placed in this remote spot to watch over China's western frontier and to safeguard the free flow of goods along the Silk Road. It was a perpetual struggle and one which, on the collapse of the Han dynasty in AD 220, the Chinese temporarily lost to their Hunnish foes. Many of the dated documents which Stein brought to light belong to the middle of the third century when the Western Chin emperor was struggling to reassert control over the western regions – a campaign in which the Lou-lan garrison played a key strategic role.

On an ancient rubbish dump (Stein was a connoisseur of these) he came upon military records which provide occasional glimpses of this frontier warfare, including reports of actions on distant fronts. That these efforts were doomed to failure we know from the Chinese annals, for the new dynasty was not strong enough to control China proper for long, let alone the outlying regions. Eventually, as Stein's rubbish heap was to prove, the barbarians succeeded in severing Lou-lan from all communication with the distant capital. But it did not die immediately, having long since learned to be independent of outside supplies or orders. Indeed, although it had lost all touch with home, the tiny garrison soldiered on for a surprising number of years. This we know from one revealing piece of evidence recovered by Stein. It is the last of the many dated documents he found at Lou-lan. Written in the year 330, it records a payment made to a barbarian (probably a mercenary) on the authority of the Emperor Chien-hsing. No one had told the beleaguered garrison commander that not only had this emperor ceased to rule fourteen years before, but that his whole dynasty had been swept away.

There is a curious, latter-day footnote to the story of Lou-lan. For it is not far from where this little outpost once stood that seventeen centuries later, in the 1960s, China's defence chiefs chose to site their nuclear weapons – pointing towards their new foe beyond the Great Wall, the Russians. Chinese historians today are particularly bitter about the documentary material removed from Lou-lan by Hedin and Stein because knowledge of this period of their nation's past is so meagre.

Lou-lan had two other surprises for Stein. One was the discovery of a metal tape-measure which Sven Hedin had left behind in 1901, and which Stein was able to return to him at a dinner given in London by the Royal Geographical

Society. The other was the unexpected arrival on Christmas Eve of his 'dak' man, or mail runner, carrying letters from Macartney and from home. Having trekked all the way westwards to Khotan with Stein's outward mail, he had then – after only one night's rest – covered the normal thirty days' journey back to Abdal in a record twenty-one. Although he had no clear idea of Stein's whereabouts, he nonetheless set out across the desert with a local tracker to look for him. On the fifth day their modest supply of ice had run out. Had they not found the party on the sixth, both men would undoubtedly have perished. Yet the 'dak' man's first request to Stein was that he should examine the seals on Macartney's letters to make sure they were intact. Grateful to him for the happy Christmas he had thus ensured, Stein feasted the men on what modest luxuries his larder could provide. That night he sat up late in his tent reading his mail by flickering candle-light, momentarily forgetting the searing cold and the pain from his badly chapped hands.

At Lou-lan he made one other discovery of significance. In addition to the rich haul of Chinese official documents and papers, he also brought to light quantities of Kharoshthi tablets. This was something of a surprise to Stein, who wrote afterwards: 'I had scarcely ventured to hope for records in ancient Indian script and language so far away to the east.' These records indicated, Stein explains, that the Chinese military authorities had allowed the indigenous administration to continue undisturbed in the hands of the local ruling family. The discovery of these Kharoshthi documents raised another interesting possibility. They seemed to indicate that, at some time in its history, Lou-lan – on the very frontiers of China – had served as a far-flung eastern outpost of an ancient Indian empire of which modern scholars had no knowledge.

By now Stein's ice supply was almost exhausted. It was time to move on again. His first call, after collecting Chiang from Abdal, was at Miran where, in a ruined Buddhist temple, he uncovered a series of magnificent murals, including one delicately painted dado of winged angels. 'I felt completely taken by surprise,' wrote Stein of this latter find. How on earth, he asked, could such classical depictions of cherubims have found their way to 'the desolate shores of Lop-nor, in the very heart of innermost Asia'? Nor was this the only painting of distinctly western character that he found at this site. Some of them were signed with the single name 'Titus' and Stein could only conclude that perhaps the artist was a Roman, trained in the classical tradition, who had somehow made his way across Turkestan to the borders of China. (Indeed, there may even have been a Roman town at that time in Chinese Central Asia. Such is the belief of one American sinologist.)

'During the next few days,' wrote Stein, 'I often felt tempted to believe myself rather among the ruins of some villa in Syria or some other eastern province of the Roman empire than those of a Buddhist sanctuary on the very confines of China.' But the icy winter winds, sometimes turning to gales, were a constant reminder of where he really was. Having stripped Miran of its finest frescoes, Stein packed these and his finds of the previous four months and dispatched them by camel to Macartney in Kashgar, a journey which would take two months. Finally, on February 21, 1907, he himself set out once more across the frozen Lop desert, this time heading north-east, for Tun-huang, some three hundred and eighty miles away. It was a journey which would cause the Chinese, in the words of one of their scholars, 'to gnash their teeth in bitter hatred'.

12. Tun-huang –
the Hidden Library

Locked away in the heart of the Gobi desert, four days' camel ride from the nearest town, lies one of the least-known of China's many wonders, the 'Caves of the Thousand Buddhas' at Tun-huang. Here, carved in irregular rows into the cliff face and filled with magnificent wall-paintings and sculptures, are more than four hundred ancient rock temples and chapels. The greatest and most extensive – it stretches for a mile – of all Central Asia's *ming-oi*, or rock temple complexes, it was for centuries renowned throughout the Buddhist world as a centre for prayer and thanksgiving. The reason for this is its geographical position. Situated in a small green valley and surrounded by towering sand dunes, it stands some twelve miles south-west of the township of Tun-huang, which, from Han times onwards, served as China's gateway to the West. Tun-huang, which means 'Blazing Beacon', was thus the last caravan halt in China proper for travellers setting out along the old Silk Road. Pilgrims, merchants and soldiers about to leave China for the spiritual darkness and physical dangers of the Taklamakan desert prayed at Tun-huang's shrines for deliverance from the goblins and other perils ahead. In the same way, travellers reaching Tun-huang from the West gave thanks there for their safe passage through the dreaded desert. Because it was the point where the northern and southern arms of the Silk Road converged, all travellers coming to or from China by the overland route had to pass through Tun-huang. As a result of this heavy caravan and pilgrim traffic, the oasis itself acquired considerable prosperity over the centuries, for its markets offered the caravanners their last chance to lay in supplies of food and water before passing out through the celebrated Jade Gate towards the first of the Taklamakan oases.

The rock temples of Tun-huang, and the origin of their name, are said to date from AD 366 when the monk Lo-tsun had a vision of a thousand Buddhas in a cloud of glory. He persuaded a rich and pious pilgrim to have one of the smaller caves painted by a local artist and then dedicated as a shrine to his own safe return. Others followed suit, and for hundreds of years more and more temples and chapels were hewn out of the cliff and decorated in the belief that this would ensure the donor protection during his travels. At one time there were more than a thousand of these grottoes, of which four hundred and sixty-nine remain today. At the height of Tun-huang's glory numerous monasteries, too, stood among the protecting groves of poplars and elms which face the honeycomb of caves. In addition to the paintings and sculptures, many inscriptions have survived which recall the pious hopes of their donors. One of these, put up by an infantry colonel on the 2nd of August in the year 947, invokes the goddess Kuan-yin's protection 'so that the district will prosper and the routes to the east and to the west will be open and free, and that in the north the Tartars and in the south the Tibetans will cease their depredations and revolts'.

Unlike so many oasis-towns further along the Silk Road which had to be abandoned to the barbarians or to the desert, Tun-huang and its cave temples survived the ups and downs of the centuries more or less intact. Enshrined there today are the paintings and sculptures of more than fifteen hundred years. 'One of the richest museums in the world,' one western art historian has called it. 'A great art gallery in the desert' is Mildred Cable's description. But because of its remoteness, until the early years of this century very few western travellers had so much as set eyes on it, and even now only a privileged trickle ever get to see it. Prejevalsky visited it in the year 1879, as also, by chance, did members of a Hungarian geological expedition.

Although Stein had no plans to excavate there, or to remove any of its magnificent wall-paintings, he had long dreamed of visiting the site after hearing of its splendours many years earlier from Lajos Loczy, a geographer accompanying the Hungarian expedition. On the morning of March 12, 1907, travel-stained and weary, and in the teeth of an icy *buran*, Stein entered the town, never thinking for a second that Tun-huang would be the scene of his greatest discovery. Indeed, at that moment his thoughts were directed towards something else he had just found in the frozen desert on the way from Miran. This was a line of ancient watchtowers which, he believed, once formed part of a long-lost west-ward extension to the Great Wall referred to in the Chinese annals. His intention, therefore, was to pay a brief visit to the Caves of the Thousand Buddhas, replenish his supplies of food and water, then return to the Lop desert for further investigation and excavation of this mysterious wall.

But very soon after arriving in Tun-huang he heard an extraordinary story from an Urumchi trader to the effect that a Taoist priest called Wang Yuan-lu, who had appointed him-self guardian of the sacred caves, had some years earlier acci-dentally stumbled upon a vast hoard of ancient manuscripts walled up in one of them. Determined to investigate this, Stein wasted no time and set out across the twelve miles of desert for the caves. On arriving there, he found that Wang had left on a begging tour of neighbouring oases to raise money for his restoration work which, Stein winced to see, had already been crudely begun. The priest, moreover, was not expected back for several weeks, and the key to the manuscript cave (which had been fitted with a door since its discovery) was firmly in his possession. Stein's enquiries, pursued through his Chinese assistant Chiang, suggested that the manuscripts amounted to 'several cartloads'. The dis-covery had been reported to the Chinese authorities at Lan-chou, and it was the Viceroy who, after seeing specimens of the manuscripts, had ordered them to be kept securely under lock and key.

Stein's excitement need hardly be described. He had found what appeared to be a long-lost extension to the Great Wall of China, he had stumbled upon an unknown library, and now he was wandering through cave after cave of magnificent paintings and sculptures which ever since he was a schoolboy in Hungary he had dreamed of seeing. It was while hurrying enthralled from grotto to grotto, with Chiang close on his heels, that he ran fortuitously into a young Ho-shang, or Buddhist monk, who, it transpired, knew of the whereabouts of a manuscript which Wang had loaned temporarily to one of the shrines. 'It was a beautifully preserved roll of paper about a foot high and perhaps fifteen yards long,' wrote Stein in *Ruins of Desert Cathay*. Together he and Chiang carefully unrolled it. Its text was written in Chinese characters, but Chiang was forced to admit he could make no sense of it. It would not be the last time that Stein would curse his own ignorance of written Chinese. However, one thing was now certain. If they wanted to examine the rest of this amazing find, there was nothing for it but to await the return of Wang. In the meantime it seemed wise to maintain their friendship with the obliging priest who had produced the scroll. Stein decided on a judicious offering, but here Chiang advised stealth. Too large a sum, he pointed out, would be likely to arouse suspicions about their motives. They finally proffered him a small piece of silver. 'The gleam of satisfaction on the young Ho-shang's face', Stein recalled, 'showed that the people of Tun-huang, whatever else their weaknesses, were not much given to spoiling poor monks.'

Having done all he could at Tun-huang in Wang's absence, Stein set out once again into the still-frozen desert to pick up the trail of his mysterious wall. He was accompanied by what he described as 'the craziest crew I ever led to digging – so torpid and enfeebled by opium were they'. Stein was lucky to have even them, however, as a rebellion by a fanatical

Moslem group some forty years before had severely depleted the local population, resulting in an acute labour shortage. During the next few weeks, although Stein's thoughts were never far from the Caves of the Thousand Buddhas and Wang's cache of manuscripts, he and his motley team of diggers made a succession of important discoveries which proved beyond question that the ruined watchtowers they had stumbled upon were the remains of an extension to the Great Wall dating back some two thousand years. They had located, moreover, the original site of China's famous Jade Gate, that historic frontier post through which all incoming and outgoing traffic along the Silk Road had to pass. The American archaeologist Langdon Warner, whose own Central Asian enterprises we shall look at later, has described Stein's finding of this stretch of the wall as 'one of the most dramatic discoveries of our time, and one which has had the most far-reaching effect on elucidating the early history of China and Central Asia'. On a subsequent expedition, Stein was to follow this wall, which he likened to the Roman *limes*, for a further three hundred miles to Etsin-gol, near the present Mongolian frontier. 'I feel at times as I ride along the wall to examine new towers as if I were going to inspect posts still held by the living,' he wrote to friends in England. 'Two thousand years seems so brief a time when the sweepings from the soldiers' huts still lie practically on the surface in front of the door....'

By the time Stein returned to Tun-huang, laden with relics and documents chronicling frontier life in Han times, the all-important Wang Yuan-lu had arrived back from his begging tour. But Stein was forced to bide his time for a further week as the annual religious fair which filled the valley with thousands of townsfolk and villagers from nearby oases was now in full swing. Finally, on May 21, 1907, he returned to the sacred caves where he found the Abbot Wang, as he is sometimes called, awaiting him. So began what was to be hailed in Europe as Stein's greatest triumph, and denounced by the

Chinese as an act of shameless trickery, not to say of theft. Like the Elgin Marbles controversy, that surrounding the Tun-huang library may very well rage on for ever, but here we are concerned only with how Stein and Chiang persuaded the guardian of the manuscripts to part with that priceless trove.

Stein records his impressions of the Abbot Wang at their first brief meeting on that May morning thus: 'He looked a very queer person, extremely shy and nervous, with an occasional expression of cunning which was far from encouraging.' Stein added: 'It was clear from the first that he would be a difficult person to handle.' Of course, nothing was said to Wang about his hoard of manuscripts. Stein – or so the little priest was allowed to believe – had come to Tun-huang to survey the principal shrines and photograph some of the wall-paintings. Indeed, it was while he was taking photographs near the side-chapel in which Wang had discovered the manuscripts that Stein noticed to his dismay that the secret chamber containing them had now been bricked up. Previously it had been secured only by a rough wooden door. At the same time an ominous rumour reached Stein's ear that the Viceroy of Kansu, in whose province the caves stood, had given orders for the entire library to be moved to Lanchou. His hopes of ever seeing the manuscripts, let alone of acquiring any of them, were beginning to look bleak. Anxious to discover what precisely was going on, Stein dispatched the shrewd Chiang to see Wang in the grotto where he lived. After a long absence Chiang returned, bearing somewhat more encouraging news. In the first place, the entrance to the cave containing the manuscripts had been walled up by Wang merely to keep out inquisitive pilgrims during the religious festivities of the previous week. Secondly, after a random selection of the manuscripts had been examined at Lanchou, the provincial capital, officials there had decided to leave the remainder where they were, in the charge of their self-appointed guardian. They were, Stein wrote, 'evidently dismayed at the cost of transport'. Whatever their reason, it would appear that the provincial authorities were well aware of the discovery of the walled-up library at Tun-huang.

Stein and Chiang, whom Stein liked to refer to as 'my literatus', now held a council of war to decide upon a strategy by which to win the confidence – and, hopefully, the co-opera-tion – of the priest. During Chiang's meetings with Wang he had asked him whether they might be allowed to see the manuscripts. The priest had been non-committal, but when Chiang held out the prospect of a 'liberal donation' to the shrine he was so zealously restoring to what he believed to be its original glory, Wang seemed more receptive. That is until Chiang, exceeding his instructions from Stein, hinted that his employer might be interested in actually purchasing some of the manuscripts. At this, Wang became highly per-turbed – a mixture of religious scruple and the fear of being found out, it seemed to Stein. Chiang quickly dropped the subject. 'To rely on the temptation of money alone as a means of overcoming his scruples', Stein writes in the *Ruins of Desert Cathay,* 'was manifestly useless.' It would be equally futile, on the other hand, to try to present to this semi-literate priest archaeological arguments for being allowed to see, or acquire, his manuscripts.

Stein decided upon a two-pronged strategy. Knowing that it was the pride and joy of the priest's life, he first asked Wang whether they might be allowed to see over the shrine he was so industriously restoring. It would incidentally enable them to study at closer quarters the lay-out of the cave. As he had expected, the suggestion was accepted with alacrity. Stein de-scribes vividly his guided tour. 'As he took me through the lofty antechapel with its substantial woodwork, all new and lavishly gilt and painted, and through the high passage or porch giving access and light to the main cella, I could not help glancing to the right where an ugly patch of unplastered brickwork then still masked the door of the hidden chapel.'

Stein knew that this was hardly the moment to express any

curiosity about what might lie behind that fresh brickwork Instead he had to show a polite yet convincing interest in the priest's restoration programme, and at the same time conceal his private horror on observing the huge and hideous new sculptures which this one-time soldier turned holy man had commissioned for the shrine. These, Stein added, showed 'only too plainly how low sculptural art had sunk in Tun-huang'. Yet he could not but admire the single-mindedness of this simple Chinese peasant 'whose devotion to this shrine and to the task of religious merit which he had set himself in restoring it, was unmistakably genuine'. From the extreme modesty of Wang's lifestyle, and everything that Chiang had heard about him in Tun-huang, it was quite clear that every penny he had left after providing for himself and his two acolytes went into restoring the shrine.

Having thus established some degree of rapport with Wang, Stein played his second card. He had been reminded 'by this quaint priest, with his curious mixture of pious zeal, naive ignorance, and astute tenacity of purpose' of the early Buddhist pilgrims who had travelled westwards along the Silk Road in search of the holy places of their religion. Perhaps if he mentioned the name of his own adopted patron saint, Hsuan-tsang, beloved also by so many Chinese, it just might touch a similar chord in Wang's affections. At once 'a gleam of lively interest' appeared in the priest's eyes. It soon transpired that both men held Hsuan-tsang in equal veneration, although their concepts of him differed vastly, Wang seeing him apparently as a sort of 'saintly Munchausen'. But such divergences hardly mattered. Stein had found what he needed. It was the way into the little priest's confidence, and thence into the cave, but it would need a great deal of time and patience. Stein began by telling Wang, 'as well as my poor Chinese would permit' of his devotion to the saintly traveller. Warming to his theme, he went on to relate 'how I had followed his footsteps from India for over ten thousand *li* across inhospitable mountains and deserts; how in the course of this pilgrimage I had traced to its present ruins, however inaccessible, many a sanctuary he had piously visited. . . .'

The effect of this was instantaneous. The little priest, bursting with pride, led Stein outside to a newly built verandah which he had commissioned a local artist to decorate with legendary scenes from the saintly pilgrim's life. Enthusiastically, Wang pointed out and explained each picture – Hsuan-tsang forcing a dragon which had swallowed his horse to disgorge it, Hsuan-tsang saving himself from a demon by the force of his prayers, and so on. However, there was one episode which Stein realised contained an omen which might have useful implications for him. This showed Hsuan-tsang standing on the bank of a raging torrent, his horse, laden with sacred Buddhist manuscripts, beside him. A large turtle swims towards him, apparently to help carry the holy writ safely across the river. 'Here was clearly a reference to the twenty pony-loads of sacred books and relics which the historical traveller managed to carry away safely from India,' Stein wrote. 'But would the pious guardian read this obvious lesson aright, and be willing to acquire spiritual merit by letting me take back to the old home of Buddhism some of the ancient manuscripts which chance had placed in his keeping?' Stein decided to keep this card up his sleeve for use at an appropriate moment. He left Chiang behind with the priest in the hope that he might now be able to persuade his fellow-countryman at least to lend them some of the manuscripts for study. But Wang remained hesitant, merely promising that he might do so later. Chiang reported this back to Stein. 'There was nothing for me to do,' Stein wrote, 'but wait.'

But not for very long, as it turned out. Late that same night Chiang came silently to Stein's tent and excitedly produced several manuscripts from beneath his coat. Stein could see at a glance that the rolled texts were very old. Concealing them again under his clothes – for the priest had insisted on absolute secrecy – Chiang slipped away to his little monk's cell at the foot of a huge seated Buddha cut out of the cliff-face. He spent

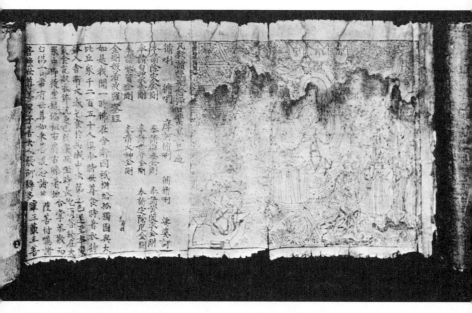

17 The world's oldest printed book from the walled-up library

8 Stein's convoy of treasures about to leave Abdal for Kashgar –
from a photograph by Sir Aurel Stein

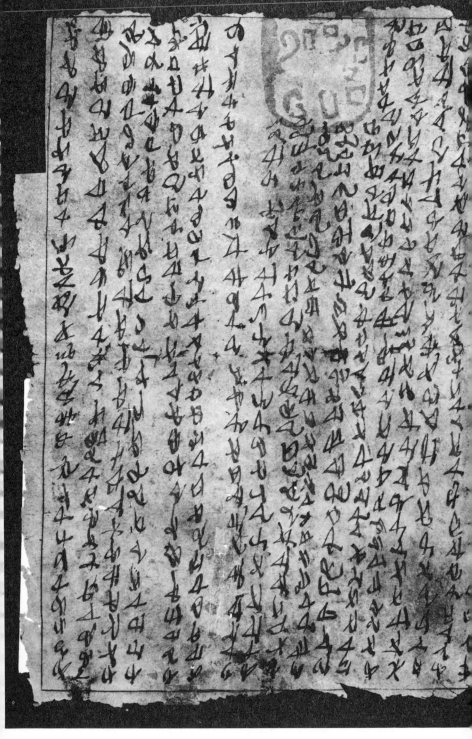

19 Example of Islam Akhun's forgery in 'Unknown Script' which had to be removed from the British Museum collection

the remainder of the night poring over the manuscripts, endeavouring to identify their texts and pinpoint their possible dates. At dawn he returned to Stein's tent, his face 'expressing both triumph and amazement'. He reported elatedly that these Chinese translations of Buddhist sutras bore colophons stating that they had been translated by Hsuan-tsang himself from originals he had brought back from India.

Here, surely, was an amazing portent – a 'quasi-divine hint', Stein called it – that even the nervous Wang could hardly fail to recognise. After all, when the little priest removed the manuscripts from his secret hoard he could not possibly have known of their link with Hsuan-tsang. Chiang hastened away to break the news to him. There could only be one possible explanation, he assured Wang. From beyond the grave, Hsuan-tsang had himself chosen this moment to reveal these sacred Buddhist texts to Stein so that 'his admirer and disciple from distant India' could return them whence they came. Chiang had no need to press the point. The omen was not wasted on the pious priest. Within hours the wall blocking the recess where the manuscripts lay had been taken down, and before the day was out Stein was peering into the secret chamber by the light of Wang's primitive oil lamp. The scene reminds one of another, some fifteen years later, when Howard Carter gazed into the tomb of Tutankhamun by the light of a flickering candle.

To an archaeologist, what Stein saw was no less staggering. 'The sight the small room disclosed was one to make my eyes open', he recounts. 'Heaped up in layers, but without any order, there appeared in the dim light of the priest's little lamp a solid mass of manuscript bundles rising to a height of nearly ten feet, and filling, as subsequent measurement showed, close on 500 cubic feet.' It was, in the words of Sir Leonard Woolley, the discoverer of Ur, 'an unparalleled archaeological scoop'. *The Times Literary Supplement* declared: 'Few more wonderful discoveries have been made by any archaeologist.'

Stein could see at a glance that it would be difficult, if not impossible, for him and Chiang to examine this mountain of manuscripts while they remained stacked inside the secret chamber. This 'black hole', as he called it, was so cramped that there was hardly room for the two of them to squeeze in, let alone work there. The obvious solution was to shift all the manuscripts to the temple's more spacious cella for scrutiny there. But Wang was quick to point out that they would be in full view there of any members of his congregation who happened to drop in to pray at this shrine whose restoration their alms had paid for. Word would get around like lightning that the shrine's sacred texts were being defiled by foreigners. Wang insisted, therefore, that he himself must remove the manuscripts from the chamber, a bundle at a time, and convey them discreetly to a small room nearby, where Stein and Chiang might examine them at leisure and unseen. Before embarking on this marathon task Stein searched for some clue which might indicate just when it was that the guardians of this ancient library had walled it up. Judging stylistically from what survived of the paintings which had once covered the entrance to the secret chamber, he cautiously estimated that this could not have happened any later than the twelfth century. Subsequent research, based upon those manuscripts found to bear dates, indicates that it took place even earlier, perhaps around AD 1000. The date when the library was walled up is one question, but *why* is another. It seems probable that it was done to save the sacred texts from falling into the hands of barbarian tribes who at that time threatened to overrun Tun-huang, and probably did, although there are other theories.

Once Wang could see that Stein's examination of the manuscripts could be carried out without risk of detection, he became bolder and began to hump load after load from the 'black hole' – known more prosaically to present-day scholars as 'cave 17' – to what Stein called his 'reading room'. Initial attempts to list all the manuscripts soon had to be abandoned.

'It would have required a whole staff of learned scribes', Stein explains in *Ruins of Desert Cathay*, 'to deal properly with such a deluge.' He examined the manuscripts for signs of damp, the destroyer of so many of man's written records. Luckily, there was not the slightest trace. As Stein observes, it would be hard to find a better storeroom for manuscripts than a sealed cave in the middle of a moistureless desert.

As day after day their work at Tun-huang continued, not only did countless manuscripts in Chinese, Sanskrit, Sogdian, Tibetan, Runic-Turki and Uighur, as well as in unknown languages, emerge from the secret chamber, but also a rich harvest of Buddhist paintings. Some, from their triangular tops and floating streamers, Stein recognised at once as temple banners, others as votive hangings. All were painted on incredibly fine silk or on paper. Many were badly crushed, their creases 'ironed' into place through lying for nine centuries beneath the heap of manuscripts. The importance of these paintings lies in their age, and consequent rarity, rather than in their quality. Paintings of the T'ang Dynasty, as these all turned out to be, are exceptionally rare – even the products of local ateliers such as these. Most were destroyed in the mid-ninth century during a wave of anti-clericalism which resulted in the closure or destruction of some forty thousand Buddhist temples and shrines throughout China. Fortuitously Tun-huang fell into Tibetan hands in AD 781 and remained in their possession for the next sixty-seven years. Its temples and shrines thus escaped the destruction wrought elsewhere in China at that time.

Some of the silken banners found among Wang's manuscripts proved to be so long when finally unfurled, that scholars believe they could only have been designed to hang from the tops of the cliffs at Tun-huang. Most of the paintings on silk Stein found it impossible to open out as they had been compressed over the centuries into hard, fragile little packets by the crushing weight of the manuscripts. Later with skill akin to brain surgery, they were successfully unfolded in the laboratories of the British Museum after first being chemically treated. It was an operation which was to take the best part of seven years.

By now Stein and Chiang had established a regular routine of removing each night to Stein's tent a selection of manuscripts and paintings for 'closer study'. Wang raised no objections to this, and before long had even agreed to allow certain categories of manuscripts to be earmarked for transfer to a 'temple of learning in Ta-Ying-Kuo' (England) in exchange for a substantial donation to his temple. He had, as Stein candidly admitted, 'been gradually led from one concession to another, and we took care not to leave him much time for reflection'. One night, however, Wang appeared to get cold feet about the whole affair, for he suddenly locked up the shrine and disappeared off to Tun-huang oasis. Stein and Chiang spent an anxious week wondering what he was up to and whether, on his return, his attitude towards them would have changed. Their fears proved groundless. The little priest had evidently been reassured by contact with his patrons that his secret had not leaked out and that, as Stein put it, 'his spiritual influence, such as it was, had suffered no diminution.' From then on things suddenly got easier, and more and more manuscripts passed into Stein's hands, including Buddhist texts in Chinese which Wang had previously excluded from any negotiations. In an account of the episode published later in his *On Ancient Central Asian Tracks*, Stein recalls: 'On his return, he was almost ready to recognise that it was a pious act on my part to rescue for Western scholarship all those relics of ancient Buddhist literature and art which were otherwise bound to get lost sooner or later through local indifference.'

The saga was now all but over, although Wang made one last condition. For his own protection, he insisted that the transaction should be kept secret for as long as Stein remained in China. It was a promise that Stein was only too happy to make, not least because he hoped to acquire further manuscripts from Wang's secret hoard. Wang and his visitors parted in perfect amity, Stein noting that the priest's face 'had resumed once more its look of shy but self-contented serenity'. Indeed, by now he had such confidence in the Englishman's discretion that when, four months later, Stein and Chiang were again in the area he readily agreed to part with a further two hundred bundles of manuscripts. Despite this, Stein felt unable to relax while his precious booty remained on Chinese soil. As he wrote long afterwards: 'My time for true relief came when, some sixteen months later, all the twenty-four cases, heavy with manuscripts, and five more filled with carefully packed paintings, embroideries and similar art relics, had safely been deposited at the British Museum in London.' All this had cost the taxpayer a mere £130 he noted with satisfaction in a letter to a friend.

Stein's second expedition was still far from over, however. Although his triumphant progress so far – the superb Miran wall paintings, the extension to the Great Wall and, now, his spectacular purchases from the Caves of the Thousand Buddhas – would have been more than enough to satisfy most archaeologists, Stein pressed on indefatigably. There was further serious work to be done on the Great Wall; large areas of the Nan Shan mountains to be mapped; and fresh sites along the northern arm of the Silk Road to be explored and possibly excavated. This was Stein's first opportunity to visit the ruins north of the Taklamakan, and he was particularly eager to see what his German rivals had been up to at the highly prized sites around Turfan. When eventually he reached the depression, and toured the sites which Grünwedel, von Le Coq and Bartus had cleared, he was dismayed by what he considered to be the crudeness of their methods. While not a hint of any criticism appears in his published works, Stein does not spare the Germans in private correspondence. To a close friend in England he complained: 'Big temples, monasteries, etc, were dug into with the method of a scholarly treasure-seeker, barely explored with any approach to archaeological thoroughness. The places most likely to yield "finds" had been reached by this system. . . .' he added. Not for nothing perhaps did Sir Mortimer Wheeler once declare: 'Archaeology is not a science, it is a vendetta.' In his *Ruins of Desert Cathay*, on the other hand, Stein refers politely to Grünwedel as 'a high authority on Buddhist art' and von Le Coq as 'a distinguished Orientalist'. He also points out – evidently for the benefit of the niggardly authorities in Calcutta – that his rivals' excavations were conducted 'with the help of abundant State means', not to mention the personal patronage of the Kaiser.

Stein decided to leave these violated sites alone. But he did discover a small group of temples at Kichik-hassar, or 'Little Castle', which the Germans had left intact, and from these he removed fragments of frescoes and stucco, and also Chinese, Uighur and Tibetan manuscripts, before moving westwards to Karashahr. At Shikchin, some fifteen miles south-west of the town, he paid a most fruitful visit to a rich *ming-oi* site, which had been only briefly explored by the Germans. Again he was dismayed at what he found. 'What distressing traces they have left behind!' he wrote to a friend. 'Fine fragments of stucco sculptures flung outside or on the scrap heap; statues too big for transport left exposed to the weather and the tender mercies of wayfarers, etc. I cannot guess what made them dig here with quite an inadequate number of labourers, and still less this indifference to the fate of all that was left in situ.' He adds, with more than a trace of self-righteousness, that despite the far greater physical difficulties of digging in what he calls 'the true desert' he always spent time and labour tidying up afterwards. One wonders whether this particular site, left looking (in the words of Stein's biographer Jeannette Mirsky) like 'a hit-and-run accident', was not in fact one of those explored by the handyman Bartus during one of his solo forays. Stein nonetheless left the site well satisfied with his ten heavy cases of antiquities.

This particular temple complex has, somewhat confusingly, come to be known as Ming-oi, although it is merely one of several such *ming-oi* ('a thousand rooms') excavated by archaeologists around the desert perimeter. As von Le Coq explains, there is no such place as Ming-oi, and the Turki term should be linked to the nearest inhabited place – thus the *ming-oi* of Kyzil, Kumtura, Shorchuk, etc. Anyone seeking to find a place called Ming-oi on the map of Chinese Turkestan will be disappointed, although the British Museum still seems convinced that it exists.

Stein's two-and-a-half-year expedition was by no means over even now, but there is no space to recount more than a few highlights. One of these was his bold southward crossing of the Taklamakan, a far more hazardous undertaking than the reverse. When Hedin crossed it he had first followed the northward-flowing Keriya-daria which ensured his water supply well into the desert. After that he knew, provided he continued to march northwards, he would sooner or later strike the eastward-flowing Tarim. A successful southward crossing, on the other hand, depended on hitting the 'mouth' of the Keriya-daria, a feat of desert navigation requiring absolute precision. The last few days of Stein's crossing were indeed anxious ones, and water had to be severely rationed. Following this exploit came two personal calamities. The first was when one of his faithful Indian assistants – Naik Ram Singh – was suddenly and agonisingly struck blind with glaucoma. Entrusted with the mission of photographing and removing further frescoes from Miran while Stein was in Khotan packing his collections, Ram Singh had doggedly insisted on continuing with his task when the sight of one eye was lost, and in spite of terrible pain. Only when totally blind did he admit defeat and allow himself to be led back to a horrified Stein. Although he could see nothing, to avoid breaking caste rules he insisted on cooking his own meals until he reached Khotan where Stein was able to engage a Hindu cook for him. Ram Singh never regained his sight, but as a result of pressure from Stein was awarded a special pension by the Government of India. Within four months, however, he was dead.

It was now Stein's turn to suffer misfortune. While mapping a glacier high in the Kun Lun mountains at a temperature of minus sixteen degrees Fahrenheit he became suddenly aware that his feet had lost all sensation. Soon this turned to severe pain, and he realised that he was suffering from frostbite. His medical manual advised rubbing snow on the afflicted area as an emergency treatment. He knew that if this failed to restore the circulation then gangrene would set in and surgery would be required. The snow treatment worked on the left foot, but not the right. Realising that his life was now threatened, Stein immediately abandoned his surveying work and set hurriedly off for Ladakh by yak, camel and finally on an improvised litter slung between two ponies. After days of agonising travel through the mountains he reached Leh where a Moravian missionary doctor amputated the toes of his right foot. The spectre which haunted him now was over his future. The pain was not so much a problem, for his stoicism was legendary. But had the operation saved his foot, or were his days as an explorer over? After many anxious weeks, during which his wounds at first refused to heal, Stein learned to his immense relief that the operation had been just in time.

The cost, in pain and anxiety, had been great, but it was perhaps not too high a price to pay for the triumphant homecoming which now awaited him. The King invested him with a C.I.E. (raised to a knighthood two years later), the Royal Geographical Society awarded him its Gold Medal, both Oxford and Cambridge conferred honorary degrees on him, while Germany (doubtless unaware of his strictures on von Le Coq's methods) hailed his achievements with a large cash prize. In Budapest he was lionised as a son who had made good. To add to his pleasure, Chiang, whose shrewd handling of the Abbot Wang had done so much to secure for

Stein the Tun-huang library, received the reward he wanted, the Chinese secretaryship to the British consulate in Kashgar.

Even now Stein's work was not over. He had to find suitably qualified scholars to work on the thousands of manuscripts and books, written in half a dozen languages, which he had either excavated or purchased from Wang, as well as restorers to disentangle and clean the several hundred temple banners and other T'ang paintings from the Caves of the Thousand Buddhas. Before long some eighteen international experts – including Hoernle, Chavannes and Lionel Giles – were at work translating and appraising the literary treasures of Tun-huang. On top of that he had to help select and prepare some of the star items from his collection for a special exhibition of it to be held at the British Museum; assist in the division of spoils between his sponsors in Bloomsbury and those in Calcutta; and finally start work on *Ruins of Desert Cathay*, his two-volume account of the expedition.

Despite the wealth of other art treasures which Stein removed from China during three expeditions (the third of which was still to come), it is with the secret library at Tun-huang that his name will always be linked. For this there are two principal reasons. The first obviously is because of its spectacular nature – the discovery has been compared to that of the Dead Sea Scrolls, also found in a cave. The second arises from the controversial circumstances in which Stein acquired the library, exposing him – like Lord Elgin – to everlasting criticism. It is perhaps for this reason that the British Museum seems to be at such pains to obliterate his memory. Unlike its other archaeological heroes, such as Layard and Rassam, whose contributions are proudly acknowledged, the visitor will look in vain for a portrait – or even a mention – of Stein in the Central Asian gallery where a pitifully small selection of his finds are currently displayed.

Regardless of the rights and wrongs of Stein's acquisition of the Tun-huang manuscripts, it is worth a brief look at some of the highlights of this great library. The most famous item to emerge from that cluttered chamber is undoubtedly the Diamond Sutra. Its fame has nothing to do with its text, for there are innumerable copies of it about (including more than five hundred, complete or incomplete, in Stein's Tun-huang haul alone). However, this one also happens to be the earliest known printed book, produced well over a thousand years ago from blocks. In a contemporary Chinese work on the history of printing, published in 1961 by the National Library of Peking, it is described thus: 'The Diamond Sutra, printed in the year 868 . . . is the world's earliest printed book, made of seven strips of paper joined together with an illustration on the first sheet which is cut with great skill.' The writer adds: 'This famous scroll was stolen over fifty years ago by the Englishman Ssu-t'an-yin [Stein] which causes people to gnash their teeth in bitter hatred.' It is currently on display in the British Museum, only a few paces from the West's most famous book, the Gutenberg Bible. The Tun-huang scroll, some sixteen feet long, bears an exact date – May 11, 868 – as well as the name of the man who commissioned and distributed it. This makes him not, as is sometimes claimed, the world's earliest known printer, but the earliest known publisher.

The bulk of the manuscripts found in Wang's secret cache were in Chinese – some seven thousand complete and a further six thousand fragments. Half a century was to pass before these (and then only the complete ones) had been catalogued. In his monograph, *Six Centuries at Tunhuang*, Dr Lionel Giles, who carried out this titanic task, calculates that in all he had to wade through between ten and twenty miles of closely written rolls of text. Because Stein could not read Chinese, and Chiang was ignorant of Buddhist literature, very many of the texts they carried away duplicated one another. For example, there were more than a thousand copies, or fragments, of the Lotus Sutra, many of them admittedly fine examples of early calligraphy. Despite this, the manuscripts included not only long-lost texts and variant versions of surviving ones, but also many totally new works in languages known and unknown to Western scholars.

Among the many curiosities to emerge from this vast archive is a thousand-year-old 'model' letter of apology in Chinese designed for inebriated guests to send to their hosts. Dr Giles translates it thus: 'Yesterday, having drunk too much, I was so intoxicated as to pass all bounds; but none of the rude and coarse language I used was uttered in a conscious state. The next morning, after hearing others speak on the subject, I realised what had happened, whereupon I was overwhelmed with confusion and ready to sink into the ground with shame ...' The letter adds that the writer will soon come to apologise in person for his 'transgression'. A suitable reply for the outraged host is suggested, which Giles translates thus: 'Yesterday, Sir, while in your cups, you so far overstepped the observances of polite society as to forfeit the name of gentleman, and made me wish to have nothing more to do with you. But since you now express your shame and regret for what has occurred, I would suggest that we meet again for a friendly talk ...' (Giles also came upon what appears to be an invitation to a football – literally 'strike-ball' – match.)

Another well-known British orientalist, Arthur Waley, has incorporated some twenty-six Chinese ballads and stories from the Caves of the Thousand Buddhas into an anthology, *Ballads and Stories from Tun-huang*. While apparently happy to make use of Stein's manuscripts, he expresses strong disapproval of the method of their acquisition, referring to the affair as 'the sacking of the Tun-huang library'. He sets out to explain why the Chinese feel so bitter about the way the manuscripts were removed to Europe by Stein 'acting on behalf of the British Museum and the Government of India'. He goes on: 'I think the best way to understand their feelings on the subject is to imagine how we should feel if a Chinese archaeologist were to come to England, discover a cache of medieval mss at a ruined monastery, bribe the custodian to part with them, and carry them off to Peking.' He ignores, however, the question of what eventually might have happened to the cache had it remained in the hands of Wang – 'that precious old humbug'.

But the Tun-huang story was not yet over. Stein's blandishments to Wang would not be, by any means, the last that the priest had to wrestle with. Hot on the Englishman's heels came the formidable Frenchman Pelliot.

13. Pelliot – the Gentle Art
of Making Enemies

Despite their colonial toe-hold on the continent (in Hanoi they even had an archaeological institute) the French were late in joining in the Central Asian treasure hunt, although they were not the last to try their luck. By the time Pelliot reached Chinese Turkestan in August 1906, the British, Swedes, Germans and Japanese had all been there at least once, the Beresovskys were nearing the end of their stay, and Stein was already back for more. The belated arrival of the French on the Silk Road is perhaps explained by their discovery, not long before, of a once-rich civilisation in the jungles of Indo-China – including the magnificent ruins at Angkor – which had been keeping their own orientalists busy. But whatever the reason for their dilatoriness, they were now determined to get their share. 'If France was to do nothing,' the distinguished French orientalist Sylvain Levi exhorted his fellow savants, 'we would be betraying our glorious tradition.' A powerful committee was set up, headed by Emile Senart, another leading oriental scholar and member of the French Academy, and backed by the Minister of Public Instruction. This had the support of no fewer than nine leading bodies devoted to scientific, geographical or cultural studies. It was decided to dispatch a three-man expedition to Chinese Turkestan as soon as possible. Chosen to lead this was a brilliant young sinologist of twenty-seven named Paul Pelliot, a former pupil of Levi's now on the staff of Hanoi's celebrated (but later to be embroiled in controversy) Ecole Française d'Extrême-Orient. His companions were Dr Louis Vaillant, an army medical officer and old friend of his, who would be responsible for mapping, collecting natural history specimens and other scientific work, and Charles Nouette, who was the expedition's photographer.

In addition to Pelliot's linguistic genius – he was at home in some thirteen languages – as a very young man he had won the Legion of Honour during the siege of the foreign legations in Peking in the summer of 1900. Trapped there at the age of twenty-one by the Boxer uprising while searching for Chinese books for the Ecole library, he was involved in two exploits which won him both praise and criticism. One was his daring capture, with the aid of two sailors, of a huge Boxer war standard, an act which greatly enraged the enemy. In his siege diary, published subsequently, there is a photograph of him proudly holding his trophy. The other exploit occurred during a temporary ceasefire when he climbed over the barricade announcing that he was going to have tea with the rebels. For several hours his fate was discussed, and his bravado condemned, by the besieged Europeans. But eventually, after being seen to take leave of the enemy with great displays of cordiality, he returned laden with gifts of fruit. He had told them, he said, that the Europeans' morale was extremely high, but that they lacked fresh fruit.

Pelliot's diary, much of it scribbled under fire, reveals a courageous but hot-headed young man always in the thick of the fray. He is fiercely critical of many of the senior diplomats, hinting at their cowardice and incompetence. It is not surprising, therefore, that some of them found him bumptious. (Even Stein, who greatly admired him as a scholar, described him some years later as 'a bit too self-centred'.) One French officer, on the other hand, wrote: 'Pelliot, the youngest of the volunteers, is adored by everybody, and, because of his youth and courage, we forgive him for getting carried away at times.' Whether one liked him or was irritated by him, it seems that it was hard to ignore him. On his return to Hanoi, and still only twenty-two, he was made Professor of Chinese at the Ecole. At the same time he began to review – often very critically – the works of other sinologists in learned journals and in the Ecole's own bulletin. 'The gentle art of making enemies ...' he once called this. Here perhaps are clues as to why, some nine years later, he would find himself victim of a vicious and concerted campaign in France when he returned in triumph from his Central Asian expedition.

*   *   *

Their preparations now complete, Pelliot and his two companions left Paris on June 17, 1906, travelling by rail via Moscow to Tashkent where they were held up for two months awaiting the arrival of their heavy baggage. Pelliot had used the time to polish up his Russian and also, as we have seen, to study Turki (or Eastern Turkish, as some scholars then called it). Thanks to his amazing gift for languages and prodigious memory, he was soon able to converse easily in the latter. It was this near-unbelievable power of recall that later was to mislead Pelliot's detractors into challenging some of his claims. The expedition finally reached Kashgar on the last day of August. There they stayed at the Russian consulate-general as guests of Petrovsky's successor, making diplomatic and other official calls on those mandarins whose goodwill and help they would require. This caused something of a stir, for few western travellers who passed through Kashgar (and certainly none of Pelliot's rivals) spoke Chinese. Dr Vaillant recalled long afterwards 'how amazed these high officials were to hear Pelliot speaking fluent and elegant Chinese, quoting from their classics and reading with ease the sentences written on the long scrolls which, in China, adorn all reception rooms'. Above all, they were impressed by his familiarity with what the doctor calls 'the refined ceremonial practised by a civilisation so proudly aware of its longevity ...'. Although all this sounds suspiciously like the young hero of the barricades showing off once again to the natives, it was – as Vaillant points out – soon to pay dividends. For a start they had decided to take with them a yurt (the circular tent of Central

Asia) and Pelliot asked the Prefect of Kashgar to try to obtain one for them. 'When we mentioned this to the Russian consul,' Vaillant recounts, 'he laughed at our pretensions.' He assured the three Frenchmen: 'They are unobtainable and even if you did find one it would take you six months to get it.' A week later, to the Russian's astonishment, the yurt was delivered, whereupon – Vaillant adds – 'Pelliot immediately got us used to erecting it and living in it in the consulate yard.'

Their plan was to travel eastwards to Kucha where they proposed to excavate at some length. This would take them past Tumchuq, where Hedin had reported seeing some ruins which he had dismissed as Moslem and not old enough, therefore, to be of interest. After six weeks of preparation at Kashgar, the three Frenchmen set out on the first leg of their journey. A few marches short of Tumchuq an amusing incident occurred when they halted for lunch at the small sub-prefecture of Faizabad. After paying their respects to the sub-prefect, and apologising for being unable to receive a return call from him, they returned to the inn for a hurried meal before moving on. Vaillant picks up the tale: 'But scarcely had we regained our camp than we heard the three shots from the cannon which meant that the mandarin had left his yamen.' Moments later Ting, their servant, shouted: 'Here is the mandarin!' The Frenchmen were aghast. Vaillant writes: 'We had nothing prepared for a visit. Pelliot greeted him with profuse apologies and invited him into the reception room. After the customary courtesies we sat down and tried not to show our anxiety. We then saw cups of tea arriving and plates laden with slices of melon and cakes.' When the meal was over, the mandarin turned to Pelliot with a smile and said: 'Really, you Europeans certainly know how to travel. I am full of admiration for the way you are able to organise such a reception in the middle of a journey. I am deeply honoured by your delicacy.' When he had gone, Pelliot immediately began to congratulate Ting on having coped so

20 Excavating an ancient house at Niya, from a photograph by Sir Aurel Stein

21 Stein and his men in the Taklamakan. Naik Ram Singh,
later struck blind, is seated on Stein's left

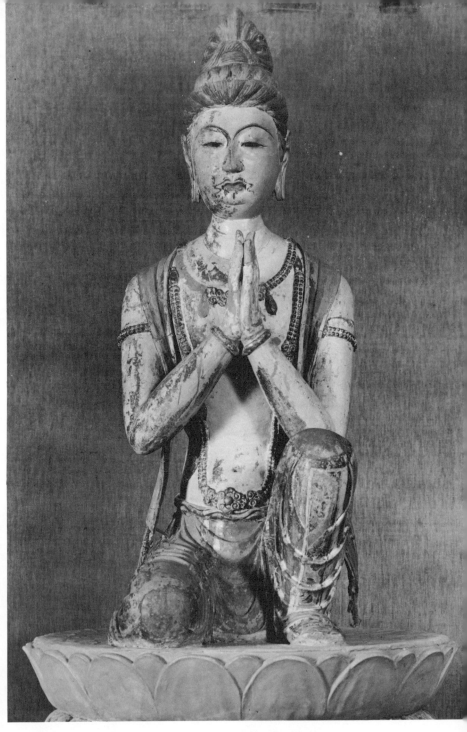

22 The kneeling Bodhisattva carried away from Tun-huang
by Langdon Warner

well. 'I did nothing,' he replied. 'Servants from the yamen brought everything. . . .'

The ruins at Tumchuq, far from being Moslem, proved to be those of an early Buddhist monastic city which had flourished until at least the year 800. It was mere chance which led Pelliot to discover this during their brief halt there. Idly prodding the ground with his riding crop, to his astonishment he turned up a figurine which was unmistakably Graeco-Buddhist. Although all their baggage, including their winter clothing, was already on its way to Kucha, Pelliot felt that they had no choice but to stay and excavate further. Six weeks later, numbed with cold but laden with painted sculptures and other finds, they hastened on to Kucha – and the comfort of their fur coats. They had been disappointed to learn that not only the Germans but also (as we shall see) the Russians and Japanese had preceded them to this archaeologically rich area. In the event they found plenty to do in the temples which their rivals had overlooked. Most important to Pelliot was their discovery of a large hoard of Buddhist documents, including many in unknown languages. Some of these proved later to be in the lost language of Kuchean, and were subsequently deciphered by Sylvain Levi.

After eight fruitful months in Kucha, the French expedition moved on to Urumchi to replenish their stores before making the desert crossing to Tun-huang. At this point their plan was merely to photograph and study the wall-paintings and sculptures in the Caves of the Thousand Buddhas, for word of Stein's great discovery six months earlier had not reached them.

While they were in Urumchi, Pelliot met an old friend – or rather foe – from Peking days. Following the defeat of the Boxers, the Duke Lan, brother of the movement's leader and himself deeply implicated in the uprising, had been exiled for life to Urumchi, where he devoted his remaining years to photography. 'We had fought one another in 1900, but the passage of time heals all things,' Pelliot wrote afterwards, adding: 'We sealed our friendship with many a glass of champagne.' When the day of their departure finally arrived, the Duke remarked sadly to Pelliot: 'You are going, but I have to stay.' Pelliot forbore from reminding the one-time Peking police chief that, some seven years earlier, there had been a day 'when he had forced us to stay when we would have asked nothing better than to leave'.

In fact, although the Duke probably did not realise it, it was an act of generosity by him which made Pelliot even more eager to get away from Urumchi and reach Tun-huang. During their stay in Urumchi they had heard vague stories about a mysterious cache of manuscripts that had been found in the Caves of the Thousand Buddhas. Pelliot knew at once that this was more than a mere bazaar rumour when the exiled Duke presented him with a manuscript which he said had come from Tun-huang. 'Pelliot had hardly unrolled this,' Vaillant recounts, 'when he realised that it dated from before the eighth century.'

When the three men reached Tun-huang and the Caves of the Thousand Buddhas they found, just as Stein had, the manuscript cave locked and Wang absent. However, before long, they ran the priest to earth in the town. Dazzled no doubt by Pelliot's Chinese, he agreed to show the Frenchman his finds. In view of the prolonged struggle that Stein and Chiang had had with Wang before being allowed to see the manuscripts, it may seem surprising that Pelliot managed it so relatively easily. Indeed, his enemies were to find it unbelievable. However, fear of discovery had been Wang's great dread, as he repeatedly told Stein and Chiang. Now, because this new visitor from Europe did not even mention Stein (Pelliot still did not realise, it seems, that his rival had beaten him to the secret chamber), it must have appeared to Wang that the Englishman had kept his vow of secrecy. The discovery that these 'foreign devils' could be trusted not to talk must have been very reassuring to him. Furthermore, he had already begun to spend Stein's 'donation' on his garish restorations, and now, no doubt, was looking for further contributions.

But even Pelliot was made to bide his time. He recounts in a letter written from Tun-huang on March 26, 1908: 'Wang arrived rather late and said he had left the key behind at Tun-huang. I had to wait again.' It was then that Pelliot learned to his disappointment that Stein had already visited the secret chamber, but – he was assured – had spent only three days there. Had he known the true length of Stein's stay he might have been less sanguine about his own prospects. As it was, he feared that in the eight years since its discovery much of the library inevitably would have disappeared. After all, the manuscript presented to him by Duke Lan, some four hundred miles away in Urumchi, was unlikely to be the only one to have escaped thus from the cave.

Finally the key arrived from Tun-huang and nearly a month after their arrival at the great *ming-oi* Pelliot was allowed into the secret chamber. 'I was stupefied,' he wrote. He estimated that there were between fifteen and twenty thousand manuscripts in the cave. To unroll each one and examine it properly, he realised, would take him a minimum of six months. However, his mind was quickly made up. 'If only cursory, examination of the entire library was essential,' he wrote. 'I must at least open everything, recognise the nature of the text and see whether it offered anything new.' He decided to make two piles: first the cream, which he must obtain at all costs, and then the desirable but less essential manuscripts.

Working by the light of a single candle, and crouched uncomfortably in the tiny space resulting (though he did not realise it) from the removal of Stein's great haul, Pelliot spent three long and claustrophobic weeks sifting through the dusty bundles. In the Pelliot gallery at the Musée Guimet in Paris there is a memorable photograph of him at work in the secret chamber taken by Nouette. Behind him, as he crouches, can be seen a daunting mountain of tightly packed manuscripts.

'During the first ten days,' Pelliot wrote in a long letter to Senart in Paris, 'I attacked nearly a thousand scrolls a day, which must be a record ...' He likened himself, somewhat flippantly, to a philologist travelling at the speed of a racing-car. It was an analogy that his critics were to fasten onto with glee.

At the end of each long session in the cave, Pelliot would rejoin his two colleagues – 'his greatcoat stuffed with his most interesting finds ... radiant with joy', Vaillant recalled years afterwards. 'One such evening he showed us a Nestorian Gospel of St John; on another a description, dating from the year 800, of the curious little lake ... situated in the high dunes south of Tun-huang; another time it was the monastery accounts.' Pelliot ruled out any hope of persuading Wang to part with the entire collection, for the discovery was too well known in the district. 'Mongol and Tibetan pilgrims came to read some of these precious documents as part of their pilgrimage,' Vaillant explains. Pelliot's great fear, however, was of leaving behind, or not recognising, any key document. 'All the same, I do not think I overlooked anything essential,' he wrote. 'I handled not only every scroll, but every scrap of paper – and God knows how many bits and pieces there were....'

Now came the most anxious moment of all, when Pelliot had to persuade the little priest to sell him the two piles of manuscripts which he had set aside. The negotiations were conducted between the two men amid great secrecy. 'We ourselves', Vaillant recalled, 'were compelled to speak of the discovery in only the most guarded fashion, even in our letters.' Finally the figure of 500 *taels* (about £90) was agreed and the hoard was carefully and discreetly packed for shipment to France. Vaillant wrote: 'Only when Nouette had embarked on the steamer with the crates containing our collections did Pelliot mention them openly and leave for Peking with a box containing samples of the manuscripts.' He added: 'They were a revelation to Chinese scholars, who could scarcely believe that such a find had been made.' But as a result, a telegram was immediately sent by the Peking authorities to the sub-prefect at Tun-huang ordering him to place an embargo on whatever remained in the cave. Vaillant observed wryly: 'The good monk must have had a bad quarter of an hour, and perhaps repented that he had accepted Pelliot's money.'

Although the acquisition of the Tun-huang manuscripts represented a great personal triumph for Pelliot – whatever one may think of the ethics involved – his two companions had also been far from idle during nearly four months there. Nouette had taken hundreds of black and white photographs of everything that Pelliot considered worthy of interest, and these were published later in six volumes. Although Pelliot never got around to writing an accompanying text, this corpus remains today the principal source of information on the paintings and sculptures, mainly because of the vandalism which was to occur only a few years later when White Russian soldiers were interned in the caves.

When Pelliot finally reached Paris on October 24, 1909, he had been away for three years. He returned to a hero's welcome, but also to find trouble brewing. This was to develop into a vicious campaign embracing not only himself but also Professor Chavannes and the Ecole Française d'Extrême-Orient in Hanoi. During his absence, the long and often graphic letter he had written from Tun-huang to Senart in the first flush of excitement had been published in the widely read journal of the Ecole, where he was still officially employed. He might well have written differently had he known what capital his foes would make of it, and almost certainly would have omitted some of his more candid, and sometimes light-hearted, comments. We have already noted how Pelliot's intellectual arrogance – as some saw it – had earned him enemies in the academic world. His letter to Senart gave them the opportunity they had been waiting for.

That part of the campaign which involved Chavannes and

the Ecole does not concern us here, but in essence it sought to cast doubts upon the former's scholarship and upon the competence of the entire staff of that prestigious institution. It was waged initially as a whispering campaign, but before long it had spread to the columns of some newspapers and periodicals, especially those concerned with Indo-China. Pelliot's involvement was on two counts. As Professor of Chinese at the Ecole, he, like all other members of the staff, had to face general accusations of élitism and – more serious – of having to rely on local interpreters for assistance with the publication of their works. But in addition to this, as leader of the highly successful expedition to Chinese Central Asia, Pelliot found himself singled out for special attention. For this triumph by one so young had inevitably aroused envy in some other French orientalists who felt, perhaps, that they instead should have been chosen.

Among his principal detractors was a senior librarian in the oriental department of the Bibliothèque Nationale in Paris, where the Tun-huang manuscripts had been deposited by Pelliot in a locked room to which only he had a key. Clearly furious (and perhaps understandably so) at being denied access to them, the librarian wrote a caustic letter to a French newspaper in which he endeavoured to cast doubts on the authenticity of Pelliot's manuscripts as well as upon the young scholar's capabilities as a sinologist. On the pretext of wishing to safeguard his own reputation as conservator of the Bibliothèque's oriental manuscripts – which those in the locked room were due to join – he announced that he was forthwith disclaiming all responsibility for Pelliot's Tun-huang purchases. Meanwhile, the other works of art brought back by the expedition – paintings, sculptures, textiles, wooden figures and terracottas – were put on public view in the Louvre, in a specially named Salle Pelliot. These, too, his detractors endeavoured to belittle. 'One wonders how it is possible that a room in the Louvre, however small, should be devoted to so little,' wrote one.

In December 1910, this 'malevolent campaign', as one French scholar has called it, reached its climax in a particularly virulent attack on Pelliot, Chavannes and the Ecole in the anti-colonial journal *La Revue Indigène*. A mixture of the unctuous and the vitriolic, and filling twenty-three pages of the magazine, it purported to analyse the Pelliot 'scandal'. The author – M. Fernand Farjenel, an old China hand and himself a Chinese speaker – first disposed of Chavannes, whose translations, he claimed, 'were inaccurate on every line when not in every word'. His main target, however, was Pelliot. The 'young explorer', as he repeatedly calls him, was accused of frittering away public money in two years of 'wandering' which, Farjenel claimed, yielded nothing of any value. He implied that by the time Pelliot reached Tun-huang he was so desperate to justify his mission that his critical judgement was seriously impaired.

In support of this, Farjenel quoted Pelliot's letter to Senart in which he admits to being 'stupefied' at what he saw when he entered Wang's secret chamber. So stupefied was he, Farjenel claimed, that he swallowed the priest's tale 'with credulous confidence', apparently unaware that, shortly before, Stein had removed 'twenty-nine cases' of manuscripts and paintings from the chamber. 'This must have pretty well emptied it,' the writer argued. But Pelliot, he went on, 'full of joy at the thought that he had just discovered a priceless treasure took no precautions whatever and made no attempt to check the monk's claims'. The obvious conclusion, he added, was that the cave had been refilled with forged and other worthless manuscripts by the local people who knew that Europeans liked to buy such things. He reminded his readers that the Far East abounded with clever rogues, as Stein's unmasking of Islam Akhun had shown. A scholar who, by his own admission, had to examine some thousand scrolls a day (Farjenel calculated that this meant two a minute) was a natural victim for such forgers, he added. The fact that the manuscripts remained even now behind locked doors, out of reach of other oriental scholars, could only reinforce his and others' suspicions. He demanded that in view of 'the very large sum that the expedition has cost', Pelliot should reply at once to his critics. But Pelliot did not reply, confident that his detractors would have to eat their words sooner or later.

The French public, of course, had no way of telling who was right. If Stein had cleaned out the secret chamber, then where *had* all these manuscripts come from? Anyway, why were they still under lock and key, unavailable to other scholars, a full year after being deposited in the Bibliothèque? It was not until 1912, when Stein's *Ruins of Desert Cathay* came out, that Pelliot's critics were finally put in their place. Had Farjenel been able to read it before launching so confidently into print, he would certainly have thought twice. For a start Stein made it perfectly clear that he had only been able to purchase part of the Tun-huang library, leaving behind him 'masses of manuscripts'. Moreover, he had not been allowed to choose freely – as Pelliot had – from the secret chamber, being limited to the bundles that Wang brought him. Furthermore, unlike Pelliot, who – as Stein put it – had been 'aided by his exceptional mastery of Chinese literature and bibliography', he himself had been gravely handicapped by his lack of Chinese. Clearly aware of the campaign to discredit his young French colleague, Stein went out of his way to praise the excellence of Pelliot's scholarship as well as to express admiration for his methods of excavation, evidence of which he had seen at Kucha.

Although the campaign had failed signally to damage Pelliot's reputation where it really mattered – in the world of learning – it had not been for want of trying. But did Pelliot's detractors genuinely believe the charges they brought so vituperatively against him, or were they seeking to destroy a man whom they clearly loathed or perhaps envied? Today, some seventy years later, and with all the witnesses long dead, it is impossible to say. But a comment by Vaillant perhaps provides the answer. During their expedition, he recounts: 'Pelliot made brief notes whose accuracy and detail astonished their recipients in France. They could not understand how, in the wilds and far from a library, he could possibly recall certain facts or texts ... His prodigious memory enabled him to do without all reference material.' This is confirmed by others. 'When Pelliot has read a book, the whole thing remains in there,' one colleague declared, pointing to his own forehead.

The fact that his enemies found him too clever by half is perhaps thus explained. Until they learned, too late, just how clever he really was, they simply assumed that he was a braggart. To some extent Pelliot appears to have brought it upon himself. Like many other archaeologists, he found it difficult to get down to the drudgery of classifying and publishing his material. As we have seen, his detractors made much of the fact that, a whole year after arriving at the Bibliothèque Nationale, the manuscripts were still in their packing cases, and that Pelliot had not so much as produced an inventory. This had enabled them to suggest that he must have something to hide – the dreadful discovery, perhaps, that his Tun-huang purchases were all forgeries.

Nor was this the only row in which he was to become embroiled, although it is the only one which concerns us here. Pelliot, who went on to carve out a brilliant career for himself as France's foremost Chinese scholar, never again excavated in Central Asia – the only one of our principal characters not to return for more. But this was not because of any lack of interest on his part. When serving as French military attaché in Peking during World War I, he told the American archaeologist Langdon Warner that he had 'several new sites up his sleeve', but no money to work them. By the time there was money available it was too late, for the Chinese had finally shut the door in the face of western archaeologists.

14. Spies Along the Silk Road

In the autumn of 1908, around the time when Pelliot was shipping his treasures home from Chinese Central Asia, British intelligence chiefs in Simla began to take an interest in the movements of two young Japanese archaeologists who had turned up on the Silk Road. Although unaware of it themselves, the men had been observed from the moment they entered Chinese Turkestan overland from Peking. In true *Kim* fashion they were shadowed for over a year by a succession of Moslem traders, native servants and others on the payroll of the Indian Government. Regular reports on their movements as they travelled from oasis to oasis, sometimes together, more often hundreds of miles apart, were compiled in Kashgar by Captain A. R. B. Shuttleworth, temporarily in charge of the consulate while Macartney was on leave in England. These were carried across the Karakoram by runner with the official mail to Sir Francis Younghusband, then British Resident in Kashmir, for onward transmission to Simla.

Ostensibly, the two Japanese – scholar-monks from Count Kozui Otani's monastery in Kyoto – were in Chinese Central Asia in search of its Buddhist past. For Otani was the spiritual leader of the *Jodo Shinzu*, or 'Pure Land Sect', a large and influential Japanese Buddhist sect which traces its origins back to that part of China. Indeed, this was not the first expedition he had sent there. As early as 1902, after learning of Stein's first discoveries, he had dispatched two of his monks on a digging spree around some of the Taklamakan sites, and they had returned home with Buddhist texts, fragments of wall-paintings and sculptures packed in wicker baskets. But that visit had gone virtually unnoticed by other Central Asian scholars, let alone by intelligence experts in Simla. For not only did they not publish their results or publicise their discoveries, but this was before the Russo-Japanese war of 1905 when overnight the Great Powers had to recognise the Japanese as a new force in Asia, and a potential threat to anyone with political or commercial interests there. Thus the first of the three archaeological missions that Count Otani was to send to Chinese Central Asia between 1902 and 1910 had been accepted by those few who were aware of it at its face value – a pious if eccentric search by Buddhist monks for their spiritual ancestry. Indeed, it was they who had first discovered the artistic riches of Kyzil. But they had been driven away by an earthquake, losing all their notes and photographs, thus enabling von Le Coq and Grünwedel to be the first to reveal its treasures to the world some two years later.

By 1908, when the second Otani mission arrived on the scene, they were regarded in a very different light. Moreover, if the British suspected that they were there for some reason other than archaeology (that well-known cover for espionage), then the Russians, still smarting from their defeat at the hands of the Japanese, were even more convinced of it. Captain Shuttleworth was assured by his Russian opposite number in Kashgar that one of the two Japanese, Zuicho Tachibana, was in fact an officer in the Imperial Japanese Navy, and the other, Eizaburo Nomura, an army officer. But besides digging up old ruins, and removing large quantities of antiquities, what were they really up to? The question was to cause considerable head-scratching in British Indian intelligence circles – and, no doubt, in Russian ones too.

The two men had reached Urumchi overland from Peking in October 1908, halting there a fortnight before pressing on to Turfan. After digging for more than two months at a number of sites in the area, including Karakhoja, they continued westwards to Korla and Karashahr where they parted. Tachibana headed for Lop-nor, excavating sites around

Lou-lan and Charkhlik before proceeding westwards along the southern arm of the Silk Road, digging at Niya, Keriya and Khotan. Meanwhile Nomura spent nearly two months excavating at Kucha before continuing westwards along the northern arm of the ancient trade route, eventually reaching Kashgar, where he awaited the arrival of Tachibana. According to a brief account of the expedition entitled *Central Asian Objects brought back by the Otani Mission*, published by the Tokyo National Museum in 1971, the two Japanese archaeologists were reunited on July 7, 1909, after five months of travelling apart. According to Captain Shuttleworth (unless the diminutive Tachibana managed to slip into town without him knowing), it was a whole week later.

The task of shadowing the two men for many weeks and over hundreds of miles had been made considerably easier by the network of *aksakals* (literary 'white-beards') which had been established by Macartney in the main population centres. They were usually the senior Indian – and therefore British – trader in each of the main oases. Officially they were responsible for the well-being and good behaviour of their expatriate community, and with assisting any British traveller who might pass through their territory. However, as Shuttleworth's secret reports (now in the so-called 'Political and Secret' files in the India Office Library) reveal, they sometimes turned their hands to the Great Game.

On June 12, 1909, for example, Shuttleworth received a letter from Badruddin Khan, his man in Khotan. Dispatched twenty-two days earlier, it contained the following intelligence. 'One Japanese traveller, accompanied by one Chinaman and a Kuchari Mohammedan interpreter, has arrived in Keriya. He lives in European fashion and can talk Chinese. He has visited all the places visited by Dr. Stein. He has also explored many ruined cities. The Amban of Keriya gave him the services of Ibrahim Beg who was with Dr. Stein. The Amban has asked me to prepare my house for his reception if he comes here. If he comes to Khotan I will report his movements and tell you what he has done in the town.' From this it seems clear that the Chinese had no suspicions that Tachibana and Nomura were anything more than itinerant scholars in search – like Stein and others before them – of the past. What was it then that made the British (and the Russians) think so differently and issue orders to Shuttleworth to have them shadowed?

The political and secret files provide the answer. It is to be found in a report on the activities of the two men sent to the Secretary of State for India, Lord Morley, in London. According to this the Indian Government had been informed by the Japanese consulate in Calcutta in September 1908 that Tachibana and Nomura, the former described as a priest and the latter as secretary to Count Otani's Buddhist temple in Kyoto, were travelling from Peking via Chinese Central Asia to India 'to make investigations in matters of religious interest'. The report goes on: 'We had some reason, however, to suspect that they were secret intelligence agents.' One reason was their connection with 'a third so-called priest', a Mr Ama, who was already suspected by the British authorities of being a Japanese spy. Ama, Lord Morley was informed, 'was in affluent circumstances, and though the avowed object of his travels was to inspect Buddhist relics, his knowledge of the subject was ascertained to be of the most superficial nature'. While on a visit to northern India in the summer of 1908 he had been refused permission to visit certain lakes on the Tibetan border, whereupon he undertook to return from Leh to Srinagar by the most direct route. 'Instead of doing so,' the report adds, 'he made an unusual deviation in the direction of Tibet' (although it was thought unlikely that he could have reached the Tibetan border in the period that elapsed between his leaving Leh and reaching Srinagar). The authors of the report do not enlarge on what they believe to be the real connection between the mysterious Mr Ama and the two Japanese archaeologists beyond the fact they all three were suspected of being spies. But if their suspicions of Tachibana and Nomura were initially founded on nothing more than guilt by association, then they must have felt vindicated as Shuttleworth's reports began to reach them through Sir Francis Younghusband in Srinagar.

The first hint that they might be right came on March 10, 1909, when the two Japanese had already been in Chinese Turkestan for nearly five months. The *aksakal* at Kucha reported their arrival there to Shuttleworth, adding that although they claimed to be 'in search of Buddhistic remains' they were also sketching and surveying. This, in fact, was not inconsistent with their being archaeologists, although neither Shuttleworth nor the *aksakal* seem to have realised this, presumably never having seen an excavator at work. Stein not only surveyed every one of the sites he dug, but also thousands of square miles of Chinese Turkestan, while Russian travellers like Prejevalsky had done likewise, not to mention Hedin. However, Chinese Central Asia was both a British and a Russian sphere of influence, and as for Hedin, what threat was a Swede to anyone? But for the Japanese to trespass there and start surveying into the bargain was definite cause for alarm.

By now, moreover, other clues had begun to emerge, adding weight to suspicions that Tachibana and Nomura were not merely archaeologists or, for that matter, even Buddhist monks. For a start there was Tachibana's behaviour towards the natives, which appeared more consistent with the Russian claim that he was a naval officer than his own that he was a holy man. The tip came from the Fu of Yarkand who complained that Tachibana had been beating Chinese subjects and making himself a general nuisance. Suspicions deepened further when Shuttleworth's agents discovered that the two Japanese were carrying with them a small library of English naval and military books – hardly the devotional reading expected from holy men, particularly when both claimed to speak no English. Nor was that all. In Yarkand, Tachibana had endeavoured to acquire maps and other records of the town, thus incurring the suspicions of the Fu, while from Kashgar they had mailed off numerous bulky letters which Shuttleworth suggested might contain maps and reports. Considering that these packages were sent through him, it is perhaps surprising that he did not discreetly open one of them. This, after all, would have settled the matter once and for all.

By now, the two Japanese having joined forces again in Kashgar, Shuttleworth was able to observe them at first hand, even inviting them to dinner at Chini-Bagh. He reported to Younghusband: 'Nomura was seen sketching around the walls of the city with what looked like a plane table. Tachibana sketched the road from Maralbashi to Yarkand ... and was also seen examining the telegraph poles and measuring the distances between them.' During their stay in Kashgar the two archaeologists (if that is what they were) did not exactly endear themselves to Shuttleworth. It had been his task to break it to them that if they wished to return home through India, then they must travel together via the Karakoram and not, as they were now requesting, by different routes. On being informed of this ruling by Calcutta, Shuttleworth reported, 'Tachibana was cheeky to me ... and I had to sit on him severely.'

If they were indeed carrying out secret intelligence work, as Shuttleworth was by now convinced, then they were a miserable advertisement for their spymasters. They even managed to run out of money and were forced to approach Shuttleworth for a consular loan of 2,000 *taels* (around £360) to get them home. He refused, pointing out that they were on Chinese territory and that the correct person to approach was the Taotai. Furthermore, they had no security to offer and since public money was involved he did not feel justified in advancing such a large sum.

Had it not been for their request for a loan, then this might well have been the end of the affair. As it turned out, it was to give the British Government the very excuse it was looking for. By now the intelligence chiefs who had instructed Shuttleworth to have the two men shadowed were as convinced as he was that Tachibana and Nomura, besides being archaeologists, were 'links in the general system of intelligence which the Japanese Government has instituted'. This was their verdict in the secret report on the two men sent to Lord Morley. They were forced to admit though that it was far from clear what Japan's interest could be in this remote backwater of China.

Whatever that interest, it is clear from the correspondence in the political and secret files that the British Government was not going to let the Mikado's Government get away scot-free with espionage, however amateur, so close to India's frontiers. An official letter was therefore sent to Count Komura, the Japanese Foreign Minister, by Sir Claude Mac-Donald, the British Ambassador in Tokyo. It complained about the overbearing behaviour of Tachibana and Nomura and made much of the fact that they had endeavoured to obtain a loan from the British consulate without first approaching the Chinese. While the ways of diplomacy never cease to amaze the layman, it is hard to believe that a complaint so utterly trivial as this would normally be brought to the personal attention of the Foreign Minister. It seems more likely that it was nothing other than a diplomatic device for warning the Japanese secret service to keep away from a British sphere of influence. MacDonald's letter ends with the suggestion that 'it would be of advantage to all concerned if Your Excellency could kindly inform me whether Tachibana and Nomura possess any claim to consideration or title to official recognition'. Count Komura's reply was short and to the point. He made no attempt to apologise for the behaviour of his countrymen and washed his hands of both of them, declaring that he had 'no concern with or cognisance of' either. To readers of spy literature his words have a familiar ring – a government disowning agents foolish enough to be caught. To those with less imagination the letter merely reads like that of a busy Foreign

Minister putting down an ambassador who has troubled him with a trifling complaint.

★ ★ ★

Tachibana and Nomura, if they were spies, were not the only ones at work on the Silk Road during this period. Nor were they alone in combining it with treasure-hunting. Another was a man destined many years later to become world-famous – Baron Carl Gustav Mannerheim, then a newly promoted colonel in the Tsar's army who had distinguished himself in the Russo-Japanese War. Mannerheim was Finnish, but at that time Finland was an autonomous state within Tsarist Russia. In the autumn of 1906, on instructions from the Russian General Staff, he set out on horseback across Chinese Central Asia to study the political and economic situation there and carry out what he described in his diary as 'tasks of a military nature'. Not a man to waste opportunities, he also undertook to conduct a programme of archaeological, ethnological and anthropological work for a new museum which the Finns were planning. The Finns, rather like the Hungarians, trace their ancestry back to the warlike hordes who once inhabited the Asian steppes, and their scholars were anxious to enlarge their knowledge of the peoples and history of this region.

As Mannerheim rode, in addition to mapping his route and recording military intelligence, he also measured human heads with callipers, collected everything from rustic surgical instruments to rolling pins, and purchased antiquities and manuscripts. Most of the latter he obtained from Khotan where by now there was a thriving market in antiquities. He also bought a certain amount in Turfan where he noted that the prices were far higher than in Khotan, and was tempted to remove three Buddhist wall-paintings from one site he visited. But he decided not to risk ruining them and to leave them to what he calls 'more qualified collectors'. Turfan marked the end of his archaeological activities and he thereafter rides eastwards out of our narrative, though not out of history. For in 1940, at the age of seventy-two and the veteran of five wars, Field Marshal Baron Carl Gustav Mannerheim led Finland's heroic but hopeless defiance of Stalin's invading armies. Today the antiquities he acquired on his lone ride across Asia thirty-three years earlier are to be seen in the National Museum in Helsinki.

*   *   *

By now rivalry between the Great Powers for the treasures of the Silk Road was intensifying. We have seen how, one by one, Stein, Grünwedel, von Le Coq, Pelliot and Count Otani's Japanese joined in the archaeological free-for-all begun by Hedin. But apart from briefly noting the presence of the Beresovsky brothers at Kucha (it was a shopping expedition rather than an archaeological one) we have paid scant attention to the Russians. There are several reasons for this. First, no single figure stands out. Secondly, they pulled off no great coups, despite the fact that the sites were more accessible to them than to anyone else. Thirdly, they were moderate in the quantities they removed. And lastly they were slow to act, despite the fact that they had been aware for years that the remains of a lost civilisation of some kind lay on their doorstep.

The first Russian to report seeing sand-buried ruins in China's great deserts, as we have already noted, was the celebrated Colonel Nikolai Prejevalsky. In 1876 – just ten years after Johnson had become the first European to see such ruins – the Russian reported finding what he described as 'a very large city' in the Lop desert. But Prejevalsky was first and foremost a zoologist and was actually rather bored by archaeology. He made no attempt to explore it, and went on his way. The next Russian to come upon traces of this lost Central Asian civilisation (which he correctly identified as Buddhist) was Dr Albert Regel, a botanist. In 1879, while on what appears to have been a spying mission in the eastern T'ien

Shan (Tsarist Russia and Manchu China were involved at that time in a border dispute), he had discovered the great walled city of Karakhoja. But due to harassment by the Chinese he had been unable to explore it further. To reach it in the first place he had been obliged to give his guards the slip in Turfan. When he returned there he found them already undergoing the punishment of slow hanging in the dreaded bamboo cage which von Le Coq was later to witness. Although he reported his discovery on reaching home, no Russian made any attempt to explore the region archaeologically for a further nineteen years.

The next to do so was Dmitri Klementz who, accompanied by his botanist wife, was sent in 1898 by the Academy of Sciences and the Imperial Russian Geographical Society to investigate reports by a Tsarist army officer that the entire Turfan area was rich in ancient ruins. Academician Klementz had been a noted revolutionary in his youth and had spent some time in prison (from which he had managed to escape) and also in exile in Siberia before settling down to become a prominent member of the scientific establishment in St Petersburg. He explored a number of sites around Turfan, including Karakhoja, Astana and Yarkhoto, taking many photographs, drawing ground plans of buildings, copying inscriptions and acquiring samples of manuscripts and antiquities. In all, he counted one hundred and thirty cave temples, many of which contained well-preserved wall-paintings. He removed several small murals, the first of so many which were to be cut from the walls of these temples and carried off to Europe. News of his startling finds was published by the Academy shortly after his return to St Petersburg, and caused considerable excitement there among Central Asian scholars and art historians. But, as we have already seen, it was in Germany that the news was to have the most immediate and far-reaching results. The Russians virtually presented Turfan to the Germans as a gift. Not only was the Klementz report published in German but a subsequent book by him contained a large folding map showing the precise whereabouts of all the sites he had discovered as well as photographs of them. This, too, was published in German (it was not uncommon at that time for Russian academics to publish in German or French). Having thus drawn the attention of potential rivals to the rich harvest to be reaped around Turfan, only just across their own frontier with China, the Russians sat back and did nothing.

It was not until 1905, when the Beresovskys set out on their buying trip to Kucha and a Committee for the Exploration of Central and East Asia was set up by the government, that they began to make up for lost time. Even then it was somewhat half-hearted. Indeed, it was not until 1908 (by which time the British, Germans, French and Japanese were already well entrenched on the Silk Road) that the Russians made their first – and only – discovery of major importance. This was Karakhoto, meaning 'Black City', and not to be confused with Karakhoja. Lying just inside China's present border with Mongolia, it is undoubtedly Marco Polo's long-lost 'City of Etzina'. It was discovered, or rather rediscovered, by Colonel Petr Koslov, a protégé of Prejevalsky's, who was leading an expedition to explore parts of the Sino-Mongolian frontier region. At a remote spot in the Gobi he and his men were astonished to see rising from the desert a huge fortress town. 'The walls of the town are covered with sand, in some places so deeply that it is possible to walk up the slope and enter the fortress,' Koslov reported. The awe-struck Russians made their entry, however, through the great western gateway. 'Here we found a quadrangular space whereon were scattered high and low, broad and narrow, ruins of buildings with rubbish of all kinds at their feet,' Koslov added.

Local oasis-dwellers told the Russians how the city came to be destroyed (in the fourteenth century, it is now known, a hundred years or so after Marco Polo's visit). The last ruler of the city – one Kara-tsian-tsiun – putting his faith in his hitherto invincible army, determined to seize the throne of China for himself. The Emperor dispatched a considerable force against him and, after a series of battles, finally cornered the rebel in his capital. Finding that they could not take it by assault, because of its high walls, the Chinese decided to sever its only water supply, the Etsin-gol river. Filling thousands of bags with sand to form a dam, they managed to divert this away from the city. (As confirmation of this story, Koslov came upon evidence of the dam.) The defenders, desperate for water, began to dig a deep well in one corner of the fortress. Finding no water they resolved to face the Chinese in one last desperate battle. Kara-tsian-tsiun, anticipating defeat, had his treasury – filling eighty carts, it was said – lowered into the well. He next killed his two wives and his son and daughter, fearing what might happen to them if they fell into Chinese hands. Finally, he ordered a breach to be made in the northern wall, and through this he charged at the head of his troops. His once invincible army was wiped out and he himself killed. The Chinese reduced the city to ruins, having first tried to find the treasury which they knew must be somewhere near. But they failed, as all subsequent attempts had. This, it was said, was because Kara-tsian-tsiun had cast a spell over the spot before charging to his death.

Koslov may not have found the royal treasure, but during the next few days he and his men brought to light enough manuscripts, books, coins and 'objects of the Buddhist cult' to fill ten chests. But they had other tasks to complete further south, for this was not primarily an archaeological expedition, and they had to press on. Determined to return on their way back, they dispatched their discoveries to the Academy of Sciences in St Petersburg. 'The ruins of Karakhoto had an irresistible attraction for us,' wrote Koslov, 'and we spoke of them daily.' The following summer, on their way home, they dug there for a further month, this time discovering a number of beautifully preserved Buddhist paintings on silk, linen or paper in the tomb of a princess. These – some twenty-five in all – can be seen today in a special room in the Hermitage in Leningrad. They also found, stockpiled on the city walls, piles of rocks evidently intended for use against the Chinese besiegers had they come within range.

As Koslov and his now heavily laden camels were leaving Karakhoto for home in the summer of 1909, a second Russian expedition was setting out from St Petersburg for the Silk Road, this time with archaeology as its sole aim. It was led by Academician Sergei Oldenburg, a leading Buddhist art historian and Indologist who some twenty years later was to incur the wrath of Stalin – and survive. Rather like Grünwedel, Oldenburg condemned the wholesale removal of works of art, preferring to leave them *in situ* and record them by means of photographs, drawings and measurements. He spent some six months visiting Karashahr, Kucha, Bezeklik and other northern Silk Road sites before returning to St Petersburg in March 1910. But despite his reluctance to remove works of art he did not return empty-handed, although he was careful to take damaged or deteriorating examples since they could at least then be saved for scholarship. It is probably due to his restraint that the Russians, whatever else the Chinese may feel about them, do not feature high on Peking's archaeological blacklist. Most of what Oldenburg did bring back – mainly wall-paintings, including one that von Le Coq had left behind as too damaged, and sculptures – can be seen today in the Hermitage together with the acquisitions of Klementz and Koslov, and the antiquities purchased by Petrovsky in Kashgar. Apart from a brief visit by Oldenburg to Tunhuang in 1914, this was the sum total of Russian archaeological enterprise in a region which lay within such easy reach of them.

*　　*　　*

In the winter of 1910, shortly after Oldenburg's return to St Petersburg, the Japanese Zuicho Tachibana unexpectedly reappears on the Silk Road. After his brush with Shuttleworth in Kashgar and the official complaints lodged about him and

Nomura by the British Government, he might reasonably have been expected to give the British a wide berth. Not a bit of it. Count Otani's man this time chose as his travelling companion an Englishman. Just who this mysterious individual was – apart from his name – and what he was doing with a suspected Japanese agent, I have failed to discover. The only thing one can be quite certain of is that he was fated to die an unpleasant and lonely death.

By now the Macartneys had returned from long leave in England and relieved Shuttleworth of his temporary duties at Kashgar. On January 13, 1911, Macartney received two telegrams from Kucha, some four hundred miles to the east. One, in Chinese, was from the British *aksakal* there informing him that a British traveller, a Mr A. O. Hobbs, had been struck down by smallpox. The second, a desperate plea for help, was from Hobbs himself who appears to have been unaware that it was smallpox that he was suffering from. In his telegram he grimly spelled out the symptoms. 'I am suffering from skin disease which has affected all organs. I can only keep my eyes open for a few minutes at a time.... My mouth and throat covered with slime and I cannot swallow any food and very little water.... For ten days I have been like this and I have not left my bed.' Neither this telegram nor the *aksakal*'s offered Macartney (who prided himself on knowing everybody's movements in Chinese Turkestan) a clue as to who this man was or what he was doing all by himself in this remote spot. After dispatching his Indian medical assistant to Kucha, Macartney signalled to Hobbs to say that help was on its way. But on January 16 he received a telegram from the Ting-kuan (senior Chinese official) of Kucha informing him that Hobbs had died the previous evening. The Ting-kuan also came up with a startling piece of intelligence. Hobbs, he informed Macartney, was the travelling companion of the Japanese archaeologist Tachibana. The two men, it seemed, had quietly entered Chinese Turkestan via Russia some four months earlier and proceeded via Urumchi to Turfan. They had dug there together for a while before separating, agreeing to meet again at Kucha. Tachibana had then made his way to the remote desert site of Lou-lan where he was excavating when, unknown to him, his English companion was struck down.

Macartney arranged with the Ting-kuan to have the Englishman's body moved to Kashgar for burial, but because of bureaucratic prevarication (or fear, perhaps, of contagion) this took the best part of three months to achieve. The funeral took place immediately afterwards, Macartney reading the burial service. At the graveside was an unexpected mourner – Tachibana. He had raced to Kashgar on hearing at Kucha of the terrible fate which had befallen his companion. In Macartney's reports on the affair, today in the political and secret files in the India Office Library, he tells us little more than just that. If he discovered from Tachibana, as presumably he must have done, precisely who Hobbs was, or why he was travelling with a man who claimed to speak no English, Macartney does not say. His references to Tachibana make no mention of British suspicions about him, merely describing him as 'the Japanese archaeological traveller'.

Reading the secret file of seventy years ago, one finds one-self wondering whether the experienced Macartney, half an oriental himself, was wholly convinced of Tachibana's double role. He nonetheless continued to have the young Japanese shadowed as he proceeded on his treasure-hunt along the southern arm of the Silk Road towards his ultimate goal, Tun-huang. Near Khotan, for example, he learned that Tachibana had struck southwards across the Kun Lun into Tibet where all his baggage animals had perished and his servants had deserted him. When the ambans of Khotan and Keriya advised him to keep to the caravan route, offering him every assistance if he did, Tachibana had threatened to lay formal complaints about their obstructiveness. Once again, it seems, Tachibana was up to his old and unpriestly tricks of being nasty to the natives.

On Christmas Eve 1911, he reached Tun-huang. There he

found another Japanese, Koichiro Yoshikawa, anxiously awaiting him. Yoshikawa had been sent by Count Otani to look for him, for the 1911 Revolution had now broken out, quickly spreading into Chinese Central Asia. Tachibana, who had been away from home for well over a year, had been reported missing – a victim, it was feared, of the revolution. The two men spent nearly eight weeks together at the Caves of the Thousand Buddhas where they obtained from Wang some six hundred religious texts, mostly sutras, from the secret hoard. These the canny custodian had hidden inside his freshly sculptured Buddhas shortly before troops arrived with carts to remove to Peking everything that Stein and Pelliot had left. At this point Tachibana disappears from the story, via Urumchi and the Trans-Siberian Express, taking his secret – if he ever had one – with him.

But before we finally leave the Japanese (the fate of their Silk Road hoard will be examined in a closing chapter), one possible explanation to the whole curious affair must be considered. Count Otani, who sponsored all three expeditions, was spiritual leader of the 'Pure Land' sect. But that is not to say that he was an unworldly cleric who spent his life in prayer and contemplation. It was a role which he had inherited on the death of his father. Before returning home to assume the leadership, he had spent much time travelling in Europe and elsewhere. He was, surprising perhaps for a Japanese in those days, a Fellow of the Royal Geographical Society. A photograph of him in their possession shows him as a relaxed and urbane-looking young man in western dress, sitting back with legs crossed nonchalantly. Even when he had taken up his spiritual responsibilities, he continued to send the Society photographs and brief accounts of the expeditions he dispatched to Central Asia. This suggests that although his primary interest may have been to find archaeological evidence of his sect's origins, he was also extremely interested in contributing to geographical knowledge, and being seen to do so. We know that shortly before the first Otani expedition of 1902, one of his young archaeologist-monks had spent a year studying geography at Oxford, presumably paid for by the Count. Otani certainly went out of his way to cultivate the handful of western explorers possessing first-hand knowledge of Central Asia, acting as host to Sven Hedin, von Le Coq and the Tibetan expert Captain (later Sir Frederick) O'Connor, to name three. The breadth of his interests is shown by the fact that he wrote two political works – one on China and the other on Manchuria – as well as one on Chinese porcelain.

This, of course, may have all been an elaborate cover for a spymaster. Indeed, it may not be too far-fetched to postulate that this sophisticated and politically conscious aristocrat may have run some kind of private intelligence service of his own, perhaps even supplying the Mikado – his brother-in-law – with the information he garnered. On the other hand he may merely have been an earnest Japanese aristocrat who, through contacts in Europe, had caught the geography bug and wished to make his own mark in that field. Certainly the cost of his expeditions brought him close to insolvency, forcing him to sell his villa and disperse his treasures. But until the Japanese choose to open their secret intelligence files, or the Otani family choose to tell us, the Count's true interests in Central Asia must remain a mystery.

*   *   *

For a while the monasteries and sand-engulfed cities of the Silk Road were left in peace, though not for very long. In Srinagar and in Berlin those two veteran rivals, Stein (now Sir Aurel) and von Le Coq, were already preparing for a fresh onslaught on the past. Stein was particularly concerned lest the Germans should reach Miran before him and remove the wall-paintings which he had discovered in 1907, but which Ram Singh's sudden blindness had prevented him from adding to his collection. 'He seems bent on getting those Miran frescoes ...' Stein wrote nervously from Chini-Bagh to a friend. He need not have worried – not about the Germans, anyway. For von Le Coq's expedition was to be dogged from the start by difficulties, including obstruction from the Chinese, a murderous attack on Bartus, financial worries and an illness which nearly cost him his life. It was to be von Le Coq's last visit to Central Asia, and furthermore it was cut short by the outbreak of World War I. The unexpected withdrawal of the German party in 1914 left Stein – at fifty-two too old for military service – in sole command of the Silk Road. All his rivals had now left the scene, although not entirely without trace. However, when he reached Miran he was in for a shock. Scattered everywhere were fragments of painted plaster. In his *On Ancient Central Asian Tracks*, written many years later, Stein points an accusing finger at 'a young Japanese traveller who lacked preparation, technical skill and experience equal to his archaeological zeal'. One only hopes that young Tachibana was more competent at spying (if that is what he was up to) than at archaeology.

But if Miran was a blow, the remainder of the expedition made up for it. At Tun-huang he acquired five more cases of manuscripts from Wang's apparently inexhaustible 'nest egg' – a few months later Oldenburg was to squeeze a further two hundred manuscripts out of him, as well as painted statues. Moving on to Karakhoto, Stein found that Colonel Koslov had not been very thorough, although the trail of smashed statues and frescoes bore witness to the enthusiasm of his excavation. Well pleased with what the Russian had inadvertently left him, he moved westwards across the Gobi to Turfan. His previous visit had been brief, and he had assumed that the Germans had stripped its sites bare. When he left the region two months later he took with him over one hundred large cases filled with frescoes, including many from Bezeklik.

But Stein had not finished yet. One more site – the great cemetery of Astana where the dead of the Turfan region were once buried – had still to yield its secrets to him. Dating from the fifth century, it consists of a series of tomb complexes lying anything up to sixteen feet below the surface. Each was approached via a sloping, rock-hewn trench leading down to a subterranean passage at the end of which lay the burial chamber. Most of them appeared to have been robbed years before of any valuables they might once have contained. Because he was not regarded as a competitor by the local tomb-robbing fraternity, Stein had no difficulty in hiring an old hand in what he calls 'this macabre line of business' to take him on an underground tour of this city of the dead before he began his grim excavation. Even the wood from the coffins had been removed in many instances, presumably taken for use as fuel in this now treeless desert region.

But the objects that meant most to Stein had not been taken. In the first place, inscribed in Chinese on a special funereal brick, was the name and date of birth of each coffin's occupant, as well as biographical data. More important still were the quantities of very early textiles in which the corpses were wrapped. These – mostly silks – displayed a remarkable variety of designs ranging from purely Chinese motifs to others of obvious Middle Eastern origin. What makes these fabrics particularly important to textile historians is the fact that they can be dated with exactness from the inscriptions on the bricks. The unearthing of these ancient and beautiful silks, which were unceremoniously but carefully cut away from the bodies, proved a fitting conclusion to Stein's career as the rediscoverer of the Silk Road. Yet when, in February 1915, he dispatched his forty-five camels laden with frescoes and other treasures on their two-month journey to Kashgar, he little realised that these would be the last he would ever remove from China.

15. Langdon Warner Attempts the Unthinkable

In the autumn of 1923, two Americans floundered westwards along the old Silk Road in blinding rain and through rivers of mud so deep that they often reached to the bellies of their mules. When they arrived at one wayside inn, the men were so encased in the clinging black slime of Central China that they had to be scraped clean with sticks by the servants. And if this were not enough to complete their misery, there was also the very real and ever-present danger of being robbed, or even murdered, by bandits. The two bedraggled travellers, both of them orientalists, were Langdon Warner of the Fogg Art Museum at Harvard and Horace Jayne of the Museum of Pennsylvania. With their modest four *mappas*, or two-wheeled Chinese carts, and their secretary-interpreter Wang, they comprised the first American expedition to Chinese Central Asia.

As far as the ancient town of Sian, where the Silk Road once began its journey to distant Rome, they had been provided by the Chinese with a military escort. From now on, armed only with a shotgun and an automatic pistol, they were on their own. To discourage Chinese troops from commandeering their carts, and, with luck, bandits from troubling them, they had been advised by a friendly Chinese warlord to fly the Stars and Stripes prominently from each vehicle. The flags had been hurriedly run up by four Chinese tailors on the instructions of Warner and Jayne, neither of whom could quite remember just how many stars their national flag should bear. The tailors, however, had settled the issue by ruling that there was only room for six on each flag anyway.

It was now eight years since Stein had left China with his final caravan-load of treasures. Between then and this first post-war expedition, no archaeologist had removed anything from Chinese Central Asia. This was partly because the war had halted all new foreign expeditions (Stein was already there when it broke out), and partly due to the ensuing political crisis in China. Not only was there a rising tide of feeling against all foreigners, which was to reach explosion point by 1925, but this was accompanied by an almost total breakdown of law and order throughout China as local warlords seized power and fought among themselves. Despite this, the Americans were determined to try their luck. The aim of this first (it was hoped) expedition was not, however, the mass removal of works of art, although Warner and Jayne certainly had no intention of returning empty-handed. It was, to quote Warner, a 'scouting trip' – in other words to discover what, if anything at all, was left after the excavators of six nations had taken first pick of the sites and their contents. They also hoped to resolve a number of art-historical conundrums. One of these was to ascertain, with the aid of the laboratories at Harvard, precisely what pigments were used by the master wall-painters of the T'ang dynasty, and from where these had been obtained.

Right up to the time of their departure from Peking there had been serious doubts about the wisdom and safety of the entire undertaking. 'But imagination flouts the counsels of prudence,' Warner wrote afterwards in *The Long Old Road in China*, his account of their journey. 'Holy men from India crossing the Roof of the World . . . Mongol hordes, embassies of emperors, emeralds from India and stuffs from Cathay, horse dealers, beggars – the splendour, squalor, suffering, and accomplishment of travel older than history – stood always before our eyes and would not be denied.' Of the squalor, especially in the filthy wayside inns with their 'hopping and crawling legions', both men were to experience about as much as they could stomach. Great suffering, too, was to test the courage of Jayne before many months were up.

The expedition had really begun in Sian on September 4, 1923, when they bade farewell to their ten-man armed escort. Shortly before, as if to remind them of the scant regard for human life in these parts, three bound prisoners had been summarily executed by Chinese soldiers not a hundred yards from where they stood. Warner recounts with distaste: '... three heads rolled off from three luckless carcasses and the soldiers shuffled on, leaving the carrion to be swept up'. But Sian – the Ch'ang-an of ancient times – has long been associated with death. Stein's 'patron saint' Hsuan-tsang is buried there beside some of China's greatest emperors and statesmen. As Warner and Jayne made their way westwards out of the walled city they noticed on either side of the road a series of ancient tumuli, or graves. 'So holy are they,' Warner wrote, 'that no man can dig near them and no one can guess what treasures they contain.' He added wryly: 'To pass among these mounds, scattered as far as the eye could reach, big and little, near and far, was an experience in self-restraint for the digger.'

Langdon Warner, leader of the two-man expedition, was not, as Pelliot had been, an unproven youngster out to make his name. A large man with red hair, he was – at forty-two – a veteran art historian and archaeologist, who had made a reputation for himself in the study of early Japanese Buddhist art. Graduating from Harvard in 1903 he had then travelled to Russian Central Asia as a member of Raphael Pumpelly's geological and archaeological expedition. There he had visited the old Silk Road cities of Samarkand and Bokhara, and also – as the first American ever to set foot there – the still independent khanate of Khiva. Shortly after his return to New England, at the age of twenty-four he had shown his mettle when he saved the life of a young soldier who had fallen in front of a train, by leaping onto the line, clasping him in his arms, and hurling the two of them clear. He had then vanished into the crowd. This daring act would never have become known had it not, by chance, been witnessed by a Harvard professor. The latter wrote to Warner's father describing what he had seen but without naming the hero. His letter simply ended: 'Possibly Langdon Warner could tell you about it.'

About this time Warner took the first of a series of museum and university posts which he was to combine with regular Asiatic travels and expeditions. At Harvard he started a course in oriental art which for many years was the only one offered by any American university. Warner was thus responsible for launching the careers of a large number of the present generation of American orientalists. Although he did not get there until 1924, he had long had his eye on Chinese Turkestan. In 1908, when he was studying Japanese Buddhist art at Nara on secondment from the Boston Museum of Fine Arts, he had been invited to take an expedition there, but although $10,000 had been set aside for this, for some reason it fell through. Then, in the summer of 1913, he was invited to go to Peking to open an American school of archaeology – to be run on somewhat similar lines to the Ecole in Hanoi – where both Chinese and American archaeologists could be trained. It was the brain-child of Charles L. Freer, a Detroit millionaire and collector of oriental art whose monument is the great collection bearing his name in Washington.

Warner travelled to Peking via Europe, where he visited London, Paris, Berlin and St Petersburg. He met Pelliot, Chavannes and other prominent orientalists, and examined the collections of Central Asian and other oriental art. After seeing von Le Coq's treasures in Berlin's Ethnological Museum (von Le Coq himself was away in Chinese Turkestan at the time), he observed: 'On the whole, without criticising the importance of the collection, the things brought back by Stein to the BM surpass them in beauty.' This is the only comparison between the various collections made by one of the contestants that I have been able to find, apart from von Le Coq's own patriotic assertion that the German collection was by far the best. Freer's dream of an American archaeological school in Peking never materialised owing to the outbreak of the war. However, it gave Warner the opportunity to travel within China and also to Mongolia, although his efforts to reach Sian were frustrated by the reign of terror unleashed by a blood-thirsty local bandit known as the White Wolf. But while in Peking he met Pelliot once again. The French scholar, tem-porarily serving as military attaché, proposed that after the war the two of them should excavate in Central Asia together. Warner, excited at this prospect, wrote home: 'If he could be attached to our expedition it would add the best known scholar in the world.' But that too came to nothing. Now, at last, Warner found himself in Sian, about to lead the first American expedition – sponsored by Harvard's Fogg Art Museum – into Chinese Central Asia. As it turned out, he and Jayne had come only just in time, for the door was already beginning to close.

Their first target was Karakhoto, the great walled 'Black City' on the Sino-Mongolian border where Koslov and Stein had both already dug. This meant following the old Silk Road via Lanchou as far as Suchou where they would turn off the main caravan route and take the lonely Gobi trail to Karak-hoto. Very shortly after leaving Sian they ran into almost in-cessant rain which made the road at times impassable. For two whole days just short of Lanchou they found themselves marooned in a dank, wayside inn. They whiled away the time reading Stein's *Ruins of Desert Cathay* – 'till we could read no more for sheer envy', wrote Warner. When finally they reached Lanchou after fourteen wet and weary hours on the road, Chinese soldiers leaped out of the dark and seized the heads of their mules, announcing that they were being con-fiscated 'for military purposes'. Warner exploded, and grab-bing the nearest corporal by the scruff of the neck he demanded to be taken to the amban, whose troops they were.

At the yamen he was told that the amban was in bed but would see them in the morning. In that case, Warner declared, it was time that the amban got up, lest the foreign devils be forced to come in and help him dress. The unprecedented threat achieved what Warner had hoped. Fifteen minutes later the startled-looking official appeared to find himself confronted by two furious foreigners, dripping mud on his furniture and carpets, and demanding that his thieving soldiery give them back their property. After much arguing he agreed to write a note ordering the soldiers to return the carts. If Warner's behaviour appears a little high-handed, it was because he knew that the whole expedition was at stake – together with the Fogg Museum's investment in it – if he failed to recover their transport.

As the two Americans travelled they occasionally met Europeans who had chosen to work in these outlandish and dangerous parts of China. One of the most remarkable was George Hunter, the legendary explorer-priest of Central Asia who (apart from thirteen months in a Soviet prison cell) for fifty-seven years preached the gospel to the Chinese and their subject peoples. Hunter, who translated the gospels into three Central Asian languages and knew more about the region than any other living man, died only in 1946 and is buried at Urumchi. He told Warner and Jayne, who met him passing through Liangchou, that he too had fallen foul of Chinese soldiery shortly before. But all they could learn of the incident from the Scottish-born priest was that: 'The puir lads are rough and it soon comes to fechtin'. They laid hands on me two-three times an' I'd a time persuading them to lat me free.' He was much more interested in learning of their own plans, for he had known Stein, von Le Coq and Pelliot from Urumchi, where he had lived since 1906. Lower down the social scale was the bearded Frenchman from Lyons, a former railway engineer who had been selling watches on the Tibetan border. He insisted on regaling them with his lurid life story. 'His loves had been many and of various races,' Warner wrote.

'Some of the raciest apparently had been Tibetans, redolent of rancid butter.'

As they continued westwards, the two men became aware of something else. 'For days now,' Warner recounts, 'there had been a strange, half-felt presence on the Great North-West Road, as of other foreigners with us.... Every chamber of every inn and many bare walls in abandoned towns were scrawled with Russian names and regimental numbers and dates not many months old.' More foreigners had trodden the Silk Road in the previous three years, he added, than in the two thousand years before. These were the White Russian refugees, civilians and soldiers, fleeing eastwards from the Bolshevik terror. Many were already living in Peking and Shanghai, while some had gone even further east. Warner wrote: '... Japanese cities saw, for the first time in history, white men and barefoot women begging from Asiatics by the roadside.' Except for the occasional straggler, almost all the refugees had now left the Silk Road. They did, however, come upon one lonely, ragged sixteen-year-old Russian boy to whom they gave what money they could spare. His 'fresh blue eyes' were to haunt Warner for the rest of his life. He often wondered what became of that boy 'in the cynical school to which I left him – a North China winter and the scant mercy of the yellow man'.

Finally Warner and Jayne came to the small town of Suchou, at the extreme end of the Great Wall, where they exchanged their mules for camels before setting out north-eastwards into the Gobi for Karakhoto, the Etzina of Marco Polo. By the time they reached their goal on November 13, some four months after leaving Peking, winter had begun to close in. But despite the harshness of the weather and the how-ling of the wolves at night, Warner was able to write home: 'The place itself is lovely beyond all my imagination of it ...' In his book he describes arriving at the great eastern gateway through which, some six centuries earlier, Marco Polo had passed into the then thriving city: 'No city guard turned out to scan my credentials now, no bowman leaned from a balcony above the big gate in idle curiosity, and no inn welcomed me with tea. . . . It was high afternoon, when no ghosts walk.' Yet, during their ten days among the silent and deserted ruins the uneasy feeling that they were not entirely alone never quite left Warner.

Almost at once they came upon ominous evidence of Karakhoto's two earlier visitors, Koslov and Stein. Their predecessors, the Americans discovered to their disappointment, had dug into all the most obvious ruins ('hacked away at' is the expression used by Warner) and removed everything of interest or value, including all the frescoes. Indeed, while in St Petersburg in 1913, Warner had seen and admired Koslov's superb finds from here. Considering he knew that the site had twice been excavated and large quantities of antiquities removed each time, it is perhaps surprising that he made it his first objective. Possibly he had not fully appreciated how much of the city lay buried beneath centuries of sand which his own small party could not even begin to clear. Although they recovered a number of minor objects, including several fresco fragments, the results were singularly disappointing. As Warner himself admitted: 'The Etzina expedition had proved that no more could be expected from the place unless we came with a large force of diggers and prepared to make a long stay. Koslov and Stein had reaped too well to make it worth gleaning behind them.' But if Karakhoto proved a disappointment to Warner, it was very nearly a disaster for Jayne.

The Americans' next objective was Tun-huang, whose artistic splendours they were so familiar with from the photographs taken by Pelliot's companion Nouette. In view of their disappointment over Karakhoto, this may also seem a puzzling choice, for they were only too aware that Stein, Pelliot, Oldenburg and Tachibana had already been there and removed everything they could lay their hands on. On the other hand Warner was an art historian rather than a philologist and therefore not particularly interested in manuscripts. Anyway, sixteen years after Stein's great coup, who knew what else might not be obtainable at Tun-huang? But there were other reasons, too, for Warner wishing to visit this remote site. As an art historian he wanted to see the great desert art gallery which so few orientalists had set eyes on. Moreover, the laboratories at Harvard were hoping that he would be able to acquire, if not entire frescoes, at least fragments on which to conduct their tests. The purpose of this expedition was to pave the way for more ambitious ventures later. There was no hurry, or so it seemed then.

To reach Tun-huang from Karakhoto meant first returning across the now frozen Gobi to Suchou and from there continuing westwards towards the great monastery complex. When they struck camp the 'Black City' was already under snow, a magical sight but the end to any further digging. The return journey across the desert proved to be infinitely more gruelling than the outward one. Snow blanketed the ground and icy winds cut through them as they plodded along beside the ice-covered Etsin-gol river. Soon the men were suffering from exhaustion and Jayne decided to ride one of the camels. It was a near fatal error. When he dismounted from his kneeling camel at the next halt, he fell flat on his face, unable to stand. Warner wrote: 'I stretched him on the snow with his back to a blaze and took off his fur boots to find both feet frozen stiff.' For the next three hours he and Wang, their interpreter, rubbed Jayne's feet with snow (the classic emergency treatment for frostbite, which had nonetheless failed to save Stein's toes). When the sensation returned, the pain was so severe that Jayne passed out. 'Still we scrubbed feverishly, hardening our hearts,' Warner recounts. Occasionally they gave their patient a drink of raw Chinese spirit which they carried as fuel for the small emergency cooker. Finally they rubbed the frozen skin with grease, in the hope that this would save some at least of the blistered skin. 'We put his soles against the bare skin inside our shirts to give them natural heat,' wrote Warner. 'All this time he had uttered no word of complaint, mustering up a feeble grin when I asked him the banal question of how he felt.'

For the rest of that night Warner lay awake trying to work out how he could get Jayne to safety from this blizzard-swept hell in the middle of nowhere. They had little fuel left, so there was no question of staying put and attempting to nurse Jayne back to health themselves. Nor was he in any fit state to endure the rocking of a camel. They had to get a cart from somewhere. Wang was dispatched to the nearest oasis, some two days away, to try to procure one at all costs. In the meantime, Jayne had developed a high fever and Warner was haunted by the fear of his feet turning gangrenous. After an absence of three days, Wang returned in the middle of the night with a ramshackle cart and its reluctant owner. The next day they set out with Jayne in the cart and the anxious Warner trudging behind, cursing himself for letting the misfortune happen and wondering how one amputated the human foot 'with a hunting knife and no anaesthetics'. Their objective was Kanchou, about ten days distant across the desert, where they knew there was a Chinese missionary doctor.

It was a nightmarish journey made even worse by the unexpectedly hostile attitude of the local population who, in one village, greeted the foreigners with jeers and catcalls, and in others tried to extort money from them or even rob them. It was their first encounter with such behaviour, and was not to be their last. Finally, on the eighteenth day, they reached the walled town of Kanchou. To their relief, the Chinese doctor was there – 'full of Christianity and antiseptics', wrote the grateful Warner. After cleaning Jayne's blistered and swollen limbs he pronounced that they had already begun to heal and that gangrene was no longer a serious risk. After a further sixteen days spent convalescing Jayne felt sufficiently better to leave for Tun-huang. However, by the time they reached Suchou it was clear that he had not the strength to go any further. 'Jayne, for all his determination, could not

even now walk more than a hundred yards,' Warner wrote.
He already had a heavy cold and in his weakened state would
be vulnerable to any infection lurking in the filthy inns along
the road. Moreover, the worst of the Chinese Central Asian
winter was still to come. Deeply disappointed, Jayne agreed
to make his way slowly back to Peking with the meagre
material they had excavated at Karakhoto. After bidding a sad
farewell to Jayne, Warner and the long-suffering Wang,
accompanied by four Turkestani ponies and one large cart,
continued westwards along the snow-covered trail towards
Tun-huang. At the small oasis town of Anhsi they left the
modern caravan route and took the once-busy but now little
used trail to where, some seventy miles across the desert, lay
Tun-huang and the Caves of the Thousand Buddhas.

Wang, the little priest, was absent (as ever), but this did
not deter Warner. He made straight for the painted caves, and
during the next ten days rarely left them except to eat or to
sleep. In *The Long Old Road in China* he recounts: '... there
was nothing to do but to gasp ... for the first time I understood
why I had crossed an ocean and two continents, plodding
beside my cart these weary months.' Warner, the most visu-
ally educated of the archaeologists to visit Tun-huang, found
himself stupefied by the tens of thousands of painted figures
in the caves. He confessed: 'I, who had come to attribute dates
and glibly to refute the professors and to discover artistic influences, stood in the centre of a chapel with my hands dug
deep in my pockets and tried to think.'

But soon, as he visited cave after cave, another emotion
seized him – blind fury. Two years earlier, four hundred
White Russian soldiers who had escaped across the frontier
into China had been interned for six months at Tun-huang
by the authorities. Evidence of their frustration and boredom
was to be seen everywhere. Warner wrote angrily to his wife:
'... across some of these lovely faces are scribbled the
numbers of a Russian regiment, and from the mouth of a
Buddha where he sits to deliver the Lotus Law flows some Slav

obscenity.' The Russians had done so much damage that the photographs taken by Stein and Nouette were now the sole record of many of the wall-paintings. 'My job', he told his wife, 'is to break my neck to rescue and preserve anything and everything I can from this quick ruin. It has been stable enough for centuries, but the end is in sight now.'

Fortuitously, he had arrived armed with a special chemical solution for detaching wall-paintings, which had been successfully pioneered in Italy. His original intention had been merely to test the solvent and at the same time remove a few small fragments for laboratory analysis. Even this was something none of his predecessors had dared attempt – inhibited, if not by ethical considerations, then by the policing of the caves by Wang. However, having seen the destruction wrought by the Cossack soldiers, Warner's scruples vanished. He wrote: 'As for the morals of such vandalism I would strip the place bare without a flicker. Who knows when Chinese troops may be quartered here as the Russians were? And, worse still, how long before the Mohameddan rebellion that everyone expects? In 20 years this place won't be worth a visit. . . .' He pointed out that every new pilgrim scratched his name on the paintings or removed a bit of 'trembling plaster'.

But even if Warner had now overcome his own moral scruples, he still had the Abbot Wang to contend with. In the event the priest was surprisingly unperturbed at the prospect of surrendering some of his frescoes – once a 'handsome present' had paved the way. He proved more obdurate though when Warner raised the question of the sculptures. However, when it dawned on him that the 'mad foreigner' had no designs on his own new and brightly painted statues, he agreed to part with one old one – a three-foot T'ang figure of a kneeling saint, today one of the most prized items in the Fogg Museum collection.

Warner now prepared to attempt what he had previously regarded as unthinkable – the removal of some of Tun-huang's priceless frescoes. Although the priest had raised no objection to this (perhaps because he failed to realise their value as nobody had ever expressed an interest in removing any before), resistance arose from a totally unexpected source – the elements. It was now mid-winter at Tun-huang and temperatures had dropped to well below zero. Whenever, brush in hand, Warner ascended his ladder to apply his fixative to a painting, he found to his dismay that the liquid froze solid before it had time to penetrate and consolidate the fragile plaster. Similarly, the glue-soaked strips of gauze (with which Warner intended to 'peel off' the frescoes rather like transfers) set hard before they could adhere properly to the paint surface. Nonetheless, after five days Warner managed to remove twelve modest-sized paintings. He was careful to leave *in situ* the earliest and finest frescoes and take only parts of those masterpieces which were already damaged. Even these, Warner claimed, '... would prove treasures the like of which we had never seen in America, and which Berlin, with its wealth of frescoes sawn in squares from the stucco walls of Turkestan, might envy'. All the same, those five days were uncomfortable ones for Warner, fully aware of the enormity of what he was doing, and haunted by the fear of causing further destruction if his techniques failed.

Finally the job was done. Still attached to its glue-soaked cloth, each of the precious, eighth-century frescoes was wrapped tenderly in felt and sandwiched between boards to cushion it against the shocks of the two-month journey to Peking by springless *mappa*. In his letters home Warner asked that no mention be made of the paintings to his sponsors, for he was far from confident that the laboratory would be able to disentangle the gluey cloths from their delicate paint surfaces. (In the event, they rescued eleven of the twelve pictures.) Meanwhile, the equally frail clay sculpture, dating from T'ang times, also had to be protected during its long, slow, bumpy ride eastwards through the badlands of Central China. There was only one answer. 'The little saint itself was wound with the oddest collection of garments that ever a

Buddhist figure wore,' Warner wrote. It was first wrapped in Warner's underclothes and socks and finally in his sheepskin trousers and blankets. Warner adds: 'If I lacked for underwear and socks on the return journey, my heart was kept warm by the thought of the service which my things were performing when they kept that fresh smooth skin and those crumbling pigments from harm.'

Warner reached Peking safely with his treasures some nine months after he had set out with Jayne the previous autumn. Despite the difficulties, and the disappointment of Karakhoto, his expedition had turned out to be a success. He had acquired works of art which no other museum possessed and which would put Harvard's small Fogg collection permanently on the map of oriental scholarship. He was determined to return to Tun-huang as soon as possible with a larger team and for a longer stay. 'On those walls', he declared, 'we should find the very genesis of the Chinese manner of painting, the beginnings of the landscape school in which she has perhaps surpassed us all....' Six months' close study of the originals would answer many of the questions posed by the master painters of Tun-huang. With luck, moreover, the expedition might add to the Fogg's small, if choice, collection of Central Asian treasures. However, as things turned out, the second Fogg expedition was to prove a fiasco.

16. The Chinese Slam the Door

Although the Americans were slow to realise it, the archaeological free-for-all in Central Asia was almost over. During the thirty years since Sven Hedin's first daring journey into the Taklamakan desert, access to the lost cities and ruined monasteries of the Silk Road had been virtually unrestricted. Masterpieces of Buddhist art had been acquired for next to nothing. To men like Stein and von Le Coq it had been one long field day. But now time was fast running out for foreign archaeologists. From the intense xenophobia he had encountered when trying to get his sick colleague to safety in the winter of 1924, Langdon Warner should perhaps have sensed that the door was beginning to close, and thought twice before deciding to return.

But on May 30, 1925, something happened which no one could have foreseen. A British police officer in the treaty port of Shanghai, faced by rioting Chinese students who refused to disperse, ordered his men to open fire. Eleven students died – most of them, it was said, shot in the back. A wave of anger against foreigners swept across China. Warner, who had recently arrived in Peking at the head of a larger expedition, reported: 'News of the Shanghai shooting on that day travelled like wild-fire through the interior.' Missionaries and other foreigners in remote stations had to be evacuated to the coastal cities. When Warner's party reached Tun-huang, where they had planned to work for eight months, they were met by a menacing mob of peasant farmers – the same people who had welcomed Warner the previous year.

The man from the Fogg had clearly been hoping this time to relieve Tun-huang of more of its frescoes, as well as to conduct art-historical studies in the painted caves. Apart from

bringing with him what Jeannette Mirsky refers to a little un-
kindly as 'barrels of glue', he had included in his seven-man
expedition Daniel Thompson, the young fresco expert who
had supplied him with the recipe for his fixative the previous
year. To avoid any risk of Thompson's concoction freezing
again, Warner had timed this visit for the spring.

Although in Peking no objections had been raised to the
expedition, the Americans now suddenly found themselves
harassed at every step by the local authorities, as well as by
a hostile populace. Forced to abandon any hope of working
at the Caves of the Thousand Buddhas, let alone removing
anything, they had no choice but to retreat to another site of
far less importance. But even here they met with a hostile
reception. 'The situation', Warner wrote, 'was one of extreme
delicacy on account of the presence of a dozen villagers who
had left their ordinary employments, some fifteen miles off,
to watch our movements and to try by a thousand expedients
to tempt us into a breach which would warrant an attack or
forcible expulsion from the region.' It took great self-restraint
on the part of the Americans to avoid violence, such was the
intensity of feeling directed against them. 'A single slip, even
an angry look,' Warner adds, 'would probably have brought
the whole hive about our ears and might well have cost us
our lives.' Friends in Peking had by now begun to send telegrams imploring them to abandon the expedition. Hostile and
inflammatory rumours, moreover, were being circulated
about their intentions. A whole year later the Russian-born
artist Nicholas Roerich, passing through Urumchi, noted in
his diary: 'Strange information reached us about the pillage
of the frescoes at Tun-huang.' The rumour claimed that some
American art dealers had visited the caves and carried away
'many cases' of frescoes.

But long before this wild version of events reached Roerich
in Urumchi, Warner had been forced to call off the second
Fogg Museum expedition, and to concede that it had been
little more than a fiasco. All that he had to show for it were

photographs of other cave temples, of minor importance compared to those at Tun-huang. Warner's anger was directed less towards the hostile local peasantry than against Dr Ch'en, a medical man and scholar who had travelled with the expedition from Peking ostensibly to aid them in deciphering inscriptions at Tun-huang and to handle any problems which might arise on the journey. Two days after their arrival he had suddenly insisted on returning at all speed to Peking where, he said, his mother was ill. Ch'en later published a slanderous book about the expedition in which he claimed that he had accompanied the Americans for the sole purpose of keeping an eye on them and preventing them from pillaging. Warner had good reason to suspect that it was Ch'en who had incited the local villagers to anger against them, then left for home knowing that his work was completed.

But despite this major set-back, the Fogg Museum had not yet abandoned hope of adding to its collection of Chinese Central Asian treasures. The trustees were perhaps encouraged by the unexpected success, some two years after Langdon Warner's return, of a German geological expedition in removing some objects (today in Bremen) from the remote and unguarded sites of Rawak and Dandan-uilik. They had only managed to get away with this because, it seems, anti-foreign feeling had still not penetrated as far west as this farthest-flung corner of the Republic. It did, however, while the Germans were still there, and they had to leave hurriedly, although the Fogg trustees may have been unaware of this.

Clearly there was little point in sending their own man Warner back to China, for he was now to all intents and purposes *persona non grata*. But then someone had a bright idea. Why not approach Sir Aurel Stein, the Grand Old Man of Central Asian archaeology, now aged sixty-seven and retired, and see whether he could be persuaded to go on behalf of the Fogg? If *he*, with all his friends and contacts in Chinese Turkestan, could not pull it off then no one could. Stein agreed to try. Some £20,000 was raised (despite the Wall Street crash) and in April 1930 the Englishman arrived in Nanking, the Republican capital, to try to talk the authorities into allowing him to take one final expedition into Chinese Central Asia. Despite fierce resistance from the self-appointed 'National Council for the Preservation of Chinese Antiquities' in Peking – a pressure group determined to keep all archaeological exploration out of foreign hands – Stein managed to extract from the Nanking authorities permission to visit and excavate in Turkestan. Considering the indignation that his and Pelliot's removal of the Tun-huang manuscripts had engendered among Chinese scholars, this was perhaps surprising. However, encouraged by his apparently easy victory, Stein hurried back to India, from where he set out for Kashgar in the summer of 1930.

But meanwhile, unknown to him, a vigorous campaign had been launched in China among the intelligentsia to try to put a stop to his expedition by getting his visa cancelled. The Chinese press, too, was demanding his expulsion and scurrilous stories about him were being circulated. Although Stein was a far tougher nut to crack than Warner, with long-standing and well-placed friends in the local Chinese administration, his adversaries eventually won the day. But not before he had travelled some two thousand miles around the Taklamakan oases, mapping and gathering for his sponsors what meagre archaeological material he could, in the face of continual obstruction. But the price of his entry to Turkestan had been a last-minute condition that everything he found must be submitted to the authorities for inspection before agreement could be given to its removal from China. Thus his few acquisitions, which included third-century manuscripts from his favourite site of Niya, had to be left behind in Kashgar when after seven months he was finally forced to abandon his expedition and return to India. It was the last that Stein would ever see of them – or, for that matter, of Chinese Central Asia. The Chinese had closed the door on him at last. His swan song had ended in failure. However, he could hardly complain when he looked back at his years of unbroken success during which he had made his name and more than satisfied all his sponsors save for the Fogg.

In retrospect, before hiring Stein the Fogg trustees should perhaps have heeded not only Warner's experience but also that of another distinguished explorer, Sven Hedin. In the winter of 1926 the Swedish traveller had returned to China at the invitation of the Government and at the expense of Lufthansa, the German airline. While his principal task was to reconnoitre a route for a new Berlin–Urumchi–Peking air link, he took with him, in addition to aviation experts, a small scientific team equipped for meteorological, geological and other work, including archaeology and palaeontology. On reaching Peking, Hedin and his men were astonished to find themselves the target of extreme hostility from Chinese scholars and press. The Chinese, they were told, did not need any help from foreigners to explore their own country. Hedin's plans to use aircraft had to be abandoned entirely after reports began to appear in local newspapers claiming that these would be used to airlift secretly out of China large quantities of art treasures. In all, it took Hedin nearly six months to renegotiate terms before the expedition could proceed. Less determined men would have packed up and gone home. In the end the Chinese had insisted that he take with him ten of their scholars in addition to his own, that the expedition be renamed the Sino-Swedish Expedition, and finally that any archaeological material he found would remain the property of the Chinese Government. By now the political turmoil in China had become so dangerous that each member of the expedition had to take with him a rifle, a revolver and eight hundred rounds of ammunition (they were to need them). Even so, Hedin's long-drawn-out expedition was to suffer a total of eight deaths from various causes. Despite their many difficulties, though, his archaeologists did make a number of finds – mainly manuscripts and textiles. But these, of course, they were not allowed to keep. The day of the free-booter was over. From now on, if one dug at all one dug for China. There were few, if any, takers.

★   ★   ★

One of the strangest episodes in Central Asian history was now at an end, but the story is not quite finished. Two questions have still to be answered. Where, today, are the vast quantities of wall-paintings, sculptures, manuscripts and other antiquities which Stein, Pelliot, von Le Coq, Tachibana, Warner and others removed *en masse* from the ancient cities of the Silk Road so many years ago? And what befell that handful of archaeological heroes (or villains, depending on your viewpoint) who devoted so much enterprise and effort and, not infrequently, sheer courage to removing it all?

The treasures and manuscripts of Serindia – to borrow Stein's term – are today divided among the museums and institutions of a dozen countries. Within those countries the material is further spread through a total of more than thirty institutions. The collections range from the very large ones – like those in London, Berlin and Delhi – to those, like the Cernuschi Museum in Paris and the Nelson Gallery in Kansas, with only the odd painting or sculpture to show. And yet, despite this incredible wealth of material from the Silk Road in the West and elsewhere, how many people have ever heard of Serindian art, of Tun-huang or even of Sir Aurel Stein? How many of us have ever seen the great Buddhist murals from Miran or Kyzil, the delicate polychrome silks from which the world's oldest trade route takes its name, or the magnificent T'ang sculptures, banners and scrolls from its temples, monasteries and shrines?

The answer, sadly, is extraordinarily few. The reason is that, with one notable exception, the few museums which possess important Silk Road collections lie beyond reach of most people. For they include the National Museum in Delhi, the Museum of Indian Art in West Berlin, the Tokyo National

Museum and the Hermitage in Leningrad. And yet the one institution within reach of almost everybody at some time or other – the British Museum – with its huge Serindian collection, has the most meagre display of all. The great bulk of Britain's share of Stein's discoveries lies, unseen by the public, in boxes in storerooms, and not a single fragment of figured silk from the Silk Road can be seen in the small Central Asian section.

All this is not so much a scandal as a sad fact of museum life. For the bigger the museum and the more comprehensive its contents, the smaller the space it can devote to any particular collection or culture. Had Stein been working for the small but ambitious young Fogg Museum, one can imagine the spectacular display his treasures would enjoy today. As it is, one cannot help feeling that he merely dug them up in China only to see them buried again in Bloomsbury. There is a strong case, it could be argued, for a museum returning to the country of origin all antiquities – like these – which it has no prospect of putting on display. For a national museum (as against an international one) can always devote more space to collections of its own culture, and often more resources to their conservation.

The Germans, on the other hand, can hardly be accused of concealing von Le Coq's treasures. Indeed, he himself was able to dictate the arrangement of his finds in the old Ethnological Museum when he became its director. Eventually he added a total of thirteen extra rooms to house what has become known as the Turfan Collection. The biggest wall-paintings, some of which stood over ten feet high, were, alas, cemented to the walls in iron frames. At that time nobody could have foreseen that this would be the direct cause of their destruction some fifteen years later during World War II. When hostilities broke out, all the movable objects, including the smaller murals and sculptures, were packed away in crates. Some were deposited for safety in the huge bunker in the Berlin zoo, others at the bottom of coal mines in western Germany, while others still were stored in the museum's basement which had been specially reinforced for the purpose.

The very largest of the wall-paintings could not, however, be moved to safety. Not only were they cemented firmly into place, but removing them would have meant first cutting them into pieces once again. Instead, the museum staff placed iron covers and sandbags over them to shield them from the effects of blast. 'Apart from that,' a senior West Berlin museum official told me, 'there was nothing they could do but pray that no harm would befall them.' Their prayers were not heeded, however. The museum, which lay close to today's Berlin Wall, was hit no fewer than seven times by Allied bombs between November 23, 1943, and January 15, 1945. Twenty-eight of the largest wall-paintings – almost all of them from Bezeklik – were totally destroyed after surviving wars, earthquakes and iconoclasts for well over a millennium. All that remains of them today are the plates in von Le Coq's great portfolio of the paintings from his first expedition – and the gaping holes in the walls of the rock-hewn monastery overlooking the Sangim gorge.

The horrifying loss of these huge Buddhist masterpieces from Bezeklik has led to the widely held belief that *all* von Le Coq's treasures were destroyed during the Allied bombing of Berlin. The Chinese themselves appear to believe it, and cite the loss bitterly to refute any suggestion that men like von Le Coq and Stein were really *rescuing* the antiquities they removed from the Silk Road. Just how much then of the Berlin collection was lost? The German art historian Dr Herbert Härtel, today director of West Berlin's splendid new Museum of Indian Art where the surviving part of the collection is housed, estimates that about sixty per cent escaped destruction. Anyone who doubts this figure should visit West Berlin, drive out to the leafy suburb of Dahlem where Härtel's museum stands, and see for himself just how much survived. Of all the collections I have seen of Chinese Central Asian art – and that includes almost all of them – the one in West

Berlin is by far the largest and most imaginatively displayed. Even the secondary pieces are well displayed in the basement, where they can be seen by arrangement.

Dr Härtel, a distinguished Indologist and former Luftwaffe pilot, estimates the wartime losses as follows. Of the six hundred and twenty complete frescoes or fragments brought back by von Le Coq and Grünwedel, some three hundred have survived in varying states (much of the damage has since been put right). Of the two hundred and ninety clay sculptures in the pre-war collection, some one hundred and seventy-five have survived. Of the remaining objects such as terracotta figures, bronzes, wooden sculptures, coins, and paintings on silk, paper and wood, Härtel estimates that some eighty per cent have survived. Very few of the manuscripts brought back by von Le Coq and Grünwedel were kept in the old Ethnological Museum, the great bulk having been deposited in the Prussian Academy for study. These were removed to safety during the war and are today in East Berlin.

However, not all the losses to the collection during World War II were due to American bombing (Dr Härtel, incidentally, spares the RAF from blame). When the bunker at the zoo, where some of the treasures were stored, fell into the hands of the Russians in 1945, its secrets were quickly discovered. It is now known that at least eight or nine packing cases of clay sculptures – only the Russians know the exact number – were removed and driven away on lorries. They also looted many important Indian sculptures, again from the Ethnological Museum, which had been deposited there for safety. Like the gold from Troy, neither the sculptures from Turkestan nor those from India have been seen or heard of since, despite West German requests that they be returned. Yet the great bulk of other art treasures looted by the Russians – particularly the European paintings – were sent back long ago. Who knows, perhaps the Russians are holding them in exchange for something they might one day want from Germany or – more appropriately – from China.

The third largest collection of antiquities to be removed from Chinese Central Asia was that amassed by the three Otani expeditions. Whatever else the Japanese may or may not have been up to, they certainly dug feverishly – usually with more energy than knowledge. Even Japanese scholars have had difficulty in piecing together what happened to the collection after its arrival at Count Otani's villa in Kyoto. Indeed, the whereabouts of part of it is still something of a mystery today (although some items, as we shall see, could well be in Soviet hands). The man who knows more about the fate of the Otani treasures than anyone is Dr Jiro Sugiyama, Curator of Oriental Art at the Tokyo National Museum. It was he who first hinted to me that Otani's men might have been carrying out other tasks besides archaeology – a suggestion which caused me to search the political and secret files in the India Office Library and thus come upon Captain Shuttleworth's curious reports.

No one knows for sure, Dr Sugiyama points out, just how large the original collection was. Otani's men – none of them trained archaeologists – kept no proper records of their discoveries and the collection was never catalogued in its entirety. Although Count Otani himself published a two-volume work on it (a sort of Japanese coffee-table book containing pictures of many of the items) there was no accompanying text, and it is therefore of little value to modern scholars. Possibly as a result of the excitement caused in Japan by Stein's discoveries at Tun-huang, part of the Otani collection – mostly frescoes and sculptures – was exhibited in the Kyoto Museum as early as 1910, although by then only two of the Count's three expeditions had been to Central Asia. As no copies of the exhibition catalogue have survived, scholars have had to rely upon the memories of those who saw or heard about it at the time to work out what was shown.

Before very long the collection began to be broken up (already Tachibana had kept back some of the finds for himself). The main reason for this was the sale by Count Otani of his villa, where the bulk of the treasures were stored, owing to sudden financial pressures. Although he personally kept some hundred pieces and gave a further two hundred and forty-nine to the Kyoto Museum, the larger part of the collection became the property of the villa's new owner, a former Japanese finance minister and a wealthy man. In exchange, it is said, for mining rights there, he in his turn gave it to the then Japanese Governor-General of Korea for the new museum in Seoul. Presumably because he had nowhere to store or display it himself, Count Otani next presented much – but not all – of what was still in his possession to the Governor-General of Lushun (Port Arthur) in Manchuria for exhibition in the museum there. As a result of these two transactions, more of the original collection was now outside Japan than remained at home. Dr Sugiyama estimates that roughly one-third went to Korea, another third to Manchuria and the rest stayed in Japan, although even the latter portion was gradually dispersed, some finding its way into private collections.

What has happened to it all now? The Seoul treasures today lie in packing cases in the storeroom of the National Museum after surviving the Korean War, during which the museum twice changed hands. They consist of some four to five hundred objects, the most important of which are sixty or so frescoes or fresco fragments. Dr Kim Che-won, who was director of the museum from 1945 to 1970, believes that the Seoul murals are the third most important collection in the world after the Berlin and Delhi (Stein) ones. There are long-term plans to build new galleries in the museum. Eventually, it is hoped, the Otani material will be displayed there. But the Koreans, less confident than von Le Coq of man's peaceable nature, have decided that the wall-paintings must remain movable and not, as in the old Berlin museum, be fixed irrevocably to the walls.

Little is known (among western scholars, anyway) of the fate of the Port Arthur treasures, or even what they consisted of. Dr Sugiyama told me that he believes they may all have been removed by the Russians when in May 1955 they finally handed Manchuria back to the Chinese. His enquiries in Moscow and Leningrad, however, have met with silence. But not all the painstaking digging done by Otani's mysterious young monks was completely wasted. If one goes to the Tokyo National Museum and visits the fine new air-conditioned Toyokan, or Gallery of Eastern Antiquities, one can see, beautifully displayed there, the remaining third of the Otani collection. It comprises those objects which stayed in the Count's personal possession as well as those deposited by him at the old Kyoto Museum. These were purchased over several years by the Japanese Government on behalf of the Tokyo National Museum after being tracked down to those private collections and institutions which in the meantime had acquired them. Finally, in 1968, they were all reunited in a special exhibition to celebrate the opening of the museum's new oriental gallery. Since then they have been augmented by a number of silk banners and clay figures brought back from Tun-huang by Pelliot and obtained from the Musée Guimet by exchange. Thus, some twenty years after Count Otani's death, he and his energetic young acolytes acquired (somewhat undeservedly, in view of their combined incompetence) a fine memorial to their archaeological zeal.

In the Hermitage, where Russia's Silk Road treasures are displayed in eight rooms, the work of Koslov, Oldenburg and the two Beresovsky brothers is similarly commemorated. In the Guimet, where a gallery is named permanently after him, Paul Pelliot too has his memorial. At the Fogg Art Gallery in Cambridge, Massachusetts, Langdon Warner's enterprise is handsomely acknowledged and his Tun-huang frescoes proudly displayed. In Stockholm, Hedin's treasures are to be given a permanent home in the city's fine new Ethnographical Museum. Only in Britain is there a complete failure to recognise the remarkable achievements of her man, Sir Marc Aurel Stein. Even the Indians have taken the trouble to hang a portrait of him in the dingy galleries in Delhi where his great Central Asian murals are to be found, while in the Indian National Museum nearby, where his smaller finds are displayed, he is generously acknowledged. Perhaps Britain – his adopted country – will one day do justice, not only to him, but also to the many unnamed Buddhist artists and sculptors whose work he rediscovered.

But it was not only paintings, sculptures and other works of art that he and the others carried off from the temples and monasteries of Turkestan and Kansu. What has happened then to the vast archive of Central Asian manuscripts and ancient block-printed books which were also removed before the Chinese finally put a stop to it? The man responsible for removing the largest quantity of these was Stein. Today the manuscripts and books from his three expeditions are divided between the British Library and that of the India Office in London. The Chinese, Sogdian, Uighur and Tangut works are in the former, while those in Tibetan, Sanskrit and Khotanese – to name just some – are in the latter. Understandably, apart from the British Library's celebrated Diamond Sutra, these are not on view to the public, for to the layman one oriental manuscript looks much like another. Moreover prolonged exposure to ultra-violet light and to the pollution of Bloomsbury (or Blackfriars) would only hasten their deterioration.

The highly prized (and still contentious) Chinese-language manuscripts and books from Tun-huang, after being stored in cardboard boxes in the British Museum for many years, have now been transferred to the British Library. There, some thirteen thousand of them live in a row of specially built cabinets amid a benign atmosphere of filtered air and in a carefully controlled temperature. Some seven thousand of them – all those that are complete – have been catalogued. The remainder, most of them little more than scraps, have still, in many cases, to be identified. Although no further work is being done on them at present by the British Library, many

Japanese scholars come to London to pore over these ancient texts, including one man who has devoted a lifetime just to the study of the Lotus Sutra. In order to protect the manuscripts from further deterioration, the British Library has embarked on a programme of conservation. In the past, the condition of many of them has been a sore point with the Chinese who undoubtedly regard the Tun-huang manuscripts – particularly those in Chinese – as their rightful property. However, relations have improved to the point where advice has been sought and obtained from Peking on what methods and materials should be used for conserving Chinese manuscripts. Experiments with ovens specially designed to accelerate ageing by as much as one hundred years in twenty-four hours have shown that man-made fibres are short-lived and generally inferior to the natural materials used by the ancient Chinese.

So much then for what one major institution is doing with its collection, or rather with just part of it. Today the thousands of manuscripts brought back from Chinese Central Asia, written in a multitude of tongues and scripts, are divided among the institutions of at least eight different countries. Very many have still to be translated. The deciphering of one script, or the translation of one collection, can take a man's entire working life. One Indologist explained to me: 'Perhaps only twice in a century does a man emerge capable of such a task. Until then the manuscripts have to wait.' Such a man is Sir Harold Bailey, the British scholar, who has spent a lifetime unravelling the mysteries of ancient Khotanese. Anyone who wishes to understand the contribution these manuscripts have made to the study of Central Asian and Buddhist history can turn to the host of translations, catalogues, monographs and other specialist studies produced by scholars such as Bailey, Giles, Waley, Maspero, Levi, Konow, Müller, Henning, Hoernle, Pelliot and Chavannes, to name just a few.

Before leaving the subject of the manuscripts, there was one particular collection that scholars (Hoernle in particular) were only too anxious to forget. These 'old books' had to be withdrawn hastily from the British Museum when Islam Akhun, the semi-literate treasure-seeker from Khotan, confessed to forging them. After being rediscovered in the British Museum basement in 1979 in two wooden chests labelled 'Central Asian Forgeries,' all ninety of them have now been catalogued and transferred to the British Library. Examining these long-forgotten relics today, one is astonished by their sophisticated appearance and the neatness and persuasiveness of their 'unknown scripts'. To the layman – and presumably to most scholars – they look all too convincing, with their well-thumbed appearance, ancient-looking paper, and faded but erudite-looking texts. It is surely not an exaggeration to describe this wily forger who so completely fooled the giants of his chosen field as something of a genius. He too has his modest memorial – that small corner of the British Library's oriental department, near the Tun-huang manuscripts, where his once-venerated 'old books' are preserved for posterity.

*   *   *

We have now considered the fate of the main collections carried off from Chinese Central Asia – those 'caravan-loads of priceless treasures ... for ever lost to China', to quote the words of Sir Eric Teichman. But the principal characters in this story have still to make their exits. Sir Aurel Stein, perhaps the dominant figure, today lies in the mud-walled Christian cemetery at Kabul, in the shadow of the Hindu Kush, surrounded by the graves of hippies for whom also Afghanistan was the end of the trail. This doyen of Central Asian archaeologists died in Kabul in 1943 at the age of eighty-two. It is a fitting resting place for him. For forty years he had repeatedly sought permission from the Afghans to explore their country – the missing link in his Silk Road travels. Finally, as he sat working in his tent on his beloved Kashmir 'marg', that permission arrived. But within a week of his arrival in Kabul he was dead – struck down by a chill which turned suddenly to pneumonia. 'Seldom', wrote Sir Denison Ross, the orientalist, 'has there been combined in one man such qualifications for exploration.' He added: 'This great Hungarian is the pride of two nations and the wonder of all.' Although a British citizen, Stein never entirely forgot the country of his birth. His frugal lifestyle had enabled him to save some £57,000, and most of this he left to set up a fund to further Central Asiatic studies. His one stipulation was that, wherever possible, the work should be carried out by British or Hungarian scholars.

Stein's greatest rival (in terms of quantity, anyway) was von Le Coq, who had predeceased him by thirteen years. The German died in April 1930, just as Stein was arriving in Nanking to negotiate his ill-fated fourth, and last, expedition. During World War I, von Le Coq had been deeply affected by the death of his only son, killed on a battlefield in France. In addition he had to endure the sadness of suddenly discovering himself, a lifelong Anglophile, on the 'other side' from pre-war friends like Macartney and Stein. On top of that, as a result of the economic collapse of Germany, he had found himself financially ruined. His solace became the arrangement of his beloved treasures in the Ethnological Museum, and even after being struck down by a painful and incurable illness he would cheerfully struggle from his bed to show off the collection to a special visitor or friend. When he knew that death was very close, he managed, unknown to his wife, to obtain some black-edged stationery and address envelopes to his many friends. In an obituary of his German colleague, Pelliot refers to the moment when he opened one of these only to discover that it contained the news of von Le Coq's own death.

Grünwedel died some five years later, a sad and broken man. His distinguished career had begun to crumble when he became involved in quarrels with colleagues, including one with his subordinate Müller over which of them had been the first to recognise some of the Turfan manuscripts as Manichaean. Other German scholars took Müller's side and consequently Grünwedel suffered a loss of reputation. He became increasingly isolated from his colleagues and soon his professional judgement began to be questioned. In the words of one obituarist, he sought refuge in obscure theories 'where the experts were not able to follow him'. It was a kind way of saying that he was approaching insanity. A less kindly reviewer described one of his later works on Buddhist Central Asian iconography as 'a religious historical novel of wild fantasy'. Grünwedel ended his days in a mental hospital, a deeply embittered, lonely and disappointed man. However, as his obituarist wrote: 'the confusion of his last few works should not be allowed to detract from his brilliant and reliable earlier works . . .' But at least he and von Le Coq – and even Engineer Bartus, who lived on until 1941 – were spared the anguish of seeing the destruction of their museum.

Paul Pelliot died of cancer in 1945, just two years after Stein, acknowledged not merely as France's foremost Chinese scholar but by all western sinologists as their master. 'Without him,' a French colleague wrote, 'sinology is left like an orphan.' That same year witnessed another death. Sir George Macartney, who was trapped by the war at his retirement home in German-occupied Jersey, died that May at the age of seventy-eight, just a few days after the German surrender.

Wang, the wily old Abbot of Tun-huang, had died long before, in 1931, and is buried close to his beloved caves. He ended his days an embittered man, aggrieved because he had been robbed of the money promised (and indeed sent to him) by the Government in compensation for the remaining Tun-huang manuscripts which belatedly it had had removed to Peking. Like so many of those manuscripts on their long journey eastwards, the money, in its turn, had been siphoned off *en route*, leaving nothing for Wang's restoration work. Perhaps Wang got the last laugh – if only from beyond the grave. During the 1940s, yet another cache of manuscripts which he had cunningly concealed from the authorities (with an eye no doubt for a rainy day) was discovered in the caves by Chinese archaeologists. When Irene Vincent, an American art historian, visited Tun-huang in 1948 she heard rumours of manuscripts and paintings still 'cached away' in houses in the area, while as recently as 1977 a Swedish oriental bookseller was able to offer several Tun-huang manuscripts in his catalogue.

Today Wang's self-appointed guardianship of the Caves of the Thousand Buddhas has been taken over by the Chinese authorities, who have reinforced the crumbling cliff-face, treated the peeling frescoes, and discovered even earlier ones beneath many of them. Honour, it could be argued, has finally been satisfied. The funds which the authorities promised the old abbot for the restoration of his shrines have at last arrived. Tun-huang is saved.

There is little more to add. Sven Hedin, the man who began it all, outlived everyone who followed him except for Langdon Warner, who was some sixteen years his junior. A lonely and forgotten figure, the great Swedish explorer died in Stockholm in 1952 at the age of eighty-seven, surrounded by the mementoes of a long and remarkable life. Within three more years Warner, the last to enter the race and the only one who really lost it, was also dead.

Today the American would hardly recognise his 'long old road'. Monasteries and caravanserais have given way to communes and tractor plants. Modern highways link the oasis towns. A new road carries motor traffic over the Karakoram. Very occasionally from the heart of Marco Polo's demon-infested Desert of Lop is heard the distant thunder of a nuclear test. Even the Taklamakan, once the swallower of entire caravans and most dreaded of all deserts, has lost its terrors. Aircraft and satellites flush out its remaining secrets. Land reclamation schemes eat away at its edges. Chini-Bagh, so long the home of the Macartneys, has come down in the world. Today it is used as a hostel for long-distance lorry drivers, though its bathroom still has its British taps – and a lavatory called 'Victory'. But the end of that era, so rich in memories, came in the summer of 1979. For that was when the first party of British tourists stepped down from their coach at the Caves of the Thousand Buddhas, blinking in the fierce sunlight. The last shred of mystery and romance had finally gone from the Silk Road.

Bibliography of Principal Sources

Many books and articles have been written about Chinese Central Asia. They embrace travel, archaeology, art, linguistics, politics and history. The following list, although far from exhaustive, includes those works which I have found particularly valuable in researching and writing this book. Obituaries and articles in contemporary journals have largely been excluded. All titles are, or were, published in London except where otherwise indicated.

SVEN HEDIN
Through Asia. 2 vols. Methuen 1898.
Central Asia and Tibet. 2 vols. Hurst and Blackett 1903.
My Life as an Explorer. Cassell 1926.
History of the Expedition in Asia, 1927–35. Parts 1–3. Stockholm 1943–4.

SIR AUREL STEIN
Sand-Buried Ruins of Khotan. Fisher Unwin 1903.
Ruins of Desert Cathay. 2 vols. Macmillan 1912.
On Ancient Central Asian Tracks. Macmillan 1933.
Mirsky, Jeannette: *Sir Aurel Stein. Archaeological Explorer*. Chicago 1977.

ALBERT VON LE COQ
Buried Treasures of Chinese Turkestan. Allen and Unwin 1928.
Von Land und Leuten in Ostturkistan. Leipzig 1928.
Chotscho. Koniglich-Preussische Turfan-Expedition. Berlin 1913.

PAUL PELLIOT
Paul Pelliot. [Obituaries and memoirs by colleages.] Société Asiatique, Paris 1946.
Une Bibliothèque médiévale retrouvée au Kan-sou. [Letter from Tun-huang.] Hanoi 1908.
Carnets de Pékin, 1899–1901. Hanoi 1904 (repr. Paris 1976).
Les Grottes de Touen-houang. 6 vols. Paris 1920–4.
Farjenal, Fernand. 'Les Manuscrits de la mission Pelliot'. *La Revue Indigène*. Paris, December 1910.

OTANI MISSIONS
Sugiyama, Jiro. *Central Asian Objects Brought back by the Otani Mission*. Tokyo National Museum 1971.
Political and secret files of period. India Office Library.

THE RUSSIANS

Prejeválsky, Col. N. *Mongolia.* 2 vols. 1876. Trans. from Russian.

— *From Kulja, Across the Tian Shan to Lob-nor.* 1879. Trans.

Rayfield, Donald. *The Dream of Lhasa.* Life of Prejevalsky. 1976.

Morgan, E. Delmar. 'Dr. Regel's Expedition from Kuldja to Turfan in 1879–80', *Proceedings of the RGS*, June 1881.

Klementz, Dimitri. *Turfan und seine Altertumer in Nachrichten uber die von der Kaiserlichen Akademie der Wissenschaften zu St. Petersburg im Jahre 1898 ausgerustete Expedition nach Turfan.* St Petersburg 1899.

LANGDON WARNER

The Long Old Road in China. Arrowsmith 1927.

Buddhist Wall-Paintings. Harvard 1938.

Bowie, Theodore (Ed.). *Langdon Warner through his Letters.* Bloomington, USA, 1966.

HISTORY, TRAVEL ETC.

Bell, Col. Mark, VC. 'The Great Central Asian Trade Route from Peking to Kashgaria', *Proceedings of the RGS*, 12, 1890.

Boulnois, L. *The Silk Road.* 1966.

Bower, Capt. H. 'A Trip to Turkestan', *Geographical Journal*, 5, 1895.

Cable, M. and French, F. *The Gobi Desert.* 1942.

Cobbold, Ralph P. *Innermost Asia.* 1900.

Dabbs, Jack A. *History of the Discovery and Exploration of Chinese Turkestan.* The Hague 1963.

Davidson, Basil. *Turkestan Alive.* 1957.

Dubbs, Homer, H. *A Roman City in Ancient China.* 1957.

Elias, N. and Ross, E. D. *A History of the Moghuls of Central Asia.* 1898.

Fairley, Jean. *The Lion River.* 1975.

Forsyth, Sir T. D. 'On the Buried Cities in the Shifting Sands of the Great Desert of Gobi,' *Journal of the RGS*, vol. 47, 1878.

Giles, H. A. *The Travels of Fa-hsien.* Cambridge 1923.

Giles, Lionel. *Six Centuries at Tunhuang.* 1944.

Hoernle, Dr A. R. 'A Collection of Antiquities from Central Asia', *Journal of the Asiatic Society of Bengal*, Part 1, 1899; Part 2, 1901.

Johnson, W. H. 'Report on his Journey to Ilchi, the Capital of Khotan, in Chinese Tartary', *Journal of the RGS*, vol. 37, 1868.

Keay, John. *When Men and Mountains Meet.* 1977.

Mannerheim, C. G. *Across Asia from West to East.* 2 vols. Oosterhout 1969.

Montgomerie, Capt. T. G. 'On the Geographical Position of Yarkund, and Some Other Places in Central Asia', *Journal of the RGS*, vol. 36, 1867.

Morgan, Gerald. *Ney Elias.* 1971.

Nyman, Lars-Erik. *Great Britain and Chinese, Russian and Japanese Interests in Sinkiang, 1918–1934.* Stockholm 1977.

Polo, Marco. *The Book of Ser Marco Polo.* Translated and edited, with notes by Sir Henry Yule. 2 vols. 3rd edn 1903.

Saha, Dr Kshanika. *Buddhism and Buddhist Literature in Central Asia*. Calcutta 1970.

Schafer, Edward H. *The Golden Peaches of Samarkand. A Study of T'ang Exotics*. University of California 1963.

Schomberg, Col. R. C. F. *Peaks and Plains of Central Asia*. 1933.

Skrine, C. P. *Chinese Central Asia*. 1926.

Skrine, C. P. and Nightingale, P. *Macartney at Kashgar*. 1973.

Sykes, Ella and Sir Percy. *Through Deserts and Oases of Central Asia*. 1920.

Teichman, Sir Eric. *Journey to Turkistan*. 1937.

Vincent, Irene V. *The Sacred Oasis*. 1953.

Waley, Arthur. *Ballads and Stories from Tun-huang*. 1960.

Wu, Aitchen K. *Turkistan Tumult*. 1940.

Younghusband, Capt. Frank. *The Heart of a Continent*. 1896. Also 1937 edition, with new preface and epilogue.

Yu, Ying-shih. *Trade and Expansion in Han China*. University of California 1967.

ART HISTORY, ICONOGRAPHY

Bhattacharya, Chhaya. *Art of Central Asia*. [Wooden art objects from northern arm of Silk Road.] Delhi 1977.

Bussagli, Prof. Mario. *Central Asian Painting*. 1978.

De Silva, Anil. *Chinese Landscape Painting in the Caves of Tun-huang*. 1967.

Gray, Basil. *Buddhist Cave Paintings at Tun-huang*. 1959.

Talbot Rice, Tamara. *Ancient Arts of Central Asia*. 1963.

Waley, Arthur. *A Catalogue of Paintings recovered from Tun-huang by Sir Aurel Stein*. 1931.

Warner, Langdon: *Buddhist Wall-Paintings: a Study of a Ninth-Century Grotto at Wan-fo-hsia near Tun-huang*. Cambridge, Mass., 1938.

Index

Index